AYODHYA
TO
AYUTTHAYA

A Relationship Transcending Faith & Time

NEERAJ VASHISTH

notionpress
.com

INDIA · SINGAPORE · MALAYSIA

ISBN
Paperback 979-8-89446-609-5
Hardcase 979-8-89475-260-0

Language – Eng (US/UK)

In memory of Lt Cdr Anant Kukreti,
Flt Lt Achudev S , Major Nisheet Dogra,
who sacrificed themselves in line of duty

May Lord of Heaven guard you!
In return, you guide us!

– On behalf of 121 Course, National Defense Academy

In praise of book

The objective of Neeraj's book is to contextualise India's historic relations with Thailand over a period of nearly two thousand years, through the prism of culture, religion, politics. Neeraj has woven a comprehensive story on historical and contemporary cultural interactions between India and Thailand. Written in a communicative and lucid style, the book will of interest to students of Asian studies, modern Asian history, learned travelers, and general readers

— Shri Amish Tripathi, Author and Former Diplomat

"India's links with South-East Asia, especially Thailand, go back thousand of years. In this book, Neeraj explores an ancient relationship that was strengthened during the freedom struggle to emerge into a modern, 21st century partnership that ranged from literature to geo-politics"

— Shri Sanjeev Sanyal, Writer & Economist

Neeraj's book provides a comprehensive exploration of India-Thailand relations, delving into diverse themes such as overland linkages, people to people interactions and religious connections

— Mrs Sonal Goel, IAS, Author, Nation Calling

Neeraj's book is a mesmerizing anthology of an immutable Thai-Indian cultural bonding, built on a credible edifice of Buddhist ideology and Indian mythology, sustained over centuries with a durable and endearing friendship till the contemporary times. Neeraj's book successfully highlights the transcending symbiotic relationship between India and Thailand which embodies a coherent historical perspective with mythological and anecdotal references. Neeraj's work provides an interesting retrospective insight into the glorious millennia, a fine manifestation of the growth-oriented development and progression in the multidimensional cultural domains of education, religion, socioeconomics, diplomacy and geopolitics.

— Lt Gen (Retd) Sunil Gadeock, Author, From War to Peace

राजदूत
**Ambassador & Permanent
Representative to ESCAP**

भारत का राजदूतावास, बेंकाक
Embassy of India, Bangkok

Foreword

'Ayodhya to Ayutthaya, A Relationship Transcending Faith and Time' is a wonderful narration of a historical relationship between two maritime neighbors, India and Thailand, bound to each other by deep-rooted civilizational linkages, over two millennia. The book brings out a unique people-to-people connect between the two countries, which is evident in their shared beliefs and traditions and linguistic similarities.

The waters of the Bay of Bengal, have physically connected India and Thailand and facilitated a vibrant exchange of goods, peoples and ideas between the two countries, even before the beginning of the Common Era. This confluence of the two cultures has created a seamless blend, which is clearly visible in everyday life in this beautiful *'Land of Smiles'*.

Given the defining influence of maritime connectivity between the two countries, it is befitting that the author, Lieutenant Commander Neeraj Vashisth, an officer of the Indian Navy and an accomplished sailor, has skillfully woven and presented to the readers, the history of Thailand and it's shared cultural and religious patrimony with India. He has spanned the period from ancient to contemporary times in a seamless and engaging manner, which keeps the reader spellbound from beginning to the end. The author has also given us a crisp *tour d'horizon* of the regional geopolitics and contemporary India-Thailand relations.

In **Section IV** of the book, the author has masterfully transited from Thai history, culture and geopolitics, to an engrossing account of his own travel experiences in this wonderful country, richly endowed with an evolved and sophisticated societal mosaic, that is firmly rooted at the same time in tradition and modernity.

Lieutenant Commander Neeraj Vashisth has written, in an easy conversational style, this excellent book which is informative, evocative and engaging for readers who wish to know more about Thailand, our civilizational neighbour. In his relatively short sojourn in this country, the author has done a marvelous job of observing, studying and deeply understanding his gracious hosts and their remarkable country.

I am confident that this literary work will prove to be a treasure trove of information for the millions of Indian and other tourists from around the world who visit 'Amazing Thailand' every year. The book will help them better understand this ancient land and its rich, complex and glorious cultural heritage.

I congratulate Lieutenant Commander Neeraj Vashisth for his commendable initiative in writing this insightful book despite his hectic training programme at the Thai Naval Command and Staff College. I believe that is also his befitting tribute to the gracious Thai people who have embraced him and all of us, with their warm friendship and an unparalleled generosity.

Neeraj's easy writing style and engaging story-telling is a testament to the fact that he also has a great future ahead, as a thinker and writer. I wish him every success in all his future endeavors, especially as an author.

(Nagesh Singh)
Ambassador of India to Thailand

Bangkok, 26 June 2024

Contents

Acknowledgments

First and foremost, my friends and family! My father and mother in particular; I dedicate this work to your dedication in raising your kids. You are my life, heart, soul, and everything else. Most importantly, an overwhelming gratitude to love of my life Nitish who gave life to the idea and offered me coffee and motivation, whenever path appeared muddy. She is the strongest pillar of support who helped me throughout the writing process. An astounding praise is reserved for Sumit, my friend, for his valuable inputs on Buddhist philosophy, owing to his higher education in Buddhist studies.

I would like to express my deepest respect and gratitude to Shri Nagesh Singh, Honorable Ambassador of India to Thailand, for agreeing to write 'foreword' for the book. Having a 'foreword' by him is an absolute honour, and that in a way has stamped authenticity to the book. I'm deeply indebted to Shri Amish Tripathi, Shri Sanjeev Sanyal, Lt Gen Sunil Gadeock(Retd), author of 'From War to Peace', Smt Sonal Goel, IAS, author of 'Nation Calling' who took out time to read and gave comments about book, for I couldn't have thought of anyone better than them on the subject.

A special mention .... A big **THANK YOU** to all people whom I met during my travels for research of the book- some of whom I kept in touch with, some of whom I introduced in this book, and some of whom have influenced my travel experiences in monumental way. It is because of these people, I reached proudest moment of my life; the moment when I typed *'The End'*. For that is my beginning!

I bow to Lord Shiva to seek his blessings, for he is the divine light within and outside. Om Namah Shivay, the five syllable mantra is ultimate wisdom, for **Na** represents earth, **Ma** water, **si** fire, **va** air and **ya** Sky.

ॐ नमः शिवाय

Preface

It was on a routine and most ordinary morning in September of 2023 (*the reckoning of the Buddhist era is 543 years ahead of Common Era, so the year corresponds to 2566 BE in Thailand*) that the idea struck me to pen down my experiences in and about the land of Thai people. The seeds were sown, watered, and were about to vanish in the aroma of morning coffee, like always. This morning was routine and ordinary in all aspects except my wife's intentions; She was not willing to let me give up on idea. Hence, the journey begun… Before this venture too, I have made honest, yet failed attempts to write a book. I have imagined myself writing, at the middle of the night, from the confines of my imagined Study, many times.For me, realisation of this work is like a traveler finding true North.

Why this book is relevant? During my one year in Bangkok, I did not find a literary work which is light and comprehensive and yet, brings out deeper understanding of ties between two civilizational neighbours across domains. There is enormous written text about Thailand and India relations but I found it little complex and scattered. When I started research about Bharat-Thailand historic connections, most often, I found larger context leading to India-South East Asia relations. Or, some covering only one aspect of relations in greater detail. In Thailand most of the written text is in Thai language or translated from Thai language which adds to the difficulty of a layman reader. This is not a scholarly work, rather I have most humbly attempted to weave the experience of traveling almost every province of Thailand, and structured reading for the sole purpose of better understanding of the land and its people in the form of a story (*Human love for stories and conspiracy is legendary*). Also, possessing an understanding of Thai language helped me a great deal in stitching pieces together. While I was undertaking this journey, I came to terms with the deep historical connections between Bharat and Thailand and a Chinese wedge that is deep and incisive. The traditional values, social pattern, religion, language, understanding of life and life after death has tremendous similarities in Bharat and Thailand despite having completely different political set up. But, larger mass on both sides is oblivion to a deeply interlinked past. This is primarily because of long period of disconnect between the people and leadership of two countries during Cold War.

This book would serve purpose of building a laymen understanding and ascertaining the connections between two countries. It subtly reflects on journey of Gurudev Rabindranath Tagore and it's political and cultural importance as well as Thailand's contribution to Indian freedom struggle. In fact, this book is fresh air and could pave way for similar books based on historic relations of other countries with India, in form of a story and travel accounts.

The book is original in matter and manner, both. This would arrest interest of readers keen on knowing India's giant and unique contribution in shaping story of one of her civilizational neighbours. The book is not simply a narration of events but, the flow of Thai story is studied in conjunction with Bharat's history. The book has a philosophical pitch while discerning cultural and religious relations between India and Thailand. Also, anyone with an honest intent of exploring or working in Thailand, this book would give a launch pad in understanding Thailand, which often swings between seemingly stable government at one end to bloodless coups at the other end of spectrum.

The book has around 70,000 words and falls under 'Read more' genre. The book starts with regularly used Thai language words loaned from *Sanskrit* or *Pali* language, followed by name of Thailand's provinces or districts (*mandalas*) which are inspired by Hindu mythology or languages. The book is imagined in five sections, each divided in various chapters. The first three sections are arranged in sequence whereas last two sections could be read independently.

Before you start ……..

Few Sanskrit Words Loaned in Thai Language

Thai language has many borrowed words, mainly from *Sanskrit*, *Pali*, *Tamil* and, *Khmer*, and more recently, English (in particular many scientific and technological terms). In and around Bangkok, Tinglish is spoken by many, which is 'Thai language heavily influenced by English'. However, it's not a language used between locals, it is only used with tourists. Some examples of loaned words are as follows:

Thai	Read	Meaning	Language	Remarks
อักษร	àk-sǒrn	alphabetic letter	Sanskrit	अक्षर/akṣara
องุ่น	a-ngùn	grape	Persian	Angur
ภาษา	phaa-să	language	भाषा/bhāṣā	
ชา	chā	tea	Chinese	chai
ภัย	phai	danger	Sanskrit, Pali	भय/bhaya

Thai	Read	Meaning	Language	Remarks
เทวี	thee-wii	Goddess	Sanskrit, Pali	देवी/devi
ฑีฆายุ	thii-khaa-yú	"long live"	Sanskrit	दीर्घायु/dirghayu
ครู	khruu	teacher	Sanskrit, Pali	गुरु/guru
กบาล	ka-baan	head	Sanskrit, Pali	कपाल/kapala
มหา-	ma-hăa-	great	Sanskrit, Pali	महा/maha
มนุษย์	ma-nút	human being	Sanskrit	मनुष्य/manuṣya
มัสยิด	mát-sa-yít	mosque	Arabic	masjid
นรก	na-rók	hell	Sanskrit, Pali	नरक/naraka
ราชา	raa-chaa	king	Sanskrit, Pali	राजा/rājā
รส	rót	taste	Sanskrit/ Pali	रस/rasa
รูป	rûp	picture	Sanskrit, Pali	रूप/rūpa

Thai	Read	Meaning	Language	Remarks
สมบูรณ์	sŏm-buun	perfect, complete	Sanskrit	संपूर्ण/sampūrṇa
ศัตรู	sàt-truu	adversary, enemy	Sanskrit	शत्रु/śatru
สิงห์	sĭng	lion	Sanskrit, Pali	सिंह/singha
สวรรค์	sa-wăn	heaven	Sanskrit	स्वर्ग/svarga
สุข	sùk	happiness	Sanskrit, Pali	सुख/sukha
สุริยา	sù-rí-yaa	sun	Pali	Suriya/ सूर्य
อุดร	ù-dorn	north	Sanskrit, Pali	उत्तर/uttara
ประถม	pra-thŏm	primary	Sanskrit	प्रथम/prathama
คชา	kha-chaa	elephant	Sanskrit, Pali	गज/gaja
ประเทศ	pra-thêet	country	Sanskrit	प्रदेश/pradesa
นคร	ná-khorn	city	Sanskrit, Pali	नगर/nagara
สันติ	săn-tì	peace	Pali	sānti

Thai	Read	Meaning	Language	Remarks
ชัย	chai	victory	Sanskrit, Pali	जय/jaya
ภูมิ	phuum	soil	Sanskrit, Pali	भूमि/bhumi
วาจา	waa-jaa	words	Sanskrit, Pali	वाचा/vaca
ภาวะ	phaa-wá	condition	Sanskrit, Pali	भाव/bhāva
กษัตริย์	ka-sàt	king	Sanskrit	क्षत्रिय/kṣatriya
ภักดี	phák-dii	loyal	Sanskrit	भक्ति/bhakti
วิจารณ์	wí-jaan	review	Sanskrit	विचारण/vicarna
พายุ	phaa-yú	storm	Sanskrit, Pali	वायु/vayu
สัตว์	sàt	animal	Sanskrit	सत्व/satva
พินาศ	phí-nâat	destruc-tion	Sanskrit	विनाश/vinasa
วิหาร	wí-hǎan	temple	Sanskrit, Pali	विहार/vihāra
เวลา	wee-laa	time	Sanskrit, Pali	वेला/velā

Thai	Read	Meaning	Language	Remarks
อาสา	aa-săa	hope (desire)	Sanskrit	अभिलाष/asha
กระดาษ	kra-dàat	paper	Sanskrit	कागद/kagada
เภตรา	phee-traa	boat	Sanskrit	वहित्र/vahitra
อากาศ	aa-kàat	air	Sanskrit	आकाश/akasa
เทศ	thêet	outlandish	Sanskrit	देश/desa
ทุกข์	thúk	suffering	Sanskrit	दुःख/duḥkha
โทษ	thôot	blame	Sanskrit	दोष/doṣa
จิตร	jìt	design	Sanskrit	चित्र/citra
ทุน	thun	fund	Sanskrit	धन/dhana
จันทร์	jan	moon	Sanskrit	चन्द्र/chandra
จักรวาล	jàk-kra-waan	universe	Sanskrit	चक्रवाल/chakravala
คุณ	khun	you, useful	Sanskrit	गुण/ghuna
สตรี	sa-trii	woman	Sanskrit	स्त्री/stri
อาคาร	aa-khaan	building	Sanskrit	आगार/agara

Thai	Read	Meaning	Language	Remarks
ปราสาท	praa-sàat	castle	Sanskrit	प्रासाद/prasada
นาม	naam	name	Sanskrit	नाम/nama
ชีวา	chii-waa	living	Sanskrit	जीव/jiva
กรุณา	ka-ru-naa	compassion	Sanskrit	करुण/karuṇa
พิเศษ	phí-sèet	special	Sanskrit	विशेष/vishesh
พุทธิ	phút-thí	intelligence	Sanskrit	बुद्धि/buddhi
หิมะ	hì-má	snow	Sanskrit	हिम/hima
เมฆ	mêek	cloud	Sanskrit	मेघ/megha
ตรีศูล	trii-sǔun	trident	Sanskrit	त्रिशूल/trisula
วิทยา	wít-tha-yaa	science	Sanskrit	विद्या/vidya
สัปดาห์	sàp-daa	week	Sanskrit	सप्ताह/saptaha
บริษัท	bor-ri-sàt	company	Sanskrit	परिषद्/pariṣad
สมาคม	sa-maa-khom	association	Sanskrit	समागम/samagama

A Selected Chronology of Thailand History

Historical Periods

Sukhothai	1238-1438
Ayuthaya	1351-1767
Thonburi	1767-1782
Bangkok (Rattanakosin)	1782- present

Chakri Kings (Bangkok Period)

Phra Phuttayotfa	Rama I	1782-1809
Phra Phuttaloetla	Rama II	1809-1824
Phra Nangklao	Rama III	1824-1851
Mongkut	Rama IV	1851-1868
Chulalongkorn	Rama V	1868-1910

Vajiravudh	Rama VI	1910-1925
Prajadhipok	Rama VII	1925- 1935
Ananda	Rama VIII	1935-1946
Bhumibol Adulyadej	Rama IX	1946-2016
Vajiralongkorn	Rama X	2016 - present

Prime Ministers

Phraya Manopakon Nithithada	1932-1933
Phraya Phahon Phonphayauhasena	1933-1938
Phibun Songkhram	1938- 1944
Khuang Aphaiwong	1944-1945
Thani Bunyaket	1945
Seni Pramoj	1945-1946
Khuang Aphaiwong	1946
Pridi Banomyong	1946
Thawan Thamrongnawasawat	1946-1947
Khuang Aphaiwong	1947-1948
Phibun Songkhram	1948-1957
Phote Sarasin	1957

Thanom Kittikachon	1958
Sarit Thanarat	1959-1963
Thanom Kittikachon	1963-1973
Sanya Dharmasakti	1973 - 1975
Seni Pramoj	1975
Kukrit Pramoj	1975-1976
Seni Pramoj	1976
Thanin Kraivichien	1976 - 1977
Kriangsak Chomanand	1977-1980
Prem Tinsulanond	1980-1988
Chatichai Choonhavan	1988 - 1991
Anand Panyarachun	1991-1992
Suchinda Kraprayun	1992
Anand Panyarachun	1992
Chuan Leekpai	1992-1995
Banharn Silpaarcha	1995-1996
Chavalit Yongchaiyudh	1996-1997
Chuan Leekpai	1997-2001
Thaksin Shinawatra	2001-2006

Surayud Chalanont	2006-2007
Samak Sundaravej	2007-2008
Somchai Wongsuwat	2008
Abhisit Vejjaijya	2008-2011
Yingluck Shinawatra	2011-2014
Prayuth Chan ocha	2014 - 2023
Srettha Thavisin	2023 - present

Indo-Thai Nomenclature and Name Connection

You Must Know

Before unfolding the book to the reader, I was very certain to initiate their interest in the text and subject. One has to understand that of the 77 provinces of Thailand, majority of the names are derivatives of Indian ancient languages or pantheon of Hindu Gods, and that we are civilzational neighbours. The names of the provinces of Thailand and their official seal, at first glance, may sound or appear Greek and Latin, but a closer understanding would disapprove all webs. Having set foot in almost all the provinces of Thailand, I can certainly say that there are inherent similarities in culture, language, costume and religious aspect of life. To a laymen in India, list of similarities ends at commonality in language and religion. Let's understand meaning and etymology of names of some the provinces along with official seals.

Most of the provinces in northern region are named after nature, animals or *Lan Na* kingdom traditions. *Chiang Mai*, literally translates to New City and *Chiang Rai,* named after King Mangrai are two prominent northern provinces. Surprisingly enough, *Chiang Mai* is called 'New City' despite more than 700 years of history and seeing its dawn almost at same time as Sukhothai Kingdom, the first true Thai kingdom. Sukhothai literally translates to 'Dawn of Happiness'. Other northern province, *Uttaradit* takes it names from north direction *(Uttar* meaning north in *Sanskrit)* and translates to 'Port of the North'.

Name of few of the southern provinces are influenced by Malaya language and history of southern part of Thailand. Ramkhamkheng stone of Sukhothai period first mentioned "*Nakhon Si Thammarat*" in 1292, which means "The City of King Sri Thammasok" or "The City of the Virtuous king Ashoka, the great of Kalinga". Post King Rama VI visit to India , in 1915, *Bandon* was renamed *Surat Thani*, a change inspired by the major port city of Surat in India. And, the river on which *Bandon* was situated was named Tapi river drawing similarity with Indian city. The name of the *Chaiya* district in *Surat Thani* province is inspired by founder of Srivijaya empire.

The first Buddhist mission sent by King Ashoka to Suvrnabhumi was received at *Nakhon Pathom* (*Nakhon - Nagar* and *Pathom - Pratham* in Pali) province which literally translates to 'First City'. On the provincial seal is *Phra Nakhon Chedi* (Stupa) where Buddha's relics are housed. *Samut Prakan, Samut Sakhon and Samut Songhram* (*Samut derived from Samudra*) are coastal cities of central region and derive their name from *Sanskrit* language meaning 'Fortress of Ocean', 'Lake Ocean' and 'War Ocean' respectively. *Nakhon Sawan* (*Sawan meaning Heaven*) province marks the point of confluence of two of Thailand's major rivers, the Ping and the Nan. These converge in *Nakhon Sawan* to form the Chao Phraya river which flows south to Bangkok and out into the Gulf of Thailand. The point of confluence of two rivers is a place of worship and, it is Thai version of *Triveni* at *Prayagraj*, India.

Phitsanulok (pronounced as Vishnulok) province literally means 'Adobe of Lord Vishnu'. For name of *Lopburi* province, there are two popular opinions. First, that it is named after Lord Rama's son Luv. Lahore in Pakistan, which predates *Lopburi*, is also named after Lord Rama's son. The other legend has it that Lopburi (which literally means Monkey city) was given to Lord Hanumana by Lord Rama after he won over Lanka. *Lopburi's* provincial seal has Lord Vishnu in front of Khmer Temple Phra Prang Sam Yod (the three holy towers). The name of another province *Nakhon Nayok* has *Sanskrit* origins which means City of Leaders (*Nayok* derived from word *Nayaka*).

The Singburi province means 'Lion City' has its name derived from *Sanskrit*, in that, Singh is Lion and *Buri (Puri)* means City. Hence, the literal translation is 'Lion City', sharing same root as Singapore. Similarly, Suphan Buri province name means 'City of Gold' where *Suphan (Suvarna)* translates to Gold. *Chanthaburi* province, a small province famous for gem trade, takes its name from *Sanskrit* word for moon, that is *Chaand*. The word *Chaiya* has roots in *sanskrit* word *Jaya* which means Victory and word '*Phum*' from word Bhumi which means 'Land'. Hence, name of province *Chaiyaphum* literally means 'Land of Victory'.

Nakhon Ratchasima province name is derivative of *Sanskrit* word (*Nakhon* derived from *nagara*; *Rajseema*, from sovereign boundary).The present city name translates to Soverign boundary City. The name of province "Sakhon Nakhon" means "City of Cities" in *Sanskrit*. The *Surin* province derives its name from *Sanskrit* words *Sura* (God). *Chonburi* province name translates to city of water (*Chon* has roots in *Sanskrit* word '*Jal*'). The official seal of many provinces has symbolic features of Hinduism. For example, some province seal depicts *Garuda*, Lord *Vishnu*, Lord *Indra* and

Holy elephant *Airawat.* Many places in Thailand derive their name and relevance from the *Ramakein* (Thai version of Ramayana).

In *Chainat* province, there exists a mountain called Khao Sapaya where it is believed that, Lord Hanuman collected a medicinal plant called *Sangkoranitrijava (Sanjeevni).* The top of this mountain is flat and smooth because Lord Hanuman swept his huge tail over the mountain to obtain the wanted plant. In *Saraburi* province, there is a mountain which has a big hole right through one side. The legend has it that *Thotsakan (Ravana)* carried Sita in his chariot, and when he was rushing past the mountain, the axle of chariot wheel hit the mountain and made a big hole. Both *Chonburi* and *Phattalung* claim to be the place where Bali (monkey king) fought with the buffalo named *Thoraphi (Dundhubi).* Legends are countless, I have mentioned few!

Relevant Maps

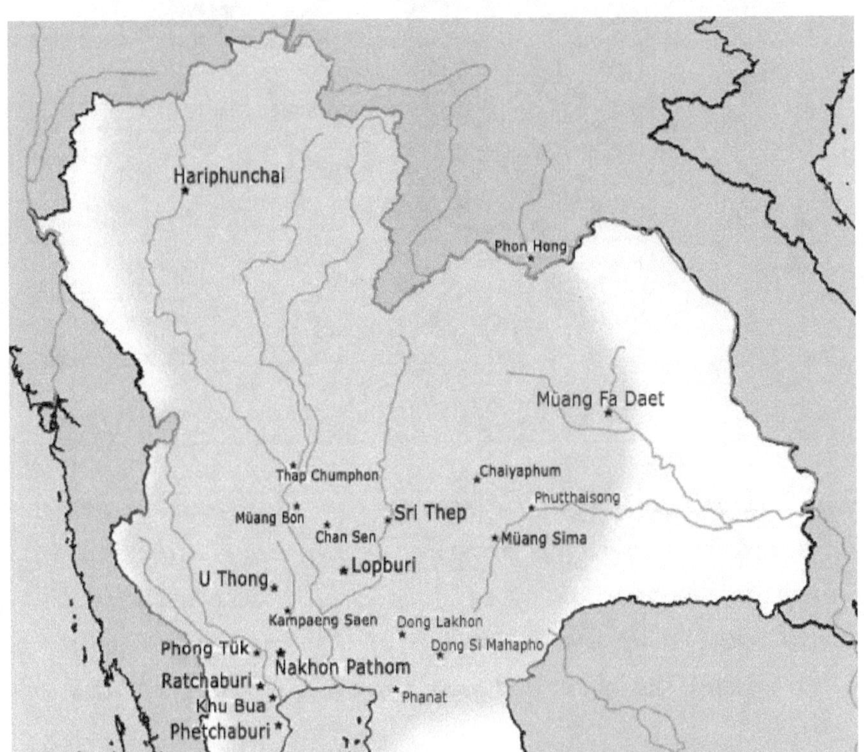

Map I Dvaravati culture settlements from 6th to 9th centuries (Heinrich Damm, spread of Dvaravati culture in early Thailand

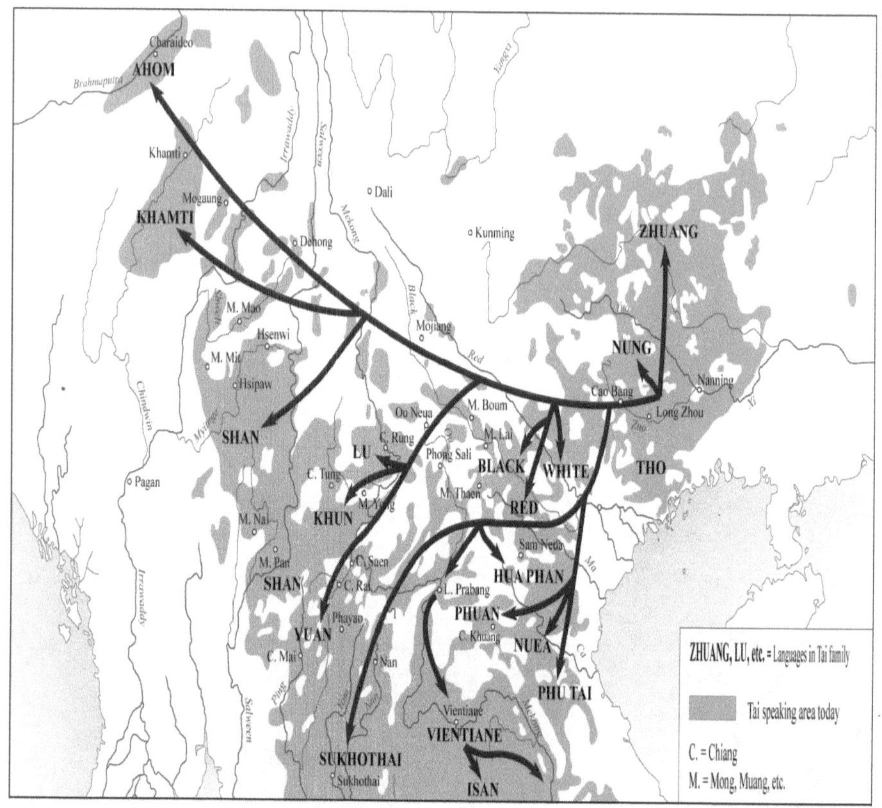

Map 2 depicting linguistic family tree classified by James R. Chamberlain (reference Siamese-heritage.org) overlaid on a geographic distribution of Tai family. The map is indicative of general pattern of the migration of Tai speaking people , not specific routes, which would have been along the rivers and other passes

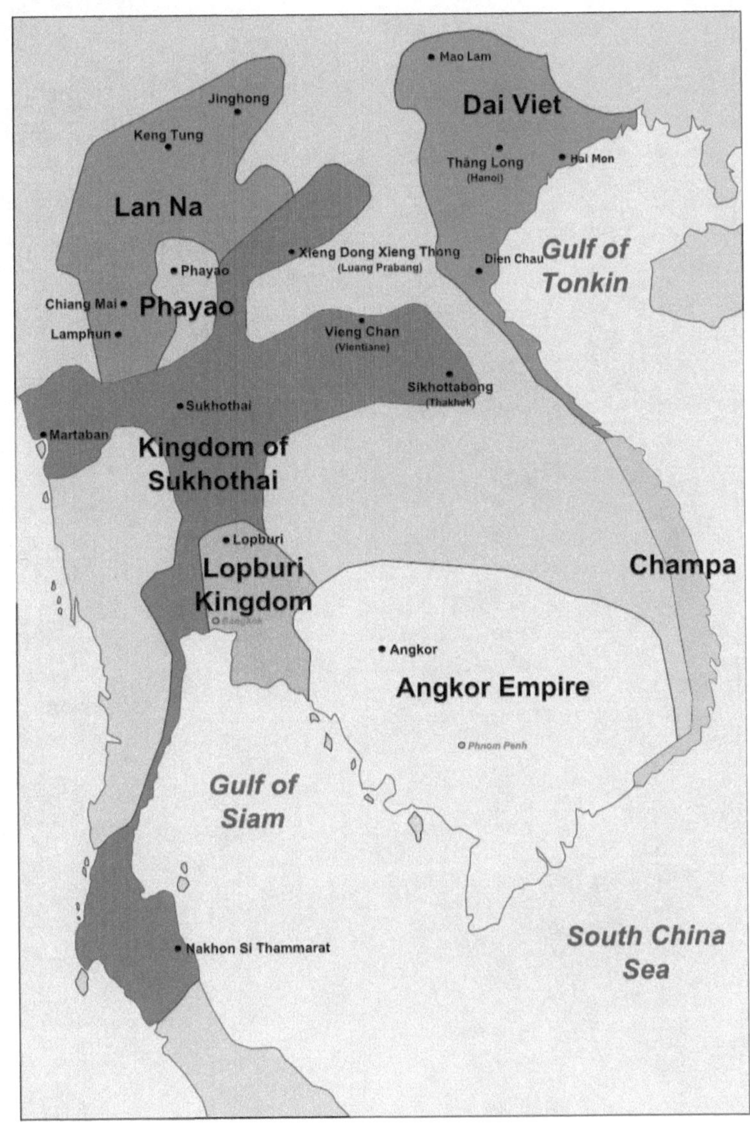

Map 3 (setting 13th century)- David K. Wyatt work "Thailand : A short history, 2nd edition Silkworm Books, Chiang Mai, page 32 and Cornell Southeast Asia program map 13th century Thailand. Depicting the Kingdom of Sukhothai, Kingdom of Lan Na and Kingdom of Phayao collaborating together to organize "The kingdom of Siam"

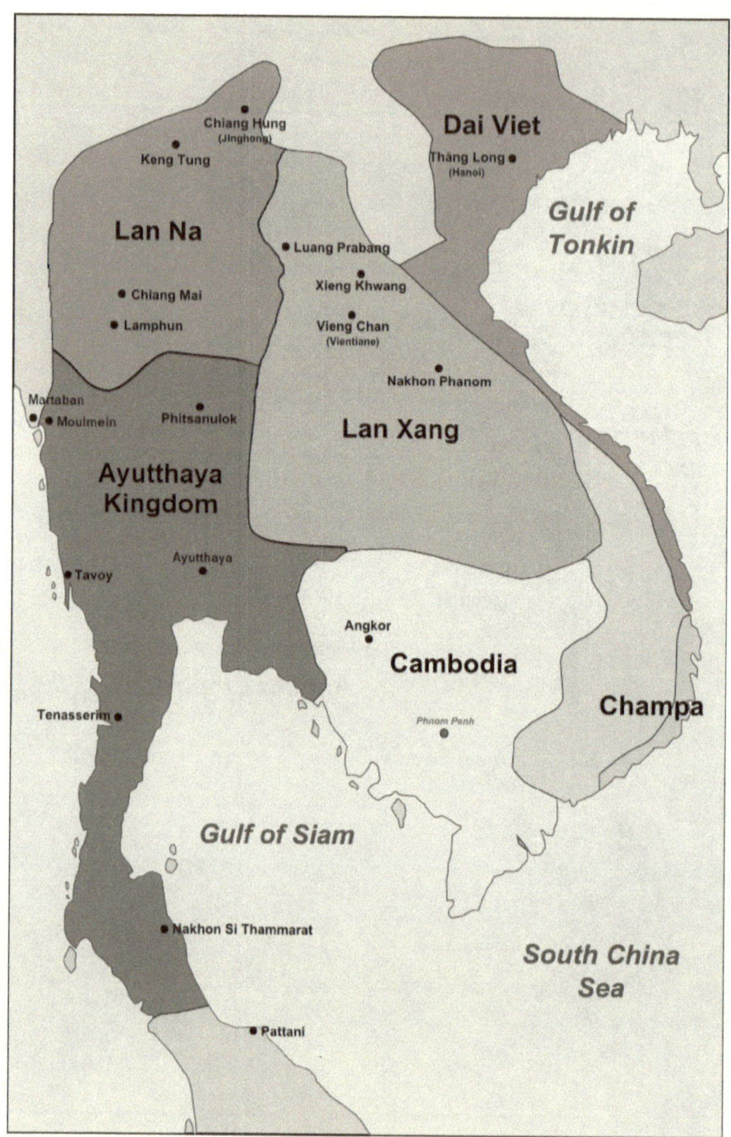

Map 4 Nicolas Eynaud- Own work based on David K Wyatt (2004), Thailand: A short history, Cornell Southeast Asia Map Ayutthaya empire 1540. Note- Ayutthaya and Mainland Southeast Asia in 1540. Southeast Asian borders remained relatively undefined until the modern period.

Map 5 Map based on a UN map. Source : UN Cartographic Section

'Over one million saw Buddha Relics'

– Bangkok Post

More than one million Buddhists flocked in Bangkok to pay their respects to the relics of the Lord Buddha and his chief disciples, Sariputra and Moggallana, between Feb 24 and March 3, according to Ministry of Culture, Thailand. The relics were brought from India to Thailand by the Indian government to commemorate the auspicious occasion of His Majesty the King's 6th-cycle birthday

Section I

History of 'Free People'

Chapter One

Geo-History of Thai People

<hr>

"There is no other happiness but peace"

– a Thai proverb

Growing up, I faced tremendous difficulty in understanding the rationale of having history and geography as separate subjects. The two subjects in question can not be understood comprehensively in isolation, and are mutually inclusive. The geographic locations are witness to many historic events, and the historic events certainly influence geography of a place. Though, two subjects are separate in their method of focus and analysis, but I feel that there is a strong need to teach these two disciplines in an integrated manner.

For the lack of integration in my knowledge of two subjects, I was almost impulsive to find out, why Lumbinigram, a small area in present day Nepal shares name with a huge park in metropolitan Bangkok? Why most of the countries in South, Southeast and East Asia celebrate *Buddha Purnima* on different dates, and most of these countries have *Buddha Purnima* as closed national holiday. Why name of many roads in Thailand are derivative of *Sanskrit* language words, which has its origins in Bharat? Why coronation

(*Rachaphisek* in Thai language) of the King incorporates many rites from ancient Hindu ceremony of anointment (*Abhisheka*)? The Thai coronation ceremony includes anointment (divine bath), the enthronement, the crowning and the investiture of the King. Why Gurudev Rabindernath Tagore undertook an unplanned journey to Thailand in 1927 and, why Netaji planned a journey to Thailand in 1943? How a small Chinese tea shop in Thailand fanned the idea of Indian National Army during WWII? The list of similarities is endless, hence meaningless to mention each one. Rather, I would attempt to discuss indissoluble similarities in all aspects of life as the journey progresses.

I rang up a good friend, Priyamwada and explained her my project. Priyamwada is an intelligent girl with a sharp intellect, South Delhi accent and fresh attitude towards life. She graduated from Delhi University in Philosophy, and grabbed an opportunity for post graduate studies in Buddhist philosophy at Mahidol university in Thailand. She is equally graceful in her physical manifestation; broad curvy lips, small nose bridge, short and narrow jaw, flawless skin, most importantly, deep and meaningful eyes. We decided to meet at mutually agreed time in Bangkok for discussing details of the book. She was certain of my uncertainty to write a book because when we met last, I had no connection with the world of creative writing. She was ecstatic with the prospect of seeing each other regularly for one year in Thailand. As luck would have it, she was in Bharat for a midterm break, and we decided to meet.

Priyamwada was waiting in company of a cup of coffee, when I entered Cafe. After exchanging pleasantries, we sat across table, and she started "I really appreciate your decision to write. I believe, reading literature is like filling a glass, while writing is oozing out of liquid from the same glass. Disclaimer: Any disrespect to monarchy is labeled as contempt in, and of Thailand. First thing, Thailand is governed by strictest Lese-majeste laws[1] and even, an alleged offense committed outside the Kingdom against these laws, can be punished inside Kingdom."

With a tinge of self-appreciation, I said "I know, I know! I have read in great detail about the country in which, I would be staying for one year. Leave alone that, I can speak their language with proficiency of an amateur. For in Thailand, King is the law and there ought to be no other."

Priyamwada, shifting bread plate towards me, remarked "You have undergone complete transformation in matter and manner, both. Next one year would be interesting with you in Thailand. Now, tell me more about your work?

I said, pulling out a piece of paper from my trendy cotton bag "I have an interesting story to tell to people. Thailand has never been brought close to common Indian, through a story. I envisage that the story would require us to travel across every part of Thailand and then, it would require glue of wisdom to piece it together"

Priyamwada said, adjusting her glasses from nose bridge to forehead "I agree in totality. A common Indian has sketchy understanding of 'the Land of Smiles'. Similarly, Thai people have vague and imprecise understanding of Bharat and its people. A large population of Thai and Indian people are oblivion to our historical linkage and contemporary re-linkage. I will visit Ayodhaya on 22 Jan for temple inauguration, would you like to be part of historical moment?

I said, with a thoughtful expression "We would meet in Ayutthaya (a city in Thailand), if visit to Ayodhaya for consecration of *Ram Lalla* at *Janambhoomi* is not possible. I would work on history of Thailand before onset of Ayutthaya Kingdom by the time you reach back Thailand. You would have joy of being part of the story starting from Ayutthaya kingdom to 10th King of Chakri dynasty(present King of Thailand)."

Priyamwada said, with no intention of discouraging me "I am afraid, the chapter on history would turn mind-numbing and tedious without interesting conversation and commentary"

I said, thanking her for cooperation and coffee "It is important to understand the historical journey to have clear and precise understanding of present. Before, I delve in politico-religious spectrum of India -Thailand relations and traveling accounts, it is necessary, by wisdom, to cover their civilization history. May Shiva bless us! May Lord Buddha bless us! We would meet at Ayutthaya temple complex in Thailand!

Pre Thai Kingdoms and Spread of Buddhism

Spread of Tai (Thai people) - The land which is Thailand today, is inhabited by human race since time immemorial, but the history of Thai people and geographic entity "Thailand" had no connection to this land before establishment of Sukhothai Kingdom in 1238 AD. Before this time, Thailand and Thai peoples' destiny was not linked. It is considered that the Tai (Thai people) originally came from Taiwan, and were interbred and culturally influenced in southern China. Thai people (literally meaning 'Free people') migrated from Southern China, probably Guangxi[2] province, because of expansionist tendency of Han dynasty. This turned out to be one of the biggest migration of human race in context of numerical strength, time consumed and spread. Thai people migrated to Thailand and other parts of Southeast Asia from 8-13th century AD. Initially, they settled in north part of present day Thailand and gradually spread to central and southern Thailand along the river plains. As of today, there are more than 60 linguistic group of Thai people spread across Laos, Cambodia, North Vietnam, North Myanmar, Assam in India with the largest ethnic groups being Dai, Thais, Isan, Tai Yai (Shan), Lao, Thai Ahom and northern Thai people. Let's briefly understand their journey ever since this migration took place. (***Chris Baker and Phongpaichit, 2017- History of Ayutthaya, Siam in Early Modern World***)

Tai (Shan) Ethnicity in Myanmar - On one of my previous visits to Shan state in Myanmar, I could glance through clear distinction between a Shan (Tai family) and Burmese local. Burmese language belongs to Sino-Tibetan family, and language of Shan people belongs to Tai Kadai family. Shan people dominated much of Burma from 13th to 16th century before they become vassal state to Burmese Kingdom. The Britishers occupied Burma in 1886, and people in Shan state became British citizens. In 1910, the British demarcated borders between Burma and Thailand. This sealed destiny of Shan people, and they were handed over nationalities depending on which side of the border they were housed in 1910. (***Dictionary of Indian Biography, Ardent Media 1906. p. 82***). Similar, trauma is destiny of many ethnicity and tribes across the world which were destroyed by the evil forces of colonization. Few ill chosen people, who had no idea about history and distribution of ethnicity of population, drew lines on small scale maps; these lines define boundaries, and bitter truth of human irrationality. Be it, the Durand Line or McMahon line, the people on both sides of these lines were not present when their destiny was sealed in close confines. It's true that sun never set on British colonial empire but, same is true about horrendous legacy of British imperialism. Today, Shan people are a minority (about 10 percent) in Myanmar and, mostly reside in Shan state, biggest state in Myanmar. As of Nov 23, 50000 people were already displaced because of military crackdown on the multitudes of ethnic groups up in arms against the military junta which took power in Feb 21(***Human Rights Watch, World Report 23: Myanmar***).

The free spirit of free (Shan people) people may be the reason for not buckling to military rule. In Thailand, Shan ethnicity reside mostly in Chiang Rai and Chiang Mai province (bordering Myanmar). On interaction with Shan people in Chiang Mai province, while on my visit to the province, it was no challenge to make out clear difference in their dialect, tone, and to an extent culture.

Ahoms (Tai people) of Assam- Tai people migrated to Assam, crossing evergreen Patkai mountains from Myanmar side, and established successful Ahom dynasty which reigned Assam from 1228 AD to 1826AD. Ahom dynasty maintained strong affiliation to Tai traditions, however, they had a long disconnect from other Thai Kingdoms. Only few dynasties in the world has seen such a long stint of unbroken rule. They are largely responsible for contours of present day Assam, and offering it a distinct culture, language and identity. I referred to ***Arup Kumar Dutta's book "The Ahoms- a re-imagined history"*** which factually and imaginatively acquaints the Reader with the fascinating saga of Ahoms. This books speaks in intricate detail, and is loud about the Ahomisation of the state and its degradation from prominence. A study was undertaken in 2015 by ***Centre for Cellular and Molecular biology, Hyderabad***

to establish genetic connection between Ahom and Thai people. Of the 22 samples taken, there were tremendous similarities in gene pool.

Ahom are great warriors, and have fought against the might of the Mughal empire and defeated them in Battle of Saraighat in 1671. Ram Singh, the army commander of the Mughal army is said to have remarked "Every Ahom solider is expert at rowing boats, shooting arrows, in digging trenches, and in wielding guns and canons. I have not seen such specimens of versatility anywhere in India". During battle, Lachit Borphukan lead with dynamism and self example to thwart Mughal attempt to capture Assam. Little did I know about Lachit Borphukan at the time of my training at National Defense Academy, that Lachit Borphukan award, given to the Cadet with best Officer Like Qualities, is named after Ahom hero, commemorating his military acumen and leadership. The state of Assam celebrates Lachit Diwas on 24 November every year celebrating his life and victory in Battle of Saraighat. *{Sarkar, J. N. (1992)}*

The kingdom grew weaker and fell to internal rebellions and repeated invasion attempts of Myanmar. Subsequently, Myanmar lost to British in first Anglo- Burmese war and reign of Ahom kingdom shifted in the hands of East India Company as a result of Treaty of Yandabo in 1826. *{Thant Myint-U (2001)}*. Today, Ahoms are largest ethnic group with a population of about 4.6 million in state of Assam, mainly settled in Jorahat, Dibrugarh, Ghoragat, Tinskia (upper Assam), Shivsagar (Bhupen Hazarika's ancestral home).

Tai Ethnicity in Cambodia A man named Jayavarman II, most probably from Java in Southeast Asia established the Khmer empire, and embraced the title of Charkrvarti in 802 AD. Khmer Empire grew in to a powerful state in Southeast Asia along Mekong river. Khmer empire was deeply influenced by Hinduism, and in later part by Buddhism in view of phenomenally high trade with Bharat. It lasted from 802 to 1431 AD and, at height of its power included much of Cambodia, Thailand (Chao Phraya Basin and beyond), Laos and Southern Vietnam. The Khmers were great builders and their cities were landscaped with huge temple complexes, reservoirs, highways and well defined road network. Khmer built *Angkor Wat* (*Wat*, literally meaning Temple) in their capital city Angkor (original name '*Yasodharapura*') which is a picture perfect microcosm of Hindu beliefs. {**Wolters, O. (1973)**}

My visit to *Angkor Wat*, along with Pancham Dham Yatra [3] entourage, was an eye opening experience, and a realization of the myopic view of present day globalization compared to the flow of trade and cultural exchange centuries back. The Khmer empire's decline is deeply associated with the Thai migration of 12th century from Yunnan province. The migration intensified further when the Mongols took over Yunnan province in 1253 AD. Eventually, Thai created small kingdoms west of Khmer Empire, and most important of them was Sukhothai Kingdom in 1238 AD established by Sri Inthrathit (distorted from Indrajeet). Later on, Thai kingdom of Ayutthaya took over Angkor in 1431 AD, and ended one the most sophisticated empire of its times. This downfall of Khmer Empire lead to synthesis of Thai and Khmers who interbred and intermixed.

Thai speakers are reduced to .01 percent of the Cambodian population primarily because of Cambodian civil war of 1975 when thousand fled to Thailand and many were displaced and killed in garb of spying on Cambodia. {**Kiernan, Ben (May 2014)**}. The realization of this episode is instant and fresh in memory of Thai people and the episode is preserved in bad taste. I'll briefly intrude in to this episode while I dissect Thailand relation with its neighbour and people to people connection. Today, Thai people are mostly found in Phnom Penh (capital city of Cambodia) primarily as families of diplomatic representatives or Thai people operating for Thai companies in Cambodia. Thai people in North Cambodia has largely assimilated in Khmer culture and are not distinguishable from Khmer villagers.

Tai people in North Vietnam The migration of Thai people was centred in the valley of Muang Thaeng which largely refers to northwestern side of Vietnam. This valley is home to the legend of Khun Borom (Khun is Thai word for paying respect). Khun Borom has a mythical standing, similar to what Christians had for Prester John, and it is believed that his nine sons were handed over reigns of different Thai kingdoms. The cultural mix and long period of association with other kingdoms divided the Thai people in valley in three groups - Black Thai, Red Thai and White Thai.

During my visit to Vietnam, I was desperately looking for the differences in costume but, couldn't register any. Though, local people can differentiate each group by customs and costumes. Black Thai name comes from the black headdresses worn by the community, especially females. They have marginally distinct traditions from the other two groups in ceremonies and rituals like marriage, death, women standing in household {*Jean Michaud (2000)*}. The white Thai are settled in Northeastern part of Vietnam and they are about 2,80,000 White Thai in Vietnam (year 2002), 2,00,000 in Laos (year 2000) and 10,000 in Yunnan province of China (year1995). Majority of Thai people in Vietnam practise Theravada form of Buddhism. However, there is practise of Animism among majority of Thai people in Vietnam. Animism is a belief that understands the spiritual essence of creatures, objects and places.

Thai people and Thailand Difficult to fix exact dates, Thai people migrated to Thailand between 8-10th century AD (though, it continued till 13th century) whereas Buddhism has been integral part of Thai region at least since 3rd century BC. I have used two words, Tai and Thai interchangeably in book but Thai people are people of present day Thailand whereas Tai refers to group of people speaking Tai language. King Ashoka, whose empire occupied present day Pakistan, Afghanistan and Bangladesh, sent a mission with Buddha's relics for spread of Buddhism at the end of third council to Suvranabhumi, most probably to the capital Nakhon Pathom. (***Ven.Phra Rajavaramuni,1984***)

PC - Author, clicked from King Narai National Museum Lopburi. Dharmachakra and Asiatic lion found in Nakhon Pathom province, oldest centre of Thai Buddhism

The more I plunged into fathomless and layered depth of knowledge, the realization was almost lightening and certain "How less I Know". A wise man from Greece said in 3rd Century BC, "I know that I know nothing" and that, crowns him as the wisest man of his time. The urge to find solutions in quest of ultimate has often pushed human beings in more problematic realms of uncertainty.

Early Buddhism in Thailand is not linked to Thai people but, the ruling kingdoms of those times. The Northern part of present day Thailand was ruled by Khmer Empire and, the central part was under control of Dvaravati (literally meaning which has gates, Dwarka) Empire. The southern Thailand was largely under the influence of Srivijaya empire and followed Mahayana form of Buddhism. A part of eastern Thailand was conquered by Burmese Kingdom and continued under influence of Burmese until Britishers settled the border. And remember, Britishers, in times of the empire, never settled a thing, in fact, dismantling and disintegrating organised societies appeared key tenets of their policy. They highhandedly drew some of the most contested boundaries of the world. Rigid borders they drew, flexible boundaries was outcome.

The spread of Buddhism and its acceptance in Suvranabhumi and Dvaravati empire is discussed in second chapter. Here, the aim is to settle the major Kingdoms in chronological order so as to set stage for comprehensive understanding of Thailand. While, understanding the life and society of these Kingdoms, I have primarily focused on seven Thai Kings titled "the Great" across the Kingdoms and Periods. The King Ramkhamhaeng, the great of Sukhothai Kingdom, King Narseuan, the Great and King Narai, the great of the Ayutthaya period, King Taksin of Thonburi period, and King Chulalok Maharj (Rama I), King Mongkut (Rama IV), King Chulalongkorn (Rama V) of the Rattanakonsin period.

[1] *In Thailand, non adherence to Lese Majeste law is a crime iaw Section 112 of the Thai criminal Code*

[2] *Guangxi, is an autonomous region of People's Republic of China, located in Southern China*

[3] *Pancham Dham Yatra aims to foster spiritual and religious connection between India and Cambodia*

Chapter II

First Thai Kingdom - Sukhothai Kingdom

Brahma, Vishnu, Shiva, golden Meru's lord,
great Yama, fine Maruti on his horse,
Viruna, Agni, demon-chief Kuvera,
the sky-illuminating sun and lustrous moon;

These gods eleven joined with one resolve
to make a holy Lord All-Knowing one
to come, protect, sustain and feed this world.
All gods vouch safe to help Him to succeed.

– Poem 'Yuan Phai'{Cushman, Richard (2000)}

The past and destiny of Thai people is engraved on the stones consumed for building the monuments in Sukhothai Kingdom. After their migration from Southern China, a phenomenon spread over centuries, Sukhothai was first truly liberated Thai kingdom. Prior to the establishment of the Sukhothai Kingdom in 1238, the area was known as Sukhodaya under Khmer empire which encompassed most part of modern Thailand at peak of its power. Sukhodaya, later Sukhothai, was a military outpost for Khmer empire at it's northwestern extent. Sukhodaya, a *Sanskrit* word, literally translates to "Dawn of Happiness". Thai people replaced the name Sukhodaya with Sukhothai, which is Thai version of Sukhodaya, with same meaning.

Pic (L) showcasing Indian style Stupa and Pic (R) Dharmachakra at Si Thep Historical Park, which dates back to Dvaravati period

I visited Sukhothai to understand the culture and the life during the times but, let's understand the sites and city first. This UNESCO world cultural site is situated in the lower northern region of Thailand, in that, the historic Town of Sukhothai and associated historic cities are located close by. Sukhothai was the political and administrative capital of the first Kingdom of Siam (now, Thailand) from 13th to 15th century. Si Satchanalai was the spiritual center of the kingdom and the site of numerous temples and Buddhist monasteries. Si Satchanalai was also the centre of the all-important ceramic export industry. The third town, Kamphaeng Phet, is located at the kingdom's southern frontier and had important military functions in protecting the kingdom from foreign intruders as well as providing security for the kingdom's extensive trading network. All three towns shared a common infrastructure to control water resources, and were linked by a major highway known as the Thanon Phra Ruang named after the king who constructed it.

In parallel world, Bharat was looted and plundered by the Sultanate period during this time. As a result of the Muslim invasion of Bharat around 712 AD, the Buddhist monks sought refuge in Nepal and Tibet. The Mughal invasion, loss of royal patronage, lack of reforms in brahmanic rituals in Hinduism lead to decline of Buddhism in Bharat {*Lars Fogelin (2015)*}. The Buddhism was almost choked in land of its birth and it revived, flourished and was embraced by kingdoms of Southeast Asia. To this account, Gurudev Rabindranath Tagore wrote a poem about Siam after his visit to the Kingdom of Siam in 1927. He wrote "I come, a pilgrim, at thy gate, O Siam, to offer my verse to the endless glory of India sheltered in thy home, away from her own deserted shrine, To bathe in the living stream that flows in thy heart, whose water descends from the snowy height of a sacred time on which arose, from the deep of my country's being, the Sun of Love and Righteousness." (*Kusalasaya, Karuna-Ruang Urai, 2001: 42*). Here, deserted shrine is referred to Buddhism in India and the sun of love and righteousness is Lord Buddha.

In Southeast Asia, Thai Kingdoms of Lopburi (literally meaning Monkey City), Sukhothai and Lan Na were competing against Indianised kingdoms like Mon, Khmer and Malay States. Si Intrahit took over throne of Sukhothai kingdom in 1238. Since kingdom was carved out of powerful Khmer empire, the general life was heavily influenced by Hindu and Buddhist rites and rituals. (***Early Thailand From Prehistory to Sukhothai by Charles Higham and Rachanie Thorasat***)

The kingdom was at peak of its spread under the reign of King Ramkhamhaeng, the great, who expanded Sukhothai to more or less present day Thailand with his influence as far as parts of Laos to the North and Malaysia to the south. King Ramkhamhaeng heavily served and mightily favoured the father and son relation between people and the King and therefore, stands tall as a respected figure across Thailand, even today. Any commoner with a grievance could ring the bell placed on the gate to seek audience with the King. The King would personally speak to the man and after examining the issue, passed the judgement. The King's approach to his subjects in Sukhothai Kingdom, by present ruling class in most parts of the world is unthinkable, even today. As I approached the statue, there was a well maintained pond in front, and a replica of the bell to the left of the statue. My Guide asked me to ring the bell, like everyone else, to seek blessing of the noble king. I rung the bell! The Sukhothai Kingdom didn't resembled present set up in tenor and texture in anyway except the geographical boundaries of land of Thai people.

In Sukhothai historical Park, King Ramkhamhaeng sits silent, watchful and hopeful that his ideas and legacy would continue to inspire generations of Thai people. I did spend five minutes carefully scanning posture of his statue holding stone tablet in one hand and, other hand postured to teach, indicating his fondness for education and diplomacy, at the historical park. The face appeared similar to Buddha image of Suhkothai period.

I asked the Guide about the relevance of two swords placed on the Thai tray next to the statue. He turned pensive, shook his head in unfamiliar fashion and said *"This statue was creatively imagined by Fine Arts Department in 1964 and human imagination, for all its greatness, has no limitations. This seems like a creative work. The place of monument was chosen near highway along old city wall based on historic relevance of the place. You, Indian people, believe in fate, how ironic, that monument was discovered in 1873 by Prince Mongkut, later king Rama IV, who at that time was an ordained monk. Mongkut while on pilgrimage to ancient city of Sukhothai, found stone tablet at the site of the old palace. The original tablet adorns the Bangkok National Museum. Almost 100 years later, his monument was inaugurated by kind and compassionate King Bhumibol; Princess Sirindhorn was in presence"*

However, if stone tablet indicates his love for literature, I assumed these swords would be his acceptance of the last mean to settle a dispute - 'Decision by the sword'. The Guide gave me to understand that the King inscribed these stone tablets to tell the story of Kingdom and his times. I was itching and struggling for the translation of stone tablets to English, when my Guide came to the rescue and standing behind me, he read *"In the times of King Ramkhamhaeng this land of Sukhothai is thriving. In the water there are fish, in the field there is rice. The ruler does not levy a tax on the people who travel along the road together, leading their oxen on the way to trade and riding their horses on the way to sell. Whoever wants to trade in horses on the way to sell. Whoever wants to trade in silver and gold, so trades...."*

My tourist Guide, an intelligent man in his sixties, was part of the minor restoration project of some of the sites. Surprisingly, these tablets remained undiscovered until 17 Jan 1833. It was during the reign of King Rama IV that the treasure was unearthed and, has been carefully guarded since then. January 17 is celebrated as the day of commemoration of King Ramkhamhaeng since 1833. The historical park is site to the yearly festival held to celebrate life and times of the King Ramkhamhaeng (Rama, the bold). When I was informed by the kind Guide about the festival in January at historical park, I vowed to return to the abode of the Brave king during festival. Return I did, and found the activities in festival culturally deep and pervasive; simulating life in ancient city, portraying fabulous prosperity of the Sukhothai.

When I traveled to Chiang Mai, the northern province of Thailand, I saw, in first hand, the huge respect and acceptance for the King Ramkhamhaeng by his people. In front of the Chiang Mai Culture Centre, is located the 'Three Kings Monument' dedicated to three founders of Chiang Mai. King of Lan Na, King of Phayao and King of Sukhothai Kingdom, joining hands together to form Kingdom of Siam. This monument has a mammoth symbolic significance for Thai people. This forms backdrop for the celebration of Thai monarchy in the northern region. I saw large number of people offering candles, flowers and incense to the three kings who came together to stitch what is present day Thailand.

My Guide injected a booster dose of history of the place, though, language was a barrier to start with but barrier fizzled out soon owing to the sign language, google translate and my B+certification in Thai language. In fact, the King Ramkhamhaeng is credited to give first Thai alphabet system which is slightly different from accepted and widely celebrated Thai script today. The stone tablet treasured at Bangkok National Museum has landed immense influence on the development of historiography of Thai kingdom. Therefore, Sukhothai kingdom is referred to as the "First Thai Kingdom". The inscription is considered, by historians, single most important document in Thai history and is inscribed on UNESCO's Memory of the World register which safeguards historical treasure from collective amnesia, wanted destruction, natural disasters and wilful neglect.

I wished the Guide well, offered my gratitude and a traditional lunch. Sometimes, a parting "Thank you" is not enough for people who willingly offer two most prestigious commodities - Time and Knowledge. And, therefore to spend some time off the site, I decided to have a meal and discussion with the Guide. I was contemplating what if stone tablet is an hagiography of King's life, orchestrated by himself.

To which Guide replied with a incisive smile and said "The stories about the historic Town of Sukhothai and associated sites are derived from a variety of sources. First and foremost among them is the authenticity of the architectural remains of temples and Buddhist monasteries which have been protected by custom since they were first constructed. Over their long history of about 1000 years, the sites, whether in use or otherwise, have been carefully maintained and timely repaired using traditional materials and methods. In 1960s, the sites were placed under direct control of Government and the Fine Arts Department has overseen all maintenance, conservation and repair work keeping in line with regulations of UNESCO world heritage site."

While relishing lunch, we exchanged ideas and notes about local food, family values, festivals, current events affecting entire world and the changes in Thai society. While I was making payment for lunch, the Guide, with puffed up chest, holding a 20 baht note remarked "King Ramkhamhaeng is virtuously seated at the back of the 20 Baht currency. His contribution to Thai script and codification of the law is remembered everyday".

Chapter III

Ayutthaya Kingdom

The whole city enjoyed happiness throughout all seasons.
Now it weighs heavily on my breast to see Ayutthaya
disappear.
Where can I find its equal?
It is as if a crystal has lost its shine,
Each day brings new destruction
How can its glory ever be restored?"

Brother of King Rama I, quoted in
Kunal Kishore (2016), Ayodhya revisited, ch 1.

In Nov 2018, Shri Yogi Adityanath, Chief Minister of Uttar Pradesh decided to rename Faizabad city to Ayodhya, eons ago which was capital city of Ikshvaku dynasty. The renaming of the city to Ayodhaya stirred emotions across Bharat, majority in favour, few went against the motion, too. Google can stimulate intellectual grains in people within some days of unstructured reading. It has grown fashionable to side with the less logical perspective under the garb of possessing 'intellectual seeds'. 'There is more than what meets the eye on this subject' or 'Ignorance is bliss' is pick up line for most pseudo intellectuals. For few lesser educated, go to phrase may vary but, the context remains unadjusted. One of the great scientists of our times Stephen Hawking very rightly said "the greatest enemy of knowledge is not ignorance, but the illusion of knowledge" By then, I was blissfully ignorant about powerful Kingdom of Ayutthaya which flourished from 1351 AD to 1761 AD in Thailand. But, I am certain that huge percent of population does not have faintest of idea about history of kingdom of Ayutthaya in Thailand.

We may, forcefully or willingly, deny our past connections, but we can't escape the truth being formed around us, because of the events in the past. In the bygone and unrecorded times of human history, all of us were together. Boundaries are, but a result of circumstances. Remember, the diplomatic relation between South Korea and Bharat were forged in 1973 AD but the cultural ties were brought to the table in 2000 AD, courtesy Ayodhya Connection which dates to 1st century AD. The time period consumed for realizing the historical connection between two countries is roughly 2000 years. Now, 2000 years appears long time to a generation which has a myopic memory and nearsighted vision. The myopic view could be because of unavailability of records, I am more worried about the nearsightedness to understand the grand design. Probably, because of this reason most politicians start their campaign only six months before, and do almost everything against the promises for next four years.

When I visited Ayodhaya in 2007, I passed by a dilapidated memorial of Queen Suriratna and it missed eye of most of the travelers to the city of Lord Rama. Since, I maintain a sustained love for clicking photographs since childhood, I sighted Queen Suriratna memorial in the insignificant background of a picture; a picture in which I had the limelight. But, the largely ignored memorial then, has gained attention of tourists from South Korea now. They come to city to pay homage to the Queen Suriratna memorial. And, of all the visitors and delegation from South Korea to visit memorial, most important delegation landed for Diwali 2018 lead by Kim Jung Sook, First Lady of Republic of Korea popularly known as 'Jolly Lady', on special invitation by Hon'ble Prime Minister Shri Narender Modi.

In first century AD, the Queen Suriratna, known as Heo Hwaing Ok in South Korea, from Ayodhaya took a arduous journey to marry King Suro of Gimhae, a town near Pusan (now called Busan) in present day South Korea. As the generations passed and lineage spread like roots of a fertile tree, today, supposedly more than 6 million people, especially Gimhae Kim, Heo and Incheon Yi clan trace their lineage to the legendary queen {*James Huntley Grayson (2001)*}. The cities are developed as sister cities for a 2000 years old connection in 21st century. My graciously growing up niece asked me if those two were husband and wife, why the cities are being developed as sister cities?

Ayodhya has better days ahead, as the city gets the gigantic temple of its most famous and cosmically celebrated King - Shri Ram (for Thai people, he is Si Phra Ram). A Indonesian friend introduced me to one more beautiful city named Ayodhaya in Indonesia. The name of the legendary city is Yogyakarta (which loosely means Maryada purshottam) which is named after birthplace of Lord Rama of Ayodhya, a city in Bharat. Yogyakarta is only city in Indonesia ruled by a monarchy and it is regarded as fulcrum of classical Javanese fine arts and culture. UNESCO world heritage site proudly has Prambana Temple compound of Yogyakarta in its list and, it is second biggest temple compound after Angkor Wat in South East Asia.

I hope sometime in near future these three cities, because of their historical linkage, are developed as sister cities. Even if this idea doesn't see light of the day, Reader must comprehensibly understand relation between the three ancient cities. Their beauty and majestic grandeur may have been injured by plunder and time lapse, but their spirit is not ravaged. We have effectively began archaeological survey, site studies and reconciliation societies a century back. That means, there is still much left to be discovered, unearth, find and connect the dots.

Let's get back to Ayutthaya story! An intelligent and kind friend Priyamwada, pursuing higher studies from International College in Mahidol University accompanied me for Ayutthaya sojourn. Remember! I met Priyamawada in India while she was on break.

While in Bharat, Ayodhya got its name and fame back recently, in Thailand the name of city itself is laden with holy titles. Phra Nakhon Si Ayutthaya literally meaning the holy city of Shri Ayodhaya (phra-Holy,Nakhon-Nagar,Si- Shri). After the death of great king Ramkhamhaeng, the Sukhothai kingdom slowly fell in to decline. In 1351, the great Kingdom of Ayutthaya, a neighbouring Thai polity till then, rose to power invading Sukhothai. Wherever and whenever, exists vacuum in power politics, power of politics is seized by another entity. Sometime, vacuum, that wholesome nothingness, is much better than the matter that replaces it. The power of polity was seized by Kingdom of Ayutthaya, and they ruled until they were made part of the same vacuum by the Burmese attack in 1767.

While the Ayutthaya in Thailand was entering age of peace and prosperity in 16th century, the soul of Shri Ayodhaya in Bharat was humiliated, sacked and caged. The Temple of Shri Ram in Ayodhaya was razed to the ground and was replaced by a mosque named after Babur in 1529. It took an overwhelming Hindu majority country 500 years to liberate birthplace of their most cherished god, Lord Rama. So much to honour democratic principles!

Priyamwada said, standing next to the ruins of Ayutthaya "Faith and Time are instrument of God; he owns them. He uses it vibrantly to teach people a lesson. Faith, like love can guide men not to be bad but, can not force them to be good. Babur, who claimed love for God by destroying a temple, died within one year of Babri construction. Don't you see? There are vibrations of both kind, positive and negative. Have you ever felt that? That, there are many ways to reach God, and no one is the final path. Now, they have constructed Rama temple, if they ever understand the law of wheel, there could be a mosque again after four centuries from now. Our societal memory has turned gilded and myopic. We don't see beyond 100 years. The people celebrating construction of temple today utterly failed to understand that the construction of mosque was approached with equal grandeur and aplomb."

I was all in appreciation of her clarity of thoughts and sophisticated understanding of the intangibles. Today, once majestic and magnificent city of Ayutthaya stand in ruins and, Ayutthaya historical park, an archaeological site, Buddhist temples and monasteries is all that is left. Simply gazing at the ruins, I gave air to my imagination - What would this city have been like at its prime, celestial! Palatial!

"A monument past its better times, like the fruits past their shelf lives, like the leaves detached from twig" said Priyamwada in a confirmatory tone. Like most students of Philosophy, she never speaks straight but in riddles and always up for dialogue heavy conversation.

Ayutthaya was strategically placed to become the capital city of the Kingdom and, it is encircled by Chao Phraya, Pasak and Lopburi rivers. The first ruler of the kingdom, King Uthong or Ramathibodi I (Ramathibodi was honorific title meaning "Overlord Rama") made two important contributions - the establishment and promotion of Theravada Buddhism as official religion and compilation of the Dharamashastra, a legal code based on Hindu sources and traditional Thai customs.(***Chris Baker and Pasuk Phongpaichit, 2017***) This was the time when Manusmriti, the Hindu legal code, was not even followed in Bharat, the land of its genesis. The Manusmriti, a legal treatise by Manu, was out of favour in Bharat until Britishers used it as a way to administer Bharat {***Donald Davis (2010) and P Bilimoria (2011)***}. It suited their divide and rule policy by having different set of legal laws for Hindus and Muslims.

<u>Foreign Encampments During Ayutthaya Period</u> While the Portuguese came to India in 1498, their first contact with Ayutthaya, known as Kingdom of Siam in West, was established in 1511. By then, Portuguese were already a established power in Bharat, and were pursuing three headed agenda of combating Islam, spreading Christianity and secure trade of spices by building a Portuguese Asian empire{***Brockey, Liam Matthew (2008)***}. In pursuance of the third agenda, Alfonso Albuquerque who was Governor of Goa sent a mission, lead by a tailor named Duarte Fernandes to Ayutthaya. King Ramathibodi II accepted the Portuguese mission honorably and, subsequently gave them trading rights and post at various places like Ayutthaya, Pattani, Nakhon Si Thammarat in exchange of guns.

"Probably, the acceptance could be act of 'Premeditatio Malorum' by King Ramathibodi II as the Portuguese successfully captured trading post at Malacca" said Priyamwada, showing me a detailed map of Ayutthaya Kingdom and trade routes.

These Portuguese settlements were occupied by military men and traders. They bravely fought alongside King in 1534 against the Burmese, offering personal protection and military advise and won many commercial and residential privileges from the King in return. They were allotted quarters in the south of the city of Ayutthaya where we were standing. Across the Chao Phraya river and opposite to Portuguese village is Japanese settlement. Up North, was English and Dutch settlement which was laid barren during the Burmese offensive of 1767. All these encampments were given place outside the city to keep them comfortably away from state politics and, near enough to avail their services to stay in power and fight wars.

The Portuguese settlement was bulldozed during the Burmese offensive of 1767. Some Portuguese were taken hostage, remaining followed King Taksin the great to area Kudi Jeen in Thonburi, and worked as language translators for the state. On a later date, I visited Kudi Jeen area with Priyamwada, and met Mr Renangkul at Thanusingha Bakery. He ordered Kudi Jeen Caucasian sweet and it tasted unlike any other Thai dessert. Mr Rengangkul said "We have cross bred with Thai and adopted Thai names. De Silvas became Ne Silawan, de Jesus become Yesu and here I am, de Reina sitting in front of you as Mr Rengangkul".

During my research for this book, I laid my hands on latest edition of "A history of Thailand" coauthored by Mr Chris Baker and his wife Pasuk Phongpaichit. He has spoken very profusely about the "The eulogy of King Prasat Thong" discovered in 1988 and, has termed it as the most important Thai literary find of 20th century. He has painstakingly translated the text from Thai to English. There was a major change fanned by the King Prasat Thong, who claimed lineage to Khmers, about the status of King and subjects. The people took solace and celebrated their reach to monarchy in Sukhothai Kingdom and Ayutthaya kingdom till this point. King Prsat Thong was a staunch believer of God King (Dev Raja) model and, this was remarkably reflected in the royal eulogy named as such. The main events are legendary- shuffling of time (literally, may be God can only stop time, he literally retarded time), a large 'alms giving' and a military parade. I have attempted to capture essence of the royal eulogy written by his *Purohit* and translated by Chris Baker and his wife, published in Journal of Siam Society. Here it is,

"He governs the people, gods and humans in great numbers and enough elephants, horses, and troops to fill the oceans.May well-being, peace and joy increase for the reigning king, the best of men, the supreme lord, enjoying bliss. Rulers from all three worlds come to offer praise, pay respect, and bow heads in prayer for favour to the feet of the great ruler, lord over all three worlds The tenth of the Buddhas, like the great boddhisatta, Metteyya (Matsya Avatar of Lord Vishnu), left the palace of the gods to be born in a royal lineage, to be a great king, whose glory spreads far and wide,decreed to be a supreme emperor of famed power in the holy city of gates, possessing the solar wealth, the royal authority, in great splendour, to strengthen the religion of the Buddha beyond reckoning, beyond imagination. According to the Pancaka, the year of the tiger, tenth of the decade, can be changed to a year of the pig. This will bring about great and complete auspiciousness, changing tiger

to pig, and establishing it as first of the decade;establishing the First Caitra,104 as indicated in the Pancaka, the first waxing in the first year of the decade, the day as a Monday." {**Chris Baker and Pasuk Pongkhongchit,2017**).

He was single highhandedly responsible to elevate monarchy in to new form of royal absolutism. His eulogy recounts the King's dream of naming his palace after Lord Indra's palace, *Vejyanta* (*Phaichaiyon* in Thai). He compared every aspect of his life to the future incarnation of Lord Vishnu. He mystified the new kingship by concealing the royal body, and glorified it through grand ceremonial, including the *Indrabhiseka* and the pilgrimage to the Buddha Footprint. *Yuan Phai* may be the oldest work of literature from Siam, most likely written after a battle fought in approximately 1475. I was privileged to attend a narration of this poem by Dr Chris Baker at The Siam Society in Bangkok. He is an authority on Thai literature, who has painstakingly translated many thai seminal works to English. The poem recounts minute details of fifteenth-century events not found elsewhere. It has the earliest and most detailed description of a Siamese army, the most luxuriant eulogy of an early Thai monarch, and a fascinating discussion of the concept of loyalty. The scenes of personal treachery, quiet heroism, bloody combat, and looting after victory give an detailed image of early Siam and its culture. Earlier kings had patronized the religion and people, but Prasat Thong made an definitive claim to divine personification and used the swollen royal revenues to dramatize his claim to grandeur.

Ayutthaya Flourishes

King Narsuen, the Great (*Reign 1590-1605*) At the King Narai National Museum in Lopburi province, there are enough documented evidence to prove that 16th century European travelers called Ayutthaya one of the three great powers of Asia alongside Vijayanagar empire and China. Unfortunately, Vijayanagar empire, which at its peak had more spread than Mughal Empire, have captured only a chapter in Indian Education curriculum and, even smaller place in our national conscience.

The Portuguese received privilege from the king Narsuen, the great, to establish Portuguese settlement in the south of Ayuthaya. Later in 1602, Dutch company established a trading post in south of Ayutthaya by royal decree. Priyanwada sighted a copy of mural painting at a defunct temple, temple Yom, in Ayutthaya, painted in 1897 (original painting in 1681) depicting a row of Japanese royal guards who accompanied the royal processions. There were many reasons for the Japanese migration to Siam - freedom to openly practice Christianity, and employment of master less Samurai who fled Japan. King Narsuen, the great, allowed Japanese to settle in Siam and establish their community on the bank of Chao Phraya river, south of city of Ayutthaya.

In Wat Suawaran Dwaram in Ayutthaya, there are fascinating details of time and exploits of King Narsuen the Great displayed on murals. Priyamawada started explaining one of these murals which depicted two kings mounted on elephants engaged in duel 'The battle scene between King Naresuan of Thailand and Mingyi Swa of Burma is a highly romanticized historical scene famous as 'Elephant Battle'. But see, to us, it's not very fascinating . We have grown up with stories of elephant fights. Remember! Mauryan King,

Chandragupta is said to have a military of 600,000 infantry, 30,000 cavalry, 8000 chariots and 9,000 war elephants beside elephants.' The elephants in "musth" fought fiercely and King Nursuen defeated King Ming wayi with a sleight of sword'{***Damrong (2001)***}

The other prominent murals in Wat (temple) depicted King entering Kingdom of Bago on elephant and his death procession. This was age of warfare and King Naresuan remains the greatest of Ayutthaya kings in battlefield. He is highly revered and, I found his name immortalized by naming dams, wild life sanctuaries, HTMS ships, schools, monuments, bank notes, movies and plays after him. His monuments stand tall and proud at Royal Thai Army headquarters, Suphan Buri (literally meaning Heaven City) and, the Ancient City. I have credit of visiting all three major monuments of King Naresuan, who fought with his men, for his country. There is a documentary filmed on the life and times of King Naresuan which became an instant hit. His stories of courage and valour are remembered with a puffed up chest by Thai people.

King Narai, the Great (1656-1688) Metaphorically speaking, if Ayutthaya is a beautiful tree, Lopburi is strong depiction of leaves of that tree. Lopburi (literally meaning "Monkey City") is one of the Thailand's continuously inhabited oldest settlements with an unbroken chronology of social and historical developments. It's colourful beginning is privy to prehistoric times, no less than 3500 years old continuing to periods of recorded history- from Dvaravati periods in 7th century to Lopburi periods under khmer control to Ayuthaya kingdom and, the present day Bangkok. At the King Narai national museum, there are enough evidence on display for authenticating the continuous parading of human civilization since prehistoric times in Lopburi.

The archaeological findings from Lopburi has human skeletons, stone, pottery and ornaments made from animal bones dating to prehistoric times. However, the Dvaravati period from 7th to 11th century is considered dawn of Thai history, when writing was put down for the first time and urban communities emerged from village level settlements. This period was heavily influenced by Indian civilization. The Dvaravati period allowed Khmers to leave their imprint on the city and which can be seen even today. The Yam sod temple and Phra Si Rattana Mahathat temple, I could see astounding similarity between Indian architectural style, which heavily influenced Khmer empire. The influence was not limited to architecture but, the religion, traditions, culture and art.

It was around the waning of the Khmer empire in 14th century that a new power centre emerged in south of Lopburi - the kingdom of Ayutthaya. And, fortunes smiled and embraced Lopburi again during the reign of King Narai of Ayuthaya. King Narai built a royal palace as his residence and renovated several temples. While renovating the erstwhile Khmer Temples, he was careful in propagating Buddhism by adding Buddhist pavilion or statue to these temples and rewriting the history. It was during his reign, Lopburi was alleviated to the status of second capital, for the king often spent up to 8 months each year. After the death of King Narai, the city went in to decline, only to rise again during the reign of King Rama IV of Chakri Dynasty.

Of the three decades King Narai reigned, first decade was consumed in uniting and consolidating on Lan Na and Mon territory. The second decade was primarily dedicated to building foreign relations with countries such as China, Netherlands, England, Iran and countries around Bay of Bengal. By third decade, he forged close relationship with the court at Isfahan in Iran and the court of Versailles in France. The close relationship with the west brought modern technology such as fortification, cannon casting, mapping the navigation, astronomy to Thailand. About more than hundred years before the reign of King Narai, Babur, founder of Mughal Empire, used gunpowder canons in the Battle of Panipat against Lodhi sultanate. That is, first recorded use of gunpowder in sub continent. Close to the end of his reign, French successfully persuaded for a military camp in Bangkok and unsuccessfully, nudged to convert King Narai to Christianity (***Chakrabongse, 1960***). History may not repeat itself, it does rhyme. If he would have embraced Christianity, Thailand today would have praised the cross and pantheon of its Gods, similar to Philippines.

I came across a intricately detailed painting in gold on a black lacquer in King Narai National Museum, depicting two figures, Aurangzeb of Mughal Empire and Louis XIV of France. The associated literature indicated close relationship between Mughal Empire, Persians and Ayutthaya kingdom. Trade unites us all, more so people with differences. In fact, standing at the ruins of Ambassador pavilion in King Narai Palace, Lopburi, I could sense architectural influence of Mughal empire. Those archways, doors, channeled water fountains are so much a claim of Mughal architecture.

Most of the literature of Ayutthaya kingdom was on non-durable material like paper and palm leaves. So, most of the literature is either deteriorated or burned during wars. However, the King Narai, the great, era is considered golden period of Thai literature.

Priyamwada said, shifting her gaze towards me "During King Narai reign, he couldn't manage trading of printing press which was discovered in China in 9th century (*Gutenberg, a German, claimed the achievement in 1434*) in spite of having good relations with west as well as China. Remember! golden age of Indian literature, astronomy, philosophy was about a thousand years back during Gupta period. They were masters of most subjects".

I consider, invention of printing press one of the biggest and most productive invention of those times. It literally pulled Europe out of Dark Age.

Priyamwada, a staunch critique of European colonization said "Europe came out of Dark age and pushed almost every part of the world in Dark Age to fend for themselves. The colonial masters, they patterned human lives in all aspects. We, humans, are not designed for a specific pattern but, we live and upgrade as we experience life. Such was, White Men Burden!"

Many famous literary works of the Ayutthaya kingdom include Jindamanee (first Thai grammar book), Anirut Kham Chan (tale of prince Anirudha), royal barge procession songs and folk songs. Chris Baker and his wife, during a lecture in Siam Society, Bangkok beautifully narrated the English version (which they translated from Thai) of five epic poems of Thai literature namely *Yuan Phai, Lilit Phra Lo, Ocean Lament, Twelve Months and Nirat*. King Narai introduced astronomy to Thailand as he himself was a keen student of poetry and astronomy. He sent an diplomatic assignment to the court of King Louis XIV to bring one telescope, a globe and astronomical equipment from Paris.

The Ayuthaya Kingdom inherited God king concept from Khmers who were highly influenced by Hindu traditions. The royal procession had strict regulations to maintain the grandeur of Kingship which was designed to portray the King as an incarnation of Lord Vishnu. M de Choisy, a member of the french mission to Thailand, writes in 1685, after witnessing one of the royal procession by river of 200 royal barge each one with 150 oars, said "The splendid procession I joined might be similar to a procession of Pharaoh of Egypt along the Nile". Also, this quote from a republican dutch suitably portrays the God King "This reverence is better becoming of a celestial deity than an earthly majesty."

Medical treatment during the Ayuthaya Kingdom and specifically during reign of King Narai was two kinds - Traditional Thai practise, and the Western Practise. A copy of the pharmacopoeia text of King Narai inscribed on palm leaves at King Narai National Museum mentions the name of the nine royal doctors who were master of Thai, Chinese, Indian traditional medicines as well as European medicine. Thai doctors did not perform any surgical operations but treated the illnesses with potions they had learnt from their ancestors. Some similarity, there!

Fall of Ayutthaya Kingdom   While coming out of the King Narai museum, Priyamwada said "The rise and fall of empires is certain, as sun rising from East. This statement in all its essence, is a cardinal truth. Most godly and established empires were uprooted and discarded to the bottomless netherworld when the time came. Precisely for this reason, I subscribe to the idea of the American political scientist Samuel Huntington that any civilization which felt that their idea of organizing a society has no scope of improvement, would be doomed. Ayutthaya was no different".

I understood her statement and emotions behind it, at once, but I wanted entire rationale behind this thought, "Why a great empire such as Ayutthaya crumbled like pack of cards with in years from her real economic, socio-political emergence?"

She continued in same vein with similar rhythm "The presence of Europeans through out King Narai's reign was reason for voluminous literature generated by Europeans on kingdom of Ayutthaya. They were all in awe and truly inspired by the beauty of Ayutthaya, and we saw literature showering exorbitant praise for the city. The Royal palaces and hundreds of temples were within the confines of the island on which city flourished. The Kings who succeeded King Narai closed the doors for foreign elements except for missionaries and conducted a modest trade with them. Ayuthaya embarked on a close door policy for next 100 years"

I remembered a similar act of 'close door policy' from William Bernstein's "A splendid exchange-how trade shaped the world". I willingly interrupted and said "After the death of Chinese Admiral Zheng He in 1431, Ming dynasty resorted to Confucianism and closed themselves to the world. The Confucian courtiers began a campaign to systematically destroy records of 'Treasure fleet' voyages. But, history has a strong character, it never dies, it subtly give lessons. The colonial history of the world would have been different than our own, had it not been for the decisive blunder of the Ming dynasty because Zheng He ruled the waves much before Europe's Age of Exploration. By shutting the door, Ming dynasty missed an opportunity to become established naval power, and perhaps a chance to replace Europeans as dominant naval power. China, when finally emerged from her 200 years of slumber, it saw a world in which ruler of 'All under heaven, Middle Kingdom' was inferior on water, while European ruled the waves."

Priyamwada continued from where she left "Perfect example (looking at me in appreciation) I suppose, close door policy reaped similar dividends for Kingdom of Ayutthaya. This allowed Kings to focus on cultural and religious affairs which ushered in Ayutthaya kingdom golden age during the reign of King Borommakot from 1733 to 1758. These years of peace turned breeding ground for literature and arts, like never before. During this period, Sri Lanka invited Thai monks to purify Sinhalese Sangha, reversing the past religious roles of the two countries. The King had wholesome control over religious affairs"

I was wondering, what on the earth a spiritual monk and King, has in common? Note that, only in Hindu civilization were religion and politics so distinctly defined and practised. In Islam, God is King; in China and Japan, King is God; in orthodox Christianity, God is King's junior brother.

Priyamwada said, indicating for a short break "While Thailand was in slumber, a village headman united the third Burmese empire, and attacked Ayutthaya in 1760 to kiss partial success and embrace major setback. His comeback was thumping in 1767 and, not only he won Ayutthaya, he set fire to the whole city and expunged four centuries of Thai civilization history. Displaying utter disregard for their common religion, Burmese set fire to rich temples and melted down all available gold from Buddha images. (***Chris Baker and Pasuk Phongpaichit, 2017***). Ayutthaya was laid to rest. In fact, the last and avoidable nail in the coffin was clearing up ruins and remains, for construction of capital at Bangkok. The annihilation was complete and metaphorical."

Chapter IV

Rise of Taksin's Cult and Self Crafted Fall

Drink water and remember the source
- A Thai proverb

During 17th century, a small fishing town of wild olive grooves found it's importance as trade and defense outpost for Ayutthaya empire. It was known as Bangkok. The human settlement straddled on both banks of Chao Phraya river, where the canal widened in to main stream river. On the west bank of river, a locality named Thonburi, grew in importance and power as the seat of power shifted from Ayutthaya to Thonburi, sooner than Burmese thought. To unravel the labyrinth of Thonburi, Priyamwada and self decided to take the story to heart of one of the many districts of present day Bangkok - Thonburi.

From her previous experience of traveling to Thonburi, Priyamwada insisted on a boat tour of Thonburi's famous spots via meandering canals. For right reasons, Bangkok is called Venice of the East. The canal system in Bangkok is thoughtful, systematic and incredibly helpful in design.

*Wat Arun, (in sight) Thonburi on a Ferry across
Chao Phraya River*

While on ferry to Thonburi seating by her side, I asked Priyamwada, who was well dressed for a long and exhaustive travel plan, "Did these canals always existed in their present form? Only nature is capable of designing beauty, as elaborate as these canals, without damaging environment."

She came close and said (the running commentary on the boat was disturbing) "Both, nature and men did it together. Chao Phraya river have two horseshoe shape canals namely Bangkok Noi and Bangkok Yai canals which slowed down trading ships. In 1542, the bight of the horseshoe was connected for both canals by digging a small canal across the base of the meandering canal. *(Steve Van Beek: The Chao Phya, p.39)* The strength of the current helped erosion of these new canal banks and the river took the present course. However, the internal canals were dug in 18th century when capital shifted from Ayuthaya to Thonburi. Although, you may have seen ferry caressing across these canals in pictures, grasping real beauty is impossible, until you visit. Agreed?" I did agree in totality.

The boating offered a view of many monuments of Thonburi lined up along Chao Phraya river on platter for visitors to relish. First among them was appealing Santa Cruz cathedral. An impressive monument featuring Italian design constructed with cream stones (renovated) by Chinese for Portuguese with permission by King Taksin in 1767. Next, the shimmering white fort on the edge of the Chao Phraya River was built in 1688 during reign of King Narai for protection of Ayutthaya from attackers. It now acts as the Royal Thai Navy Headquarters. A prominent flagpole flying Naval Ensign is on display since 1971 and a fellow passenger informed that the fort serves ceremonial purpose of firing gun salutes since 1979, when Memorial bridge was permanently lowered, preventing RTN ships to sail upriver to perform the task. The most prominent and important feature of the skyline towards Thonburi are five towers dotted with colourful tiles of the Temple of the Dawn, Wat Arun. This temple was within the Taskin's residential complex, and is one of the monuments that lure tourists from around the world. We could smell and sense the traditional Thai way of life in local villages hugging the canals, quaint floating markets. We disembarked the ferry and foot walked our way into the heart of Thai way of life.

We encountered a Mosque, temple, Gurdwara within a good sprint distance of each other.

I observed "Before this, only in Bharat, I experienced not only the close proximity of religious places of various faiths but, their acceptance in totality"

Priyamwada said, making way for a speeding motorbike "Problem is never with religion, but with the fanatically religious. A religion to a man is what tea is to an Indian, absence of it creates a serious sense of disability"

We reached a 200 year old wooden house on canal edge, known as Artist's house, in time for the Thai puppetry show. At the backyard of Artist's house, we sat with legs dangling in water and hands holding cup of coffee.

I said "I visited the cave in Nakhon Si Thammarat province that sheltered King Taksin when he fled from Burmese and rebounded like a true warrior. Does Taskin really shifted capital to this beautiful place because he saw old king prophesying in night dream."

Priyamwada said, throwing a crumb of bread in water to feed fishes "Not certain, but strategic considerations were more weighted in his decision rather than supernatural ones. Thonburi proximity to sea facilitated trade, procurement of arms, and make defense and withdrawal easier in case of re-attack by Burmese. In fact, even in contemporary times, Myanmar shifted capital from Yangon to Naypyidaw citing Yangon's overcrowding and vulnerability to natural disasters as primary reason. Indonesia also plans to shift from Jarkarta to Nusantara in East Kalimantan to diversify economic activity and reduce congestion.(**New York Times, 16 May 23**) For Taskin, who expelled the Burmese occupation with in seven months, it would have been more than mere allegiance to a dream."

I asked her instantly, as she finished "Why he could not seed an empire or initiate a dynasty rule like his predecessors?"

Priyamwada said "His own arrogance and imbecility! In last years of his reign, he relied heavily and entrusted absolute command on two brothers Chao Phrya Chakri and Chao Phraya Sarasih for military campaigns. They brought laurels and huge lands as price to King Taskin by liberating Chiang Mai and rest of northern Thailand from Burmese rule. In fact, they brought Cambodia and most of the present day Lao under Thai sovereignty. It was from this Laotian campaign that Phraya Chakri brought famed Emerald Buddha from Vientiane to Thonburi in 1779 *{Eric Roeder(1999)}*. Emerald Buddha called so because of colour and not composition, has an faith defining journey. Emerald Buddha is most sacred of Buddha images for Thai people, and their faith has it that the Buddha ensures independence and prosperity of their nation."

I said, gently ruffling water with my legs "I don't know much, but Emerald Buddha has historical connection with Bharat. Did the two Generals defected and removed Taskin?"

Priyamwada said, finishing her Coffee "He, for no reason or rhyme, turned paranoid and self declared himself as Bodhisattva (future Buddha). The transition from a strong and just leader to cruel and insane leader was probably because of overexertion or strain of continuous war. He flogged monks who didn't paid obeisance to him and brutally tortured his family and officials to make them confess to imaginary crimes.*{Journal of M. Descourvieres, 21 Dec,1782}*. A well planned revolt sidelined Taksin; later executed and General Chakri assumed Kingship on 6 April -a day celebrated annually as Chakri Day- and established the reigning Chakri dynasty."

We came back from the pier, richer and satisfied.

Chapter V

Chakri Dynasty

"I don't care if they protest against the government but they cannot touch the monarchy."

**– Titipol Phakdeewanich,
Dean Of Political Science, Ubon Ratchathani University**

I was soaking tremendous pressure to meet timelines for the book. Priyamwada, while we were headed towards Grand Palace said "Pressure is normal state of nature. Everything that exists here is under pressure of some kind, it is law of equilibrium. A diamond is a piece of charcoal that handled pressure exceptionally well. Honestly, every journey is about taking next step. Just do that."

We entered the Grand Palace, the seat of Chakri dynasty. It was amusing to read notice "Foreigner-500 Baht, Thai national and children below 120cm height – Free". This is the only place which offers free entry not as per age or sex, but height. The Grand Palace complex, a huge compound in the heart of Bangkok, consists of royal and throne halls, a number of government offices as well as renowned temple of Emerald Buddha. We were to meet, Professor Purushottam, an octogenarian who is almost as old as constitutional monarchy in Thailand, near Amarindra Hall in Outer Court. The Grand Palace has Outer and Inner court. Outer court has many impressive buildings such as Amrindra Hall where as in Inner court royal family lived and conducted private affairs. Priyamwada, rightly, dedicated two seating with Professor each covering five kings of Chakri dynasty. Priyamwada and self, bowed (Wai gesture) in respect to the Professor, who was on wheelchair and appeared strong and positive.

Rattanakosin Era (1782-1932)

Professor spoke, tilting his neck slightly towards us "Amarindra Hall was residence of the King Rama I, but now it houses collection of historical artifacts."

I was stuck at the rationale for the name "Chakri" and need to shift capital from Thonburi to Bangkok.

Professor replied with immense calmness "Prior to General Chakri presiding over the throne, Rama I held title of Chakri, the civil chancellor for many years. The king himself chose "*Chakri*" as the name for his dynasty. The emblem of the house is composed of the discus (*Chakra*) and the trident (*Trishul)*, the celestial weapons of the Lord *Vishnu* and Lord *Shiva*. Rama I accomplished the shifting of capital and Emerald Buddha across the river from Thonburi to Bangkok (Bangkok literally means 'Place of Olive Plums; in Thai Ban means house and Makok means Olive Plums). As Emerald Buddha was shifted, a new word was added to official name of the city[1] – Krung Thep Phra Maha Nakorn Amorn Rattanakosin… (Bangkok, city of Angels, Abode of Ratan). The shift of capital was ordered due to its better strategic location in defenses against Burmese invasions from the West, the area was protected from attack by the river to the west and by a series of canals along other three directions. The eastern side was surrounded by low marshlands inhabited by the Chinese, who were shifted to present day Chinatown."

Priyamwada asked with the intelligence of a brilliant student "Professor, what is his legacy other than commissioning Chakri dynasty."

Very politely, Professor replied "He gave Bangkok to the world and Emerald Buddha to Bangkok, Isn't that sufficient? But, modern Thailand is indebted to him for his outstanding and courageous effort for cultural revival programme. He appointed commission of experts to assemble fragments of historical and religious importance which survived destruction of Ayutthaya."

Priyamwada said "He gave heart and lungs to Bangkok, if we consider Bangkok in human form. But, I think , King Rama I would have been proud to list written version of Ramakein (Thai version of Ramayana) as his proud legacy *(Lipi Ghosh, 2017).*"

Professor rolled his hand over head, cleared his eyeglasses and throat and spoke "Old age is getting better of me. Agreed! The Indian epic Ramayana had played an important role in mooring Indian culture in Thailand. In fact, no other piece of literature has more profoundly affected the way of Thai life than Ramayana. The Thai version of Ramayana known as *Ramakien* (Rama's story) is part of Thai folklore since 13th century as mentioned in stone Inscription No. 1 and No. 2 of Sukhothai ruler Ramkhamhaeng, who took his name from Lord Rama. A number of versions of the epic were lost during annihilation of Ayuthaya in 1767 by Burmese. Rama I painstakingly collected the literature and prepared present Ramakein version in 1797. You would see Ramakein story portrayed through beautiful murals around Temple of Emerald Buddha, at walking distance from where we sit. Oh! I mean, wheel chair distance too. Remember, breathing and walking are two supremely neglected and underrated acts of humans. In fact, Rama II (ruled 1809-1824), a great artist and poet, completed the Ramakein, with large section composed by him. At his court, he introduced classical dance troupes of *Khon* and *Lakorn,* largely influenced by Ramakein.

Carefully shifting Professor's wheel chair to tree shed, I asked "Tell us more about reign of Rama II and Rama III"

Professor conveyed gratitude for the gesture and said "Rama II and Rama III consolidated the boundaries of the Kingdom. Rama II established relations with the West which were in limbo since end of King Narai's reign. During his reign Portuguese opened first western embassy in Bangkok in 1820. Rama III continued to open Thailand borders to foreigners and promoted trade with China. Did you notice tiles at temple Arun? The easy availability of Chinese porcelain led him to decorate temple Arun (and other temples) with porcelain fragments. He also incorporated western medicine to Thailand and small pox vaccination."

I asked , carefully, without annoying Professor "Is the story in Hollywood movie 'The King and I' and 'Anna and the King of Siam' true about King Mongkut, Rama IV (ruled 1851-1868)?"

Professor said, with a grin expression "Nothing could be farther from truth! He became most famous king of Thailand because of these movies where he was portrayed as a bald-headed, frivolous and insane despot. He wanted his children to benefit from English language and he hired services of Anna Leonowens *(**Habegger, 2014**)*. The self-elevated governess greatly exaggerated her role and dehumanize King Mongkut in her autobiographical writing. Look, how the information changed hands - 1956 film *The King and I* is based on the 1946 film *Anna and the King of Siam* which is based on a 1944 novel by an American author, drawn from Leonowens' memoirs from her years (1862-1867) at King Mongkut's court. What do you think now? (smiling)

I said, handing over a bottle of water to Professor "Reel and real life are different and there exits gulf of mismatch in stories about King Mongkut. But, the most infamous German chancellor once said 'If you tell a lie big enough and keep repeating it, people will eventually come to believe it'. But Rama IV life as ordained monk and post voluntary defrocking has lot of contrast?"

Priyamwada said, taking bottle back from Professor, and after having a sip herself "Simply put, it could be a result of different responsibilities on both sides of the spectrum. We all change roles and character in this one big act called Life, right? As a king, his focus would have been to manage a sense of stability and continuity, national identify, unity and pride whereas as a monk it would be been very different but, not without challenges.

Professor said, who have a very deep understanding of Buddhist way of life "I only partially agree that he was different in two roles. As a monk he practised celibacy whereas on becoming king he fathered 82 children. In that, he was different. He practiced austere monkhood for 27 years and had unique experience to roam as a commoner among the populace. He began a reform movement for reinforcing the Vinaya law that evolved in to Dhammayutta Nikaya sect, most powerful sect. As a King, he realized that traditional Thai values would not save his country from western imperialism. He sensed possibility of outbreak of war with European powers, taking cue from Anglo-Chinese war. He ordered the nobility to wear shirts while attending his court to show that Thailand was a "modern" nation. Previously, Siamese nobles were forbidden to wear shirts to prevent them from hiding any weapons in it and met the king bare-chested. He saw Chinese succumbing to British during second opium war and drew his lesson. He proactively signed Bowring Treaty in 1855 with British granting extraterritorial privileges, a duty of only 3 percent on imports, and permission to bring in Indian opium duty free. And, as a result, when King Mongkut lifted state monopoly on rice, it suddenly became Thailand's go to export product"

I said, occupying a seat at a lower pedestal than Professor "So, he brought western education and methods in Thailand to keep Europeans at bay. I understand that King Mongkut had seed for history, geography, sciences and especially astronomy."

Priyamwada said, pointing at me "This was time when Lord Macaulay introduced English education to Bharat, and made an inroad in the strong and successful civilizational traditions. They had blessings of the Queen of England to spread the idea of British supremacy and shed a bit of 'White men's Burden'"

Professor said, cutting her short "But King Mongkut, Rama IV acted wise and never allowed shadow of colonization to fall on the Kingdom of Thailand. Will you buy that his favourite hobby, astronomy, was the indirect cause of his untimely end."

Priyamwada said "My all time favourite holy text Bhaghwad Gita emphasizes the concept of 'detached attachments. An excess of everything is an invitation to suffering"

Professor said, clearing his throat, and waiting for a few seconds before he responded "But a King is a King! From observatories at his favourite palaces, the Summer Palace at Bang Pa-in and the palace on the hill at Petchaburi province, he successfully calculated and predicted a total eclipse of the sun on 18 Aug 1868. Mongkut triumph raised his esteem and standing among western residents and eastern astrologers alike. But, this jubilation was short lived. Both, King Mongkut and heir to the throne, Chulalongkorn, later Rama V contracted Malaria during this trip down the coast and King Mongkut died two months later. Chulalonglorm survived and adorned the throne as King Rama V."

With a sense of elation, I said to Priyamwada "Remember, Khao Sam Roi Yot (Mountain of 300 peaks) park in Petchaburi province! The sky above this park is witness to the exact astronomical calculation (four minutes off) shown to the governor of Singapore and other member of Bangkok court by King Mongkut.

Professor continued, sipping medicinal beverage from his tumbler "Chulalongkorn, Rama V (ruled 1868-1910) was only 15 when he ascended throne but reigned for 42 years with honour and authority. He transformed the fate of Kingdom from a backward Asian land to a modern 20th century Kingdom. He revolutionized his court by ending regressive custom of prostration and allowed officials to sit on chairs during royal audiences. He replaced the age old custom of corvee labour *(Chris Baker, Phasuk Phongpaichit (2017)* with direct taxation. Like these, he embarked on the path of social revolution of his court. You understand corvee labour? You believe Rajayog in a Kundalini?"

I replied instantly, leaving nothing to chance "Corvee labour was a state imposed law according to which selected individuals would serve as unpaid forced labour, lasting for limited period of time, generally only a fixed number of days each year. This was a form of slavery. And, slavery is an indelible and abysmal blot on human conscience. In Bharat, the British slaved people with debt bond, by which millions of people from Bharat were transported to British colonies to labour in British farms on a minimum wage"

Priyamwada remarked "Leave British or any other colonial master, today there are more number of slaves around the world, in some form, than any other time in human history. Some are forced into physical labour and others choose mental slavery. Back to Rajayoga, the lines in palm has destiny inscribed on them. There is Amla yoga, Gajalakshmini Yoga , Indraraja Yoga and many other. King Rama V would be rich with Indraraja yoga which destines a person to become King like, courageous, intelligent, skilled and famous.

Professor passed a satisfied look and said "He triggered a true revolution from the throne for his people. When he took reign, Thailand had no school,hospital,roads, railways or well-equipped military forces, only seat of learning were monasteries. He oiled the process of modernization by bringing in foreign advisors and sending his sons and other young people abroad for education. He opened schools and vocational centers for aristocracy as well as common people. Chulalongkorn's brothers and sons spearheaded the modernization by putting their education to effect. In 1892, he expanded his cabinet from 4 to 12 ministers. Importantly, a post and telegraph office was established and construction of first railway line begun. His elder son contributed immensely to modernization of Army and Navy and came to be known as 'Father of Thai Navy'. Most of Thai people preferred herbal medicine to western medicine. Chulalongkorn electrified education reforms to overcome shortage of doctors and opened first hospital Siriraj in 1886 after years of opposition. Chulalongkorn established the hierarchical system of Monthons (Mondals) in 1897 which composed of province, city, district, sub-district, and   village in descending order, thereby reducing power of local dynasties"

I asked, referring to my notes "These are all values and essentials of a great and beloved king. But, my notes suggests that he bargained Thai territory with Western powers and gave up 1,20,000 square km of fringe territory, in total?

Professor countered my question with facts "Foreign policy was rational but, compromising. Rama V found himself sandwiched between British Burma and French Indochina. French resorted to Gun boat diplomacy, on one occasion French gunboat entered the Chao Phraya river and anchored near the French consulate, ready to attack. On northern front, Rama V bargained with Laos and western Cambodia. Similarly, a part of Malay peninsula territory was ceded to Britain in exchange for renunciation of British extraterritorial rights in Thailand. But, understanding the complex situation and vulnerability of Rama V to geopolitics of the time, this was a small price for maintaining freedom and peace of Thailand"

Priyamwada said, adjusting her Sarong "When Kings make way for the next King, they are gauged through the critical lens of development, with one eye on improving life of the people and other eye on international relations. But, I assume, he was not one of those kings, who would bring progress through judicious exercise of their absolute power?"

Professor reluctantly said "Ahh! Difficult to say that. History is kind to most kings. His reforms bore fruit for Thailand and her people. The economy flourished! Thai farmers were better off in comparison to their French Indochina and British Burmese counterparts, and no wonder people posthumously titled him Piya Maharaj 'The Beloved Great King'. In fact, he was aware of the democratic trends around the world, but felt his country was not prepared for a change, yet. Since you are from one of my beloved country, Do you know about Rama V connection to Bharat?"

We, both gave a surprised look. Sometime, we read more from face and eyes than words. Professor did exactly that and said "Rama V travelled to Bharat by sea from 13 Jan to 26 Feb 1872 *(Sachchidanand Sahai 2002)*. In Calcutta he stayed for maximum time and visited many important landmarks namely the Government House, the Indian Museum, the Asiatic Society, the Silver and Copper Mint, St. Paul's Cathedral, Fort William, other military facilities at Barrackpore, the Alipore Prison, a weapon factory, a cotton and jute mill, water work facility, a hospital, and a literary association, - among others. The Thai Monarch stayed at Great Eastern Hotel, Asia's oldest Hotel since 1840 (now, the Lalit Great Eastern Hotel), and at No. 7 Wood Street (now, the Saturday Club). Calcutta has played a pivotal role in Thailand-India relations, in that Calcutta, inspired his reforms that would, in turn, result in the modernization of the Kingdom of Thailand"

I said correlating with Professor's narration "I have been to both, Saturday club and the Lalit, but these places are largely ignorant about this legacy. Since Rama V educated his children and brothers in western education, certain thing is, Rama VI (1910-1925) must be all western in taste and colour?"

Professor signaled his assistant , desire for a break to attend nature's call. The signal was subtle and soft. Sometime, I wonder, are we all capable of communicating without using mouth? We took a stroll while Professor was guided to Restroom. The Grand Palace is rightly named so, every building inside is tempting, adorns alluring splendor and is drenched in culture and history. The story of Grand Palace is in some way story of Thailand. Priyamwada and self, exchanged an emotion and smiled as laughter and unfamiliar phrases from tourists bombarded our ears. Human rush was high and selfie sticks were everywhere.

Professor joined us and said "Yes, he was Oxford educated and thoroughly anglicized. He resorted to west inspired reforms to modernize Thailand which considerably altered the structural fabric of Thai society. One of the first and key shift came in 1913 when he commanded Thai people to adopt surnames. In the absence of a clan or caste system, the lineage name was not inherent in Thai society. The Thai people especially in rural areas were baffled initially, but embraced the new law. By another order, women were encouraged to keep long hairs instead of cropped hair, as Thai standards of beauty does not confirm to western style of femininity. And, Thai women were ordered to adjust their dress from *dhoti* to *Panung*, a Thai style sarong. He made primary education compulsory throughout the Kingdom. He gave Thailand first university, Chulalongkorn university and many schools and vocational centers"

Priyamwada said, knowing fully Professor's attachment to Thai literature "But, he was an accomplished writer and he used literature as a tool to bring in immense sense of nationalism by glorifying Thai legends"

Professor laughed and said "He believed in 'Let me rule you, reign you and I would say that in good sentences'. He translated many literary works from English and French into Thai language. You are correct! He wrote many literary pieces promoting Thai nationalism like "The honour of Tiger soldier.""

I asked, a question from the list I prepared for Professor "Did he translated or read Hindi or *Sanskrit* literature, too? Or his love for French and English was because of his western education?"

Professor said, commandeering arm rest of his wheel chair "The king was conversant in Hindi and *Sanskrit* literature, including the Ramayana and the Mahabharata epics. He translated many stories from these two Hindu epics into Thai language and also wrote theatrical plays inspired by Indian literature. Before him, no King of Chakri dynasty adorned title of Rama. He, in honour of Lord Rama, took dynastic name Rama, followed by standing in ruling order. Following the sequence, he proclaimed himself as Rama VI. In 1915, King Rama VI, paid a visit to the port city of Surat. Reportedly, he was mighty impressed with the vibrancy and culture of the city that on his return, he renamed Chaiya province in southern Thailand as Surat Thani or City of Good People and the Phum Duang river as Tapi river after Tapti river in Surat."

I exclaimed "Wow! That is some story." And took down crisp notes about it.

Priyamwada asked, in awe of Professor's in depth knowledge of the subject "When WWI struck world, which camp he chose, and did Thailand benefited from his decision?

Professor replied with clinical precision "He chose, what you chose during Cold War, - neutrality but, in a more informed way. He joined Allies by sending a small expeditionary force to fight in Europe in 1917, only Southeast Asians in the European theatre of World War I, thereby securing Thailand's admittance to the 'League of Nations'. Thai contingent did not see much action, as they joined towards the end of the war but, it allowed Thailand to negotiate with the Western powers as a junior partner. 19 Thai soldiers died, most because of Spanish Flu. During WWI only, he changed Thai flag from white elephant on red background to red, white and blue stripes representing, the nation, religion and monarchy- elements that are essential to soul of Thailand, today *{Stefan Hell (2017)}*."

Priyamwada said, with a tone of appreciation "In that, he maneuvered cautiously and circumvented the ruins of war with his prudence. There was massive spread of 'toxic positivism' among our political leaders in Bharat during WWI. We fed the second largest contingent in WWI, and were rewarded with thousand of deaths of our soldiers. The political leadership missed the lessons of feeding young people of Bharat to flames for British interest in two Anglo Afghan wars, three Burmese wars, Opium wars and many more. The Great war engulfed large population, directly or indirectly in its fiery furnace, this was when large part of Indian population didn't fit in their '*theory of marital races*'."

Emotions got better of me and I continued in same vein "During WWI, Germans accused British for a breach of 'civilized' norms in bringing uncivilized Indians in conflict between European nations. Indian soldiers died defending British interests at the cost of Indian resources. And, leave freedom, they gave us Jallianwallah Bagh Massacre on 13 Apr 1919."

Professor interrupted "Study of history can offer you results, not intentions. War is like sex, some do it for love, some for power, some are dragged in it. I hope, you understand that. Rama VI enjoyed company of his courtiers more than the family and in that, he was generously draining state resources. His extravagance dried up state treasury towards end off his reign. He married late and his only daughter was born two hours before his death in 1925. Prajadhipok, Rama VII followed him to the throne and reaped benefit of his elder brother's controversial yet brilliant reign.

Professor took a sigh of relief and with that, he called it a day. We shared same feeling; bowed to Professor and exited after visiting Grand Palace. While we were departing, Professor said "We meet at Temple of Emerald Buddha for our next meeting".

On our way back home, I had a look at Professor's visiting card and shocked I was, to know that Professor has a Masters degree in Indian astronomy and is a palmist, too. Professor was very calmly listening to Rajayoga episode from Priyamwada, and didn't attempted to prove his knowledge.

Priyamwada said "Intelligent people thrive on this philosophy, they stay calm and make other people appear intelligent. Ensure that you put the story in good sentences and attractive English. I smiled and said "I shall and I will."

We prepared a set of questions for second meeting with Professor. Priyamwada saw my notebook, and said "Why have you struck off the questions marked tough (questions with three stars)"

I said,paying ticket amount to bus conductor "I can not afford to disappoint Professor."

Priyamwada said, shifting notebook to her lap "Don't bend or twist your idea; don't tame it down; don't yearn for logic in that; don't edit your idea according to someone's comfort. Rather, follow your most intense passion and idea mercilessly. When you write, readers expect you to offer mind-blowing, naked and, even irrational idea. Take chances. It may be stupid, but it's the only way you can do anything really good."

That was encouraging to hear! For our second seating, we chose a date near to the summer 'Ceremonial Change of Cloth' ceremony. We reached the temple of Emerald Buddha, and found Professor reading a book and taking down notes. We bowed to Professor, and sat at a distance from temple of Emerald Buddha.

Professor said, looking at his watch "I promise to spare you in time so that you can maximise walk around time through Grand Palace complex. Have you heard about the ceremonial change of cloth ceremony for Emerald Buddha? Let me simplify it for you! A royal ceremony rich with royal regalia takes place, three times a year, with entourage of monks, Brahmins and dignitaries. Temple of Emerald Buddha is to Thai people, what Kashi Vishwanath is to Indians, Notre-Dame cathedral to France, and Mecca to Muslims. The King sprinkles water over Emerald Buddha to harbour good fortune for Kingdom. Three such customs a year, one each in Summer, Rainy and Winter season. Each custom costs a huge fortune." (Professor backed this with a subtle smile).

I said, pulling out pen and paper from bag "As per Hindu temple customs, Priests change clothes, feed deities at regular intervals and keep temples closed for the duration. The tradition of keeping Bal Gopal (childhood form of Krishna) with strict priestly discipline at home, is on the rise. But, this is voluntary, a matter of faith and reverence of the people for their God justifies it."

Professor said, looking at the scores of tourists around "All religions are good. Humanity is the religion and that, elevates human to status of Gods. Let's get back to God- King Prajadhipok, Rama VII. He honestly attempted to arrest the downward spin of economy triggered by his predecessor by axing public expenditure, the Civil list and royal household expenses drastically. His economic policies combined with increased revenue via foreign trade, averted economic depression in Thailand. But, the approaching 'Great depression' of 1931 reduced Thailand's rice export. The Government resorted to lean army and cut down on salaries of junior officers, which sent a wave of resentment and discontentment among army officials and bureaucrats."

Priyamwada inquired "How did King reacted to this discontentment among army officials and bureaucratic circle? Did he already accepted that the time for absolute monarchy was nearing? Was he weak or rational?"

Professor was impressed by Priyamwada's intellect "History may not repeat itself but, it certainly rhymes in different narratives. To me, he was rational, and by no measure weak. In many public speeches, he favoured democracy but only when democratic consciousness could effectively be introduced. Two months after the 150th anniversary celebration of Chakri Dynasty, few tanks, and about 100 people finished absolute monarchy. The country celebrated introduction to Constitutional monarchy. The King returned to the capital from retreat palace, and accepted the provisional constitution by which he *ceased to rule but, continued to reign.*"

I could not hold sense of accomplishment "I have been to retreat palace of King Rama VII, named Klai Klangwan (meaning, far from worries) in Hua Hin province. He was far from all worries when few people conspired to put an end to absolute monarchy"

Professor connected a call to his wife, who is an imminent historian and graciously requested her for an hour in the evening on topic "The King -a symbol from distant past and a man vital to the present." We could make out by his expression that she kindly consented.

Professor said, handing over cellphone to his help "Democracy in itself is not a solution to all problems. We have come dramatically far from the origins of democracy. Within six months, the King signed a constitution promising universal suffrage and general election every four years. But, the abrupt infusion of western style democracy to a traditional society resulted in rudderless and aimlessness in political system. Out of a situation of nothingness, two strong characters emerged namely, Pridi and Pibul (Pibulsongram), and Thai politics was dominated by these two for next two decades. Both of them were from *Khana Ratsadon* (the People's party) party, Pibul had military backing whereas Pridi's supporters were from intelligentsia"

At this point, Priyamwada grew impatient, and asked "The King ceased to be the powerhouse? The revision of constitution several times and rampant experiments with legislature didn't outraged the King?"

Professor's paused for a brief moment and said "Rama VII was finding his changed role increasingly disturbing and painful. This lead him to abdicate in 1935, the only instance of this kind in Thai history. (Professor pulling out his red colour diary) In his farewell speech to the nation he said that 'he had given up power to whole of Thai people and, not to any particular group'. He stayed back in England with title 'Prince Sukhothai' and, Ananda Mahidol, his 10 year old nephew, studying in Switzerland at that time, was proclaimed King. Second, the King will never be out of relevance in Thailand. He is both, a godly symbol and a man"

"Professor, how the saga unfolded with a 10 year old King on throne?" I wanted to learn how 10 year old King warmed up to the throne. We have various instances in Indian history when young kings surprised everyone with their decision making and ability to rule.

Priyamwada answered "King Ananda Mahidol ! I study in the prestigious university named after him. It has an wholesome environment for learning which breeds innovation and seeds wisdom. King Mahidol returned when he turned 20, WWII ended and political instability was norm; to such setting he arrived in Thailand. A year after his return, the young King was found shot dead in his bedroom. His tragic and unsolved death remains a mystery till date"

Professor listened carefully adjusting his hearing aid, and spoke in a very soft tone "King never dies! I was about 12 year old when King Mahidol was assassinated, and I faintly remember that entire Thailand almost stopped for his funeral. Pibul began a 'civilizing campaign' by which he gave 12 mandate for every Thai citizen. He changed name of country from Siam to Thailand, banned chewing of betel nut (favoured by Thai since time immemorial), made wearing of hat and shoes compulsory. I remember, my expectant aunt was refused a bed in hospital because she was not wearing hat. Forced westernization, it was! By the way, first mandate was 'The country, people and nationality are to be called 'Thai'. Rest, you read!"

This subject is very close and dear to my heart. I couldn't resist "We, too, are facing forced westernization of a kind, Under appreciation for everything indigenous and reverence for all things, 'Foreign'. God is kind, my country recognised it and, is in gradual process of arresting the downfall of a civilization."

Professor said, landing a soft and affirming pat on my back "Nothing can kill Sanatana Dharma, in brief, it is immortal and closest to finest principles of human conscience. Thailand had doused immense internal turmoil and time of uncertainties till today, but they all maneuvered subtly and successfully in International Relations. They always put Thai interest before theirs. King Rama IX, Bhumibol Adulyadej reigned for almost 71 years. For present generation of Thai people, including people of my age, King Bhumibol has come to be synonymous with the throne. Standing true to my promise, I leave you to yourself for next two hours to visit remaining part of the Grand Palace. Drive me to Chakrabongse Villas, where my wife has planned 'family chat over dinner' for four of us"

We, both smiled, carried our bag, and bowed to the wise Professor. Moving around Grand Palace was exhausting physically, but more so mentally as every part of it is has a story.

Priyamwada occupied the driver seat, and we occupied rear seats for ease of conversation. I saw Professor scribbling in his red diary "What is occupying your mind and diary, Professor?"

"Ideas are like Ants. If few Ants handle the dead insect well, soon they are joined by dozen. If you don't allow ideas to flee, soon you have a dozen of them. And, I write because writing allows you to live a moment twice, in the moment and in retrospect." We underestimated Bangkok traffic and therefore, had to stretch our conversation.

I added "I, too, have noticed that sometime if you don't latch on to idea immediately, it vanishes. That, is a leaf, I pick up from your company, Professor. I like to write late night, in isolation and boost sense with a cup of coffee, maybe"

Professor smiled "Blessing is, you, often, don't have to change anything to what you get in middle of night. Those ideas are, mostly, original. And, when you write, a cup of coffee perfect so that real life considerations cannot destroy the idea"

This was my second time in Chakrabongse villas. First time, I came to attend closing session of Bangkok Literature Festival; and ambience was exquisite and filled with literary grandiose. But, second visit was to instill purpose to life that is, in relation to my book. The Villa was former residence of HRH Prince Chakrabongse in 1908. This is truly one of the most beautiful place to dine out along Chao Phraya river, and offers resplendent view of famous Wat Arun across the river.

We sat across table, and Professor did the introduction formalities for all of us.

The lady broke the ice "This place savour authentic royal Thai cuisine using original recipes from palace kitchens, idea engineered by King Bhumibol Adulyadej. And, they have permanent menu that changes daily." We all laughed.

Priyamwada expressed gratitude for invitation "Why so much effusive emotion for Rama IX, almost all shops, every house and most street vendors have a photo of him placed with love and respect? I came across few pictures from his death ceremony and I realized that entire Thailand was bruised and broken; almost entire world felt it. 70 years on throne is a long time! To draw relevance, he took throne before Bharat got its independence"

Alarmed us of a monologue, the lady said "He was my favourite king too, our generation could not imagine life without him. But,

I shoe away pessimism and, hope that future would be better; for without hope, we would be doomed."

We all braced for the monologue. And, the lady continued "Thailand's history is mired with military coups, probably most in any country of the world. Let me touch upon some important events! We saw Thailand's version of Tienanmen Square in 1973 ***{Suwannathat-Pian, Kobkua (2003)}***. The king proclaimed a new constitution in 1968. But, the internal situation soon deteriorated due to terrorist insurgency, resulting in abrogation of constitution and proclamation of martial law. (Showing pictures from 1973 Student revolution) Look, this is me! The size of gathering was similar to size of discontentment among students. Through peaceful protests, students demanded end to military rule and sunrise of parliamentary democracy. This reasonable wish of ours produced 69 deaths and 800 wounded students. The uprising unleashed a range of political forces from 1973 to 1976, not seen in Thailand before, and the country gradually became more polarized. There was strong resentment among students for return of General Thanom Kittikachorn from exile. Two activists were beaten to death, their bodies were hung from a gate in October 1976. You would see a famous picture of crowd looking, few smiling, at a student hanging from a tree and a man hitting him with chair on head. Heart wrenching and cold ! A dramatization of this hanging was staged by student protesters at Thammasat University on campus, but the student at the end of the noose allegedly bore a resemblance to Crown Prince Vajiralongkorn, and thereby violated Lese Majeste rules. This lead to another broad daylight massacre. World opinion considered Thailand the next 'Domino' to fall under the communist garb. But, the unity of the king and Buddhist religion ensured that Thailand's interests are honoured."

I finished scrolled through thick menu brochure "These were testing times for many countries of the world. In Bharat too, ghastly emergency was enforced in 1977 leading to mass demonstrations, protest rallies and in many cases, illegal arrest and torture. But, we learnt our lessons. This was the time, when world was engulfed by darkness raised by two superpowers of the time. They collectively destroyed infrastructure, killed men and inflicted damage to national conscience of many countries. There should be protest against tyranny and bad humanism because nothing strengthens authority like silence"

The lady always had in mind her position as host for the dinner, and she promptly ordered genuine Thai food for us, She explained "The coronation pledge of King Rama IX was 'We will reign with Dharma (righteousness) for the benefit and happiness of the Siamese people. During turbulent times for Thailand politics, the King and Queen tirelessly traveled around the Thai villages and ruled the heart of the people. He maintained neutrality as constitutional monarch but intervened firmly, when interest of the people were at stake"

Briefly interrupting, I said "I second it! Having traveled across Thailand, there is no part where I have not heard stories or seen photographs of their visit. Their photographs loudly convey warmth and reverence of people towards their King and Queen."

Lady gave a confirmatory smile, and continued "The King's firm decisiveness and moral authority was at display during 1981 coup. Read more about it! During bicentennial celebration of Chakri dynasty, the King proudly remarked 'We still stand here, we stand here for the good of the world.' He was one of the most respected and noticeable rulers of the world; regularly opening fairs, presiding over ceremonies, diploma award ceremonies, Buddhist holidays,

Armed forces day parade and opening of parliament to name a few. I have a memorable photograph with the respected King and Queen. Imagine! Clanking of swords, snapping to attention and from the ornately decorated doors appears a slim man dressed in white uniform followed by a woman of breath taking and awe inspiring beauty. (closes her eyes and with a wai gesture) Their majesties, King Bhumibol and Queen Sirikit have arrived"

Professor, drew a sip from his glass, "In most countries, kings or equivalent are restricted to ceremonial positions but, in Thailand, king is a unifying figure."

Looking at me and then at Professor, Priyamwada said "People stand in reverence for the King and national anthem at the end of every movie that I have watched in Thailand. Thai people have no appetite for any disrespectful remark towards their King. King Rama IX has respect of Thai people."

The lady said with a pleasant smile "We, the Thai people have traditional respect for our king as a symbol but Rama IX is blessed to have same respect as a man, too. King Bhumibol made Thai monarchy stronger than at any time since King Chulalongkorn, Rama V. I bow to the King in heavens!"

Priyamwada remarked "It is startling though that the King Bhumibol never visited Bharat during his reign of 70 years. Though, he visited Pakistan on a 12 day state visit in 1962. Remember, relevance of 1962! I am happy that his children, King Rama X and HRH Princess Maha Chakri Sirindhorn have visited Bharat many times. HRH Princess Maha Chakri has made most number of visits—15 since 1987. She was in India for a week in November 2016 for receiving 'World *Sanskrit* Award'."

I said in a self-laudatory tone "Some bragging rights! I had the honour to meet HRH Princess Maha Chakri Sirindhorn during this visit"

Professor gave a rationed smile, and said "The King's decision had no pattern in decision making and in fact subtly, maneuvered during coups of 1957, 1973,1976,1981,1992, 2006,2008, 2014 and many internal disturbances throughout his reign. Also, the practice of crawling in front of royalty during audiences, banned by King Rama V, was revived in certain situations and the royal-sponsored Dhammayutta Nikaya sect was revived in power. For the first time, since the absolute monarchy ended, a kingly procession was conveyed up the river in a Royal Barge Procession to offer robes at temples. The two English-language books, with no veracity in some details, —*The Revolutionary King* (2001), *The King Never Smiles* (2006) bring out indifference in King's decision and life. These books highlight relationship between the military and the monarch. During one of his birthday speeches, the King flaunted his love for democracy and said 'Actually, I must also be criticized. I am not afraid if the criticism concerns what I do wrong, because then I know. Because if you say the king cannot be criticized, it means that the king is not human' And, when a widespread barrage of criticisms resulted, non-obedience to *lèse-majesté* prosecutions increased. Although *lèse-majesté* officially applies only to current kings, but King Bhumibol remains protected by *lèse-majesté* even after death. Remember, the King never dies and the King never smiles!"

The lady was visibly furious at her husband for presenting a skewed narrative of life and times of her favorite King. Professor, could at best avoid it, rather taking her head on. Professor, immediately put the lid off the pressure cooker by changing topic of conversation, and switched to the King Rama X.

I said, shifting my focus from plate to the Lady "Does King Rama X, present king, stays in Germany, permanently? His personal life is all, but controversial or is it largely byproduct of media gossip? I could glance through few pictures available on internet, he appears to have colorful life"

The Lady said in composed manner "He is different at so many levels compared to my favorite King. On death of the King, King Vajiralongkorn, Rama X graciously accepted the invitation by Government, saying in a televised statement that "I would like to accept in order to fulfill his majesty's wishes and for the benefit of all Thais."

Professor continued from where his wife left, and said "The king has accomplished a lot in field of medicine, agriculture, education for his people. He makes political intervention, too whenever required . In an unprecedented move, the King's elder sister announced her candidacy for the prime ministerial candidate in 2019 elections. Later that day, the King issued a strongly worded statement, terming her candidacy "inappropriate and unconstitutional". The Election commission then disqualified and formally put an end to her candidacy."

Priyamwada said, placing her both elbows on table "I think, there is an indomitable free spirit in Thai people. The younger generation will not allow sovereignty of Thailand and their freedom to be bartered, sold, stolen or taken by force. It is the logical and cherished way of human existence. In every men, there exists a space for sense and logic in dormant state, and which, unless excited, will remain in that condition till he meets the final truth 'Death'.

Until, we have Kings who possess political acumen, wisdom, understanding of philosophy and a strong sense of grace and virtue, the societies will face the evil eye"

I could make out, Priyamwada has written these dialogues in her diary only minutes back, rehearsed it and then spoken like a master orator. We finished our dinner and paid gratitude to the old couple for sharing experience. The lady assisted Professor to wheel chair and two left for their home, almost fighting with each other.

I praised Professor and his wife for they share immense understanding, interests and ability to care for each other. It is fact, that all happy people resemble each other but, each unhappy people have its own kind. Having accomplished the goals for first chapter that was to bring out history of Thailand in condensed and simplistic terms, let's delve in to the complex mixture of Hindu and Thai faith. To learn the importance of religion in the state politics and inter linkage of two religions, it is a necessity to understand the spread of Buddhism, its amalgamation with Hindu rituals and its central role in shaping the Thai society that we see today.

While sitting in Tuktuk, I could read scribble on a page which missed Priyamwada's bag and attention. It read "Reason is complete in itself; and ignorant submits to dictatorship. But, such is the irresistible nature of Life, that all it seeks is the liberty of appearing."

[1] *Official name of Bangkok is biggest name of any city in the world*

Hinduism and Buddhism - An Odyssey

Chapter I

Birth of Buddha and Buddhism

"Peace can be established in world only through Hindu Values of Life. World which is struggling with turmoil should take inspiration from Hindu values."

– Srettha Thavisin, PM of Thailand

Initially, I was not certain if this chapter was necessary for the progress of this section in particular and the book, in general. But, Priyamwada was dead certain that understanding of Thai religious polity is a non negotiable, if we have to understand politics. Her friend at Mahidol University suggested Baan Taad monastery, Udon Thaani (a northern province in Thailand) to understand Buddhism, where wise and venerable monks meditate, far from worldly pleasures. Also, it gave us opportunity to cut loose from heat, concrete and congestion of Bangkok. The view of the northern Thailand was breathtaking, and was very different from southern Thailand which prides itself in trademark pristine beaches and azure sea. I could see conical -hatted farmers toiling in rice fields while vehicles leisurely caressed on the carefully designed roads. I could sense peace and tranquility in air as life seems to be crawling at unhurried pace in this part of the country. Even midst urbanization, city radiates feeling of an overdeveloped village with the essence of it intact.

Baan Taad Monastery About 8 Km from Baan Taad Village, we reached a lush green patch of land, Baan Taad Monastery, which is shady, quiet and protected from intrusions by a concrete wall that encircles it. Passing through the gate in to the monastery, we found thick hardwood forests lining both sides of the driveway. It resembled the idea of *Ashram* of ancient Bharat - clean, orderly and tailor made for meditative environment. As we entered, there was a meeting hall (called Saal, Pali language) which is used for monastic functions, and there was no excess and extravagance in its design. It is used as a eating hall, and as a place to lodge monks or lay people who come to stay for a short time. We utilized services of the hall for daytime. The clean and polished wood floor had reflection of the Buddha statue and pictures of senior teachers and highly venerated monks addressed as Ajahn (pronounced as *Aacharya* in *Sanskrit*). A meandering trail from meeting hall lead us to the Kutis (*Kutirs* in *Sanskrit*), which were dwelling places for monks. These *Kutis*, blended with natural settings, were single-room hut constructed of simple bamboo and spread so that inhabitants can not see each other, straight from the sets of Ramanand Sagar's epic serial. In front of each *Kuti*, there was a path for walking meditation. The 25 to 30 steps path was level and smooth and candles were placed at both ends to provide adequate light for walking at night. Walking meditation is an important part of daily lives for forest monkshood. This pretty much is setting of the all forest monasteries.

We met one 90 year old Ajahn (Aacharya) by sheer luck, when he broke his meditation for only meal of the day. His face was radiating, and his body had an aura of immortality. But, his humility was the star attraction of his personality. He saw us and remarked "India is a beautiful and complete place, what you want to know?" I was startled 'how on earth he came to know that we are here for a purpose? As we got along in conversation, he spoke a lot about my past and present, and most of it was true. He said "Future is best left to God and you."

At Baan Taad monastery with revered Ajahn (Guru)

We sat in a "Nameste posture" and posed first question to Aacharya- "Oh revered, please tell us about Buddha and Buddhism"

He smiled, sat where he was standing "Around 2500 years back, religion had complex character in Bharat. It was cocktail of indigenous cult practices derived from Indus Valley civilization and Brahmin priests ensured their grip successfully highlighting meaningfulness of these practices. Only the Brahmins could learn the sacred scriptures and, believed in sacrificial rituals to many

Gods. To condense it for you, the religion was meant for only few and common people had no access to Gods (smiles). Also, this period saw the new republics Kapilvastu, Rajagraha, Ujjain (his pronunciation was little different for these cities) flourishing with ideas. The society either decided to cut off from orthodox views or dissatisfied, looked for new orientations to their religious concerns. Both, the Brahmins and the Shamans (Tantriks) responded to this emerging threat by leading radical intellectual and religious movements. *{Lars Fogelin (2015)}.* In this setting, in northern Bharat, the son of a ruler gave up his worldly pleasures and, after six years of spiritual striving, convincingly declared himself the "Buddha" (Awakened one). It was this Buddha who introduced Buddhism, a religion that was a middle path between a materialistic pursuit of sensual desires, and a life of extreme ascetic self-denial. It was neither focused on pleasing the gods through sacrifice nor on pursuing the kind of extreme asceticism as a way to forcibly control the desires. Siddharth's, later Buddha, teachings did not demand submission or blind faith, but reflection and contemplation. He, when requested, gave a set of teachings and doctrines for his disciples but, he never imposed himself."

Priyamwada asked inquisitively "Aacharya, but the Vedas and other religious scriptures offer same teachings. As a matter of fact, it is the hand that holds power, which decides the outcome. Lord Buddha gave idea of rationality, self contemplation but, the difference in opinion in Buddhist councils, the religious teaching he so proudly preached, manifested in three different vehicles - Theravada, Mahayana and Vajrayana. Can you please enlighten us, Aacharya."

He incautiously looked her in the eyes, and said "That, is no-brainer. The split is a simplistic view of human nature. The divide of Islam in to Shia and Sunni, Hindus in Vaishnavism, Shavism, Christian in to Catholics and Protestants speaks more about human nature than any scripture or faith. Faith is a personal matter. First Buddhist council, held immediately after the Buddha's death in 483 BC to preserve his teachings under the patronage of King Ajatsatru. At this council, Ananda, Buddha's famous disciple composed Suttapitaka (Buddha's teachings) and Mahakassapa composed Vinayapitaka (monastic code). This council gave Theravada vehicle of Buddhism, that is based on teachings of the elders (Thera in Pali). This vehicle has kept itself close to the earliest teachings of Buddha which is to attain liberation using Dhamma (Dharma in *Sanskrit*) as guide. The second Buddhist council to settle disputes over codes of Vinayapitaka at Vaishali, saw major split of Buddhism in to Theravada and Mahasanghika (great community,which interpreted the Buddha's teachings more liberally). The third and most defining Buddhist council was organized under the hand of King Ashoka, the great, in 250 BC at Patliputra. This council is known for composition of the *Abhidhamma Pitaka* and weeding out opportunistic factions and corruption in the *Sangha.* It was King Ashoka who was responsible for seeding Buddhism in Thailand in 3rd century BC *{**Karuna Kusalasaya (2006)**}.* "

Aacharya saw me turning impatient with questions. I asked Aacharya about the Sangha and form of Buddhism practised by King Ashoka.

Aacharya said "A visit to Phra Nakhon Chedi (Holy City of Stupa) in Nakhon Pathom province will unlock the questions regarding spread of Buddhism. By the way, in fourth Buddhist council in 72 AD in Kashmir, all Abhidhamma texts were translated from Prakrit to *Sanskrit.* But, the council is known for further division of Buddhism in two sects namely, Mahayana (the greater vehicle) and Hinayana (the Lesser vehicle). By definition. King Ashoka followed Hinayana version of Buddhism. Mahayana sect believed in idol worship, rituals, *Sanskrit* scriptures and regarded Buddha as God. Whereas, Hinayana continued the original teachings and practise of Buddha and adherence to Pali scriptures." How important is Sangha in Buddhism ? I posed next question with all humility.

He wiped sweat off his head, and laughingly said "I am aged now, not sure of the importance of Sangha in Buddhism but it has lot of credibility in Thailand. The Sangha Supreme Council (*Sangharaja* is head of the council) is a body of highest ranking monks from both, Dhammayutta order and Maha Nikaya order **(Stillness Flowing, (pdf) pp. 57-58)**, and it consults Supreme Patriarch of Thailand, who is headquartered in Nakhon Pathom province, for administrative and theological matters"

Priyamwada and self exchanged confirmatory glance because we found the Supreme Patriarch of Thailand Headquarters, coincidentally. I enjoyed running at Phutthamonthon state park in Nakhon Pathom province on a regular basis and one day, we reached a forlorn placard that read "Supreme Patriarch of Thailand"

The revered monk continued "Anyone who does not follow Dhammayutta order is part of Mahanikaya order. What forms Dhammayutta order? Your minds must be spinning with injections of heavy dosage of theoretical knowledge? The Dhammayuttika Nikaya was originally started as a reform movement against the corruption and dilution of Theravada monastic code which later lead to the development of the Thai forest Tradition. You are seating in a Thai forest tradition monastery which advocates strict adherence to the monastic codes. The order has played a significant political role in Thailand since its origins as the Dhammayuttika Nikaya has historically been the preferred choice of the government machinery and monarchy. Having been started by a Thai prince (later King Mongkut, Rama IV), the order always had close ties to the monarchy and has historically played a key role in upholding public support for the palace. The two sons of India have defined the religious landscape of most of the Asia and truth be told, its revival in Bharat and spread outside of Asia is on a progressive track"

I recollected from my visit to one of the temples in Thailand "Yes, there are temples dedicated to King Ashoka across Thailand and what more, a train station and streets are named after him. There are huge Ashoka statues in Samut Prakan (Sea Fortress, in *Sanskrit*) and Nakhon si Thammarat (City of Righteousness) province and almost, revered in divine status. The other son of Bharat, undoubtedly is incarnation of God."

For no reason or rhyme, Priyamwada made incisive comment "Respected teacher has gracefully given credit to Bharat for the birth of Buddha and Buddhism. But, truth is, the religious setting of Buddha's time could not accommodate teachings of the noble son of the land, and his ideas has to find refuge in other parts of Asia. The significance of the Lord Buddha and King Ashoka is that the Lion capital of Ashoka placed above the motto, Satyamev Jayate (Truth alone Triumphs) is state emblem of Bharat."

I wasn't amused at this untimely remark but, showed approval for her narrative with a nod of head. We bowed to the respected Monk and gleefully left the monastery premises, of course, after satisfying our palates. The pilgrimage to the monastery was successful and supremely satisfactory. Our next stop for sorting the religious maze of Hinduism and Buddhism in Thailand was 'Phra Nakhon Chedi'

Phra Nakhon Chedi, Entry Point of Buddhism We boarded train from Bangkok to Phra Nakhon Chedi (Holy city of Stupa) in Nakhon Pathom province which is located about 70 km North West of Bangkok. Phra Nakhon Chedi is the heart of the city and is known as the place where Buddhism was introduced to Thailand from Bharat.

Phra Nakhon Chedi , first centre of Buddhism in Thailand

Priyamwada, when we were about to reach destination, asked if it's time for an interesting story. Observing my face for response, she started "A day after Japanese signed instrument of surrender in WWII, a bloody massacre was averted near Phra Nakhon Chedi"

"You mean 16 Aug 1945? Japanese instrument of surrender to Allied powers was signed precisely two years ahead of independence of Bharat. Where you get this story from?" I asked, as we got down at Nakhon Pathom railway station.

She continued "Remember, the personal letters of Prisoners of War (who constructed infamous 'Death Railway') from JEATH war museum at Kanchanaburi province. On 16 Aug 1945, while the Japanese were retreating to Singapore, Japanese soldiers got in trouble with Thai police over petty stealing. The dispute between disgusted Japanese soldiers and Thai police grew out of proportion. Both, the Japanese and Thai soldiers stood face to face with guns in hand on either side of the railway track, when a Japanese solider brought a cannon, and took aim at Phra Nakhon Chedi in front of them."

She held my hand and said "On 16 Aug 1945, they were standing across this track, where we are standing now. Look at Phra Nakhon Chedi now, distance is no more than 300 m. That cannon, if fired, wouldn't have missed the target. The military police sergeant ran up to the Japanese side, stood in front of the gun, and talked the blood shot Japanese officer out of firing the gun. Phra Nakhon Chedi is the genesis of Buddhism in Thailand. It is very sacred and close to every Thai heart. If its not for the wisdom and wit of the Military police Sargent, a total of 1,20,000 Japanese soldiers in Thailand wouldn't have returned to Japan safely. This incident would have been bone of contention between two countries forever."

'Wow, That is scintillating and is good appetizer,' I said in admiration of her penchant for stories.

We did our homework before reaching Chedi, and exactly knew the spots of our interest. The history of the Buddhism in Thailand is pictured on intricately crafted murals before entering main Chedi premises. We went inside and the lady at the desk gleefully exchanged a wai gesture (Nameste).She recognized at once that we belonged to Bharat, the land of the Buddha and Ashoka.

She was over joyous to meet us and said "I will travel to the Land of the Buddha soon for ordination as *Bhikhuni* (female monk). In Thailand, officially, under a Buddhist order passed by Sangharaja in 1928, ordination of female to monkhood is forbidden (***Bangkok Post,11 Jan 2017***). One option for aspiring female monks is to accept becoming white clad Buddhist nuns, who are relegated to lower pedestal than monks, and assigned housekeeping tasks in temples"

Priyamwada was seemingly disgusted to hear it repeatedly since the time she came to Thailand. Priyamwada said "How they expect God, on whose name they oppress, to be kind to them? What surprises me more is human ability to endure oppression than method and process of oppression."

The Lady said "Now, women have started defying the tradition by getting ordained overseas, in India or Sri Lanka. Let me help you in demystifying Chedi through the murals. (Pointing at murals) Ashoka sent council of prominent monks to expand Buddhism in Suvrnabhumi, which included Nakhon Pathom. This is the stupa built around 193 BC"

To me, the stupa looked similar with the Great Stupa in Sanchi, Bharat, with a hemispherical brick structure built over the relics of Buddha topped with *Chatra* symbolizing high status.

The Lady said, pointing at another mural "During reign of Khmer empire in 11th century, Khmer type prang (tower) was capped on the existing stupa. The city was plundered by the Burmese Kingdom and consequently, the stupa was abandoned and wooded by the forest; it remained so for centuries. It was in 1831 that the then Prince Mongkut discovered the ruins of Phra Pathom chedi. After his coronation, King Mongkut (Rama IV) passed royal decree to built the stupa in Sri Lankan style, and it was completed during the reign of King Chulalongkorn (Rama V). King Chulalongkorn is credited with adding belfries and covering of whole stupa with golden brown tiles from China that you see today"

How did it spread to other parts of Thailand from this sacred place? And, when did state and religion merge?

To which Priyamwada said "Most religions had at some point accepted and exercised "Divine Right of Kings Theory" and Europeans, in dark ages, claim copyright for it in letter and spirit *{Allen Brent, Brill (1999)}*. The dark ages in Europe helped concept of "Divine right of kings". It was a belief fed to common people that a King derive temporal power from Gods, and can neither be questioned nor held accountable by humans. Difficult to digest, great scientist Galileo was sentenced by Church because he told publicly that Earth moves around the sun. Could people be found in more darkness than this in 17th century in any part of the world? In Bharat, Hinduism shunned the God King concept around the turn of the first century. Though, Buddhism borrowed the idea of God King(Dev Raja) from Khmer empire who were highly influenced by Hinduism."

The Lady said "This conversation would be time consuming and heavy on philosophy. Help yourselves with tea and refreshments, and we will continue dialogue. The taste of our tea could be different, but word for Tea is same in Bharat and Thailand- Cha."

The Lady continued, delicately holding cup in her hand (a unique way of handling cup, though) "Humans organised themselves in society to bring order, and grew oblivion of the fact that the order in humans is a myth, unachievable but, desirable. The heart of societal disorder lies in the humans appreciation of false promise and hoaxed hope. When God King promises Bridge, most of the time, there is no water body"

We saw Dharma Wheels, Buddha footprints, crouching deer and Pali inscriptions excavated from Nakhon Pathom province in King Narai Musuem, Lopburi and then the shape of Phra Pathom Chedi authenticate the centrality of Nakhon Pathom for spread of Buddhism.

The Lady said "In fact, Mahavamsa, a Sri Lankan scripture brings out the council of monks sent to Suvrnabhumi by King Ashoka. **Buddhism in Thailand is much older than Thai people who migrated and adopted Buddhism in and about 7th century.** The first accepted Thai Kingdom, Sukhothai Kingdom, ruled from 13-15th century, practised Theravada, Mahayana as well as Khmer Brahmanism. The Theravada form of Buddhism flourished during Sukhothai Kingom because of the Thai monks who traveled to Sri Lanka brought Lankan sect of Theravada Buddhism. They made Nakhon si Thamaarat (a southern province) as its center. That is why, you would see King Ashoka statue, temples, and continuation of this sect even to this day"

We already saw it during our visit to south of Thailand, and passed approving nod of head.

The Lady continued, relishing her tea "The famous and respected King Ramkhamhaeng offered royal support, which is a priceless commodity, to Therevada Buddhism. He built monasteries and sent more more monks to Sri Lanka to learn Lankan sect of Theravada Buddhism. Also, he created the position of Sangharaja, whose decree of 1928 continues to haunt aspiring female monks to this day. The King promoted study of Pali Buddhist texts and inherited the concept of Dharma King (rule by 'Just be Just')."

I requested her to wait as I was struggling to keep pace with the story, and my slow pace of writing was aggravating the situation "King Ramkhamhaeng's policy of propagating Pali Buddhist texts lead to influence of Pali language over Thai language script. The Thai script was written by King himself, and the influence of Pali was therefore inevitable"

The Lady continued "Di Maak (very intelligent)!, During Sukhothai Kingdom, another group of Sri Lankan monks brought in Sri Lankan forest tradition, prevalent to this day in northern provinces of Thailand. Are you remotely aware about the organised process of strangulating Buddhism in Bharat by invaders around same time?

I put words in mouth, as I saw an instant urge in Priyamwada to reply; Priyamwada said, addressing both of us "It would be imprudent to define and bind the decline of Buddhism in Bharat to dates and events. It lacks authentic archaeological evidence, and a shocking lack of indigenous text on the subject. But, let me attempt to share my side of truth, politely. For the initial few centuries since the genesis of Buddhism, both religions grew together. The kings and royal family donated for building monasteries and Viharas, (Present day state of Bihar derive its name from large number of Viharas in the state) and offered support and protection. The donations were particularity necessary for Buddhism because of heavy reliance of monks on alms. In fact, during Gupta empire (4 to 6th century), the ritualistic Mahayana Buddhism grew, the difference in Buddhism and Hinduism blurred and popularity of Brahmanism increased. Also, during this period, Gupta kings built Buddhist temples and monastic universities such as at Nalanda."

I kept tea cup aside and intervened "This was the time of the rise of Sanatana Dharma, through lens of Vedic philosophy by a legendary man from south of India named Jagadguru Adi Shankryacharya (Teacher of the world). During his journey through Bharat, he deflated ritualistic Buddhist experts and Brahmans in religious debates at various locations. One such debate between Adishankarcharya and Mandana Mishra has a mythical standing. Mandana Mishra's understanding of Vedas was based on brahmanic teaching, and soliciting men to perform rituals to reach God. Whereas, Shankaracharya believed Vedic philosophy as vehicle for eternal bliss, the unity of existence, liberation of soul from worldly circle. Ubahaya Bharti, wife of Mandana Mishra, who presided as empire for debate, accepted Shankaracharya's ideas over the contentious and irregular understanding of Mandana Mishra *{Kuppuswami Sastri, S. (1984)}*."

Priyamwada was eagerly awaiting for her chance "This debate is supreme example of dignified dialogue, acceptance of dissension and mutual respect for each other. Secondly, the fact that wife of an opponent was accepted as Umpire, holds that women were held in high esteem and respected for their erudition in ancient Bharat, too. And, Mandana Mishra's graceful acceptance of Shankaracharya as his guru reveals that Teacher-Student (Guru- Shishya) association had nothing attached with age. Chinese travelers of 5-8th century speaks about the decline of the Buddhist Sangha in the wake of the Hun invasions from central Asia. But, the Muslim invasion of Bharat around 712 AD was the first major iconoclastic invasion in to South Asia. As a result of these invasions, the Buddhist monks sought refugee in other parts of Asia. And, interesting point to note is that Hinduism embraced Buddha as Lord Vishnu's incarnation, and abandoned regressive ceremonies and rituals. Also, Buddhist monks assisted derailment of their faith by accepting material donations, exercising corrupt practices, abandoning Pali language (People's language, then), in favour of *Sanskrit* (the intellectual's language). Around 12th century, Buddhism was completed faded from the land of its birth and in parallel world, Sukhothai Kingdom was established."

The Lady was listening with all her heart with dropped jaws. She collected herself and carefully started "That was simply exceptionalism blended with genius! Courtesy this discussion, I am firm to choose Bharat for my ordination (she laughed heartily). So, the Buddhism continued on a Bull Run during Ayutthaya Kingdom in Thailand. The Ayutthaya Kingdom was major centre of Buddhism and was coloured with both Sukhothai and Khmer Hindu elements. More importantly, Ayutthaya Kings continued to offer royal patronage to Lankan Theravada sect. The main sect of religion remained Theravada Buddhism, but many elements of political and social system were borrowed from Hindu traditions, and numerous rites were conducted by Brahmins which continues to this day.(the Lady took a deep breathe).

The evening tea was more meaningful today. Sometimes, its not what we eat but how we felt, while we ate. You, both, are on a fulfilling mission, I bow to you. Rest part of Buddhist history flows from Bangkok. My evening meditation time is nearing. Allow me to excuse myself"

We were immensely satisfied with proceedings of the day, and were utterly thankful to the Lady, whom we never met again.

Author's Lounge, Bangkok Priyamwada arranged a meeting with a student from Chulalongkorn University who recently finished his doctorate in Buddhist studies. His articles have occupied respectable place in leading newspapers in Thailand, and has a sizable fandom on YouTube. We chose Authors' Lounge in Bangkok to meet for our humble literary quest, for there is not one place in Bangkok where so many literary giants have stayed fleetingly or have called it their home. We entered and saw the elegance of architecture, richness of aura and photograph gallery of authors who have walked the Lounge. Raman underestimated Bangkok traffic and that gave us time to move around the Lounge. We stumbled on a Coffee Table Book titled '*The Oriental: The Amazing Tale of Bangkok's Legendary hotel*'. It is a pictorial book showcasing Kings and Queens, Diplomats, Astronauts, Actors, sporting greats, Authors' who have walked Authors' Lounge. I picked up a relevant and powerful quote by James Kitchener from that book "If your book doesn't keep you up at nights when you are writing it, it wont keep anyone up at night reading it". If that is true, I am not worried.

Raman hurriedly entered cafe with huge bundle of books, and recognised Priymwada at once. We chose the comfortable comer of the Lounge for the conversation between a student of history, a student of philosophy and an ambitious writer.

Quickly, I rushed through my notes, and explained Raman about the journey so far. Raman (shifting his glasses on nose bridge to look closely at the book in hand) started "During the initial period of Chakri Dynasty, there were major reforms brought in for strenghening Buddhism in Thailand. Every King has contributed in a significant way but, none more than the King Mongkut, Rama IV. Rama I period saw construction of temple of Emerald Buddha, appointment of first Supreme Patriarch (*Sangharaja*). He ushered in era of strict governance for conduct of monastics such as putting monks through a rigid examination including the oral translation of Pali text to Thai. In fact, ordained monks were listed on a register and were issued identification card. The King reserved the right to defrock monks who deviated from the decree issued by the State"

Priyamwada was not an advocate of State control over religion "We have shockingly defined parameters and essentials to attain liberation of soul from worldly suffering. In fact, soul has no destination, it only appreciates journey. We have defined boundaries, even clothes for respective faith and religions. Filth in human mind has crossed all barriers. If there is God in universe, humanity is the only possible religion"

Raman continued (visibly amused about what he was about to say) "Rama II further put strictness in exams by putting in nine grade of exams for ordained monks; the practise continues to this day. The king that followed Rama II, was a devout Buddhist and his reign saw construction of major temples like the Stupa at Wat Arun (Temple Arun dedicated to sun god),the Golden Mount at Wat Sraket and Wat Pho (which is also site of first university)"

I could hear and sense songs of praise for King Mongkut, Rama IV in every part of Thailand. Raman couldn't resist, cut me short "He was a monk for 27 years, a long time by any yardstick.

He was a scholar educated in western science and humanities. The establishment of Dhammayutika sect which preaches strict adherence to even stricter monastic discipline, is his legacy carved in stone. He advocated return to the older version of Buddhism. His successor, King Chulalongkorn (Rama V), continued the administrative reforms in Sangha, and made the Sangha hierarchy formal and permanent by passing the Sangha Law of 1902. The act was intimidating as the monks have to carry identification documents when traveling. The Abbot of the monastery was given carta blanca rights to run monastery and mediate or punish offenders"

Very carefully, I remarked , addressing Raman directly "Your narrative is consuming, direct and sensible. It has telltale sign of the boiling Frog Theory. The restrictions put on the monkshood were gradual and calculated, and therefore, the monks were not realising that they were being pushed to the corner. Since, monks derive their power more from the monarchy then the God himself, and therefore, acceptance of the chains. How Hitler gradually developed an ecosystem to put Jews to trash before WWII? German people were handed the packaged idea of supremacy of race and Lebensraum. Similarly, history is full of examples where in people were gradually suppressed, and they didn't realised the last elastic limit of oppression"

Priyamwada was making notes as Raman continued "But the community of monks don't look at it this way. If the monarch is a car, the community of monks is engine"

Priyamwada jokingly, with a tinge of sarcasm said "And, military must be wheel."

Raman knew what she was hinting at, but regardless, he continued "During the reign of Rama VI, there were successful efforts to centralize the control of the Sangha from capital. Also, the King introduced the official use of the Buddhist era dating system on 01 Apr 1912. A new organized system of written exams was introduced for the monks to increase awareness, and raise the standard of doctrinal learning. During the early part of 20th century, there was a gulf between forest monks and city monks because the forest monks weighed meditation and awakening more than the text book approach of city monks. The Rama VII reign was break from usual, and he was last absolute monarch before transformation to constitutional monarchy. He organized 10th Buddhist council for discussing new Pali canon. I Know, In Bharat we recognise three Buddhist councils only and a smaller section recognize four Buddhist councils *{Louis de La Vallée Poussin (1976)}.*"

Slowly the noose was tightened on the monks, but their appreciation for the noose grew as it made them powerful. The faith of a person has no boundaries, it knows no fear, it commits no allegiance to a culture or a nation. That is why, when a soul has its moment of truth, nationality does not matter to him. That's why soul has no great literature, and faith has no exact explanation."

Priyamwada smirked at me and looks of her indicated that I was unnecessary trying to philosophize the moment. Raman got the essence of my remark "Constitutional monarchy did not washed away the power struggle , in fact it worsened. Thailand has seen 13 successful coup attempts (and many unsuccessful attempts) more than most nations. General Sarit Thanarat who seized power in 1957, removed most of the democratic provisions around Sangha administration, centralized powers around Sangharaja and affirmed absolute rule of the Sangharaja . But, its not all darkness. That is not the natures dictum; there is a glimmer of hope, always. This land and its people have tremendous ability to heal themselves. Since the 1950s, there is rise in interest for practise of meditation among lay persons in Thailand that points to peoples' faith in their faith. This period also saw reposed faith in forest monasteries which arose as a response to massive deforestation. That is the reason, almost around whole of Thailand you will see large number of trees ordained and wrapped in a monks robe."

Priyamwada was eyeing for a break, and a breather from continuous bombardment with facts and stories. I saw Raman pulled a bundle of papers to continue his part. Without Priyamwada wholly involved in conversation, I would risk missing a perspective which is more varied, different and thoughtful than mine. I gently interrupted and requested for a walk to pickup a glimpse of sunset at nearby Chao Phraya river.

I prefer watching Sunset over Sunrise I Standing and holding iron bars at view point, a feeling of completeness engulfed me. For most part of this journey, I was swimming like a duck appearing calm and composed on the surface while peddling hard underneath to keep the idea and ray of hope alive. I allowed Thailand to not only surround me, but I licensed it to change my mental orientation about this beautiful Land of Smiles. Thailand kindly obliged! These fleeting reflections passed quickly, and I shitted my sight to the beautiful sunset view. From this vantage point, the city and the Chao Phraya river appeared like a celestial palace covered with gold flakes. Some of these moments come inexpensively to us. While sunset was nearing, those golden stupas were glittering, and appeared quite surreal and majestic. These stupas, they are art , they are beauty and they are secretive!

We geared up for another round of discussion on Buddhist customs and practices. Priyamwada set the ball rolling "How the people, self- supposedly close to God, subject others to a writing and oral examination for becoming monk? How is this wretchedness justified? A religion which has its genesis against the rituals and orthodoxy has immersed in it ?

Ramana said "There is one *Atman,* and there are many paths to achieve it. This is Sanatana Dharma for you! If Yoga works for you, do it; If prayers to deities works for you, do it; If you don't trust in God, so be it. You are not alive and therefore, not you but, physical body dies. We revere death as *Mahaprasthana*, the great journey which ensures perfect oneness with Om."

Priyamwada and Ramana were both getting warmed up for the discussion, I added "This is straight from a article written by Lisa Miller for Newsweek titled '***We all will be Hindus now***'. She writes on seeing huge swath of land in America covered with cemetery '…Then there's the question of what happens when you die. Christians traditionally believe that bodies and souls are sacred, You need both, in other words, and you need them forever. Hindus believe no such thing. At death, the body burns on a pyre, while the spirit—where identity resides—escapes. In reincarnation, central to Hinduism, selves come back to earth again and again in different bodies. So here is another way in which Americans are becoming more Hindu: 24 percent of Americans say they believe in reincarnation, according to a 2008 Harris poll…. More than a third of Americans now choose cremation, according to the Cremation Association of North America, up from 6 percent in 1975. So let us all say Aum."

Priyamwada asked, with a tinge of sarcasm, 'how can I become monk in Thailand ?'

Ramana got the essence of the question and Priyamwada's sarcasm,both "The decision to become a permanent monk rests with individual, but introduction to monkshood is no choice for Thai people. Thai tradition entail all men to live as monks, at least for sometime, at time of their choosing before turning 20. Three months is expected, though people stay monks for as little as one to two days. I don't claim veracity of the statement but some parents put this as criteria for their daughter's marriage. On ordainment, they must shave their head and eyebrows as well as take part in number of ceremonies. They are to engage in cleaning, sweeping and care for temple, they stay in. In fact, many Thai people start their day by offering alms to the monks. Thai lay people have a relationship of respect and gratitude towards monks. They ensure that a monk does not compromise on his bindings with monastic conventions, and are keen to support him because choosing to accept monkshood is not an easy calling. There is an exhaustive list of regulations that every monk has to abide by. Some requirements are clearly evident, such as monks always have to wear a robe, not drink alcohol, no swimming for leisure, monks can not laugh or speak loudly. They practice strict celibacy, and even a lustful intent is a serious offense for monks and nuns. And, Thai people, considering monks have only one meal a day,offer enough without asking as monk will take what he needs and leave the rest."

I have found monks very friendly for a chat. But, I have read about soldier monks and their capability to wield guns.

Priyamwada replied "Do not see it in isolation, Every religion has warring sect for defending their religion if push come to shove, whether they are *Nihang* in Sikhism, monks in Chinese Shaolin monastery, *Naga Sadhus* in Hinduism or Mujaheddin in Islam."

Ramana interrupted calmly and said "The rise of ultra nationalist Buddhism in Southern Thailand is premised on tensions between Buddhists and Islamic separatists. Some of these monks carry weapons, and they even called for burning of mosques to achieve objectives. It appears that, the assimilation and acceptance of cultures is copyright of Indian civilization."

Next chapter brings out, how Hinduism has peacefully merged with Buddhism in Thailand. Icing on cake is that they consider it their own because it is theirs, too!

Chapter II

Hinduism in Buddhist Thailand - Concocted Religious Faiths and Liberal Gods

"Thailand was built on Compassion"

– King Bhumibol Adulyadej, Rama IX

Whatever generates economy, is a festival for Thai people. Economy is fueled by tourism and tourism propels the economy. Thailand packet festivals from across faiths, gives them a brand value, and commercialize them to generate commerce. Fortunately, the Hindu festivals, because of their spiritual nature and cultural binding could be commercialized in limit, whereas Christmas, Thanksgiving Day and Chinese New year Festival can enhance tourism and spin money. For example Navratri, for right reasons, could not be commercialized beyond a point. In this section, we would discuss relevance of Trinity (Brahma, Vishnu, Mahesh) and other gods from pantheon of Hindu gods to Thai populace.

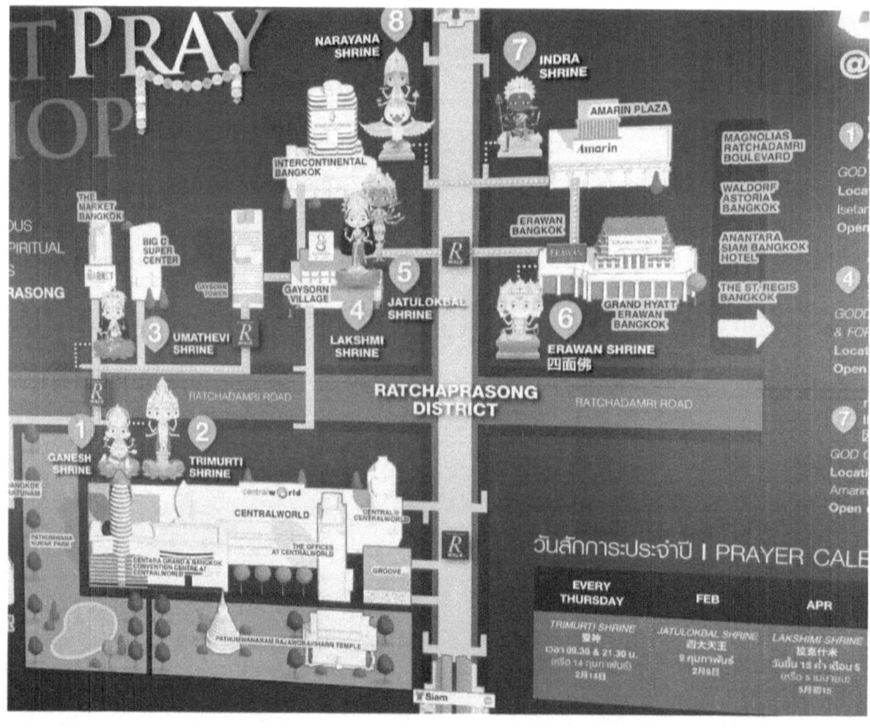

A maze of Hindu shrines in centre of Bangkok, pic by Author

Navratri Festival -Maa Parwati (Uma) and Thai Society

The rush was gigantic and nothing actually moved on Silom road, Bangkok around Marriamman temple as we struggled to straddle our way through public engaged in procession of the deity. The sight was very different from my previous visit on a regular day to Marriamman temple. It was startling to find out that majority of the people offering prayers to Goddess Uma (Parwati) were Thai Buddhists. The temple is heaped with motifs of ancient south Indian art and the sanctum sanctorum of the temple is graciously occupied by Sri Maha Marriamman surrounded by Vishnu, Lakshmi, Kali,

Ganesha, Kartikeya, Krishna and a small shrine that house Yoni, symbol of Maa Parwati. There is a Buddha image inside, and a section for placing Chinese fortune sticks (Chi Chi Sticks). The devotion on display, of Thai people to Hindu deities was immense, deep and imitable. Most Thai people offer marigold garlands, coconut, bananas and other major puja essentials.

On an average, most Thai people were spending 100 baht (about 230 INR) which was more than what an average Indian spends on prayers at a temple. Their method of prayer is to kneel before the gods, put incense sticks and oil lamps, lit them and close eyes for prayers. This is no different than taught by my grandfather when I was a kid. Hinduism,which is rooted in history of Thailand for centuries, permeates Thai religion and culture. Take a cue, that the King has his own Brahmin priest of Thai ancestry and a chief Hindu priest of Indian lineage who plays an important role during official and ceremonial functions. For now, we struggled our way through, and reached the temple.

This was first for me, but Priyamwada was part of Navaratri festival previous year, too. Priyamwada was attired in traditional peacock green long skirt (*lehenga*) paired fashionably with matching blouse and *dupatta*. She was looking irresistibly beautiful, and had my unbroken attention and admiration for her attire. I asked her about selection of specific colour by everyone in temple, and women who were part of procession. She looked over her shoulders and gleefully replied "this colour is dedicated to Maa Siddhidatri, ninth manifestation of Goddess Durga, and represents perfection and fulfillment. And, she rides on a lion and wears peacock green clothes."

The legend of Maa Uma (Parwati) entered Thailand through South Indian immigrants and Thai people embraced it, lovingly.

In fact, Maha Marriamman temples around the world are loud about the historically strong and established maritime traditions of South India. The major Maha Marimman temples could be found in South Africa, Sri Lanka, Singapore, Malaysia and Indonesia.

I asked in a loud tone as the decibel reading was high at temple "Is devotion of Thai people less than devotion to deities in any part of Bharat".

Priyamwada continued, bowing to Goddess Uma "There is a dichotomy, here. Thai people in this Hindu temple can not differentiate between Hinduism and Buddhism. Hindu and Buddhist rituals are conducted simultaneously. In fact, you would be surprised that few Buddhists even think that Hinduism is just a ritual and, not a religion. Some think that Hinduism is a derivative of Buddhism and, that is the reason they happily participate in Hindu rituals. Also, Thai people visit the Marriamman temple because she is regarded as Goddess of Protection. During World War II, when a lot of places were destroyed around temple, this temple remained absolutely safe."

This was revelation for me. The procession approached and special fire ceremony (*Havana*) was started by the priests seated on a raised platform. Upon completion of fire ceremony, hundreds of Thai people and many Indian descent people lined up for traditional circulation of *aarti* lamp among devotees. I was wondering about what Priyamawada told me minutes back "Do they know whom they are praying to? But it's perfect as long as they know what they are praying for- Peace and Happiness"

Brahma, the Creator at Erawan (Airavat) Shrine

We decided to attend a lecture at Foreign Correspondent Club of Thailand. Since we had time in hand, we decided to visit near by Erawan shrine before attending lecture.

Priyamwada said "How same gods are prayed and understood in different countries in completely different ways. Nobody knows the truth and everybody lay claims to it. Only Shiva is truth"

I said, manoeuvring to make way for a pedestrian "May be, even he is not the truth. The seventh and the final verse of the famous *Nasadiya sukta from 10th Mandala of Rigveda* says 'He from whom this creation arose, he may uphold it, or he may not (**no one else can**);he who is the superintendent in the highest heaven, he alone assuredly knows. For this is well known; if he knows not (no one else does). However, Al Basham's wishful and incorrect westernized version is direct translation which says 'He, who surveys it from Heaven, he knows-or may be even he does not know'."

I have crossed it many times before I got opportunity to pay homage to Lord Brahma Shrine. Confusing though, Erawan Shrine is the name, and Brahma is deity worshiped in shrine. Erawan word is derived from *Airavat,* the four tusk and seven trunks white elephant offered to Lord *Indra* during *Samudra Manthan.*

Priyamwada said, shfting her bag to other shoulder and taking quick steps towards shrine "There is no confusion in this world, in fact, truth and knowledge is wooded. Truth is, knowledge is a guarantor of unhappiness and destruction since people can not handle a speck of it. According to lore, the construction of Erawan hotel was mired with misfortunes and mishaps. An astrologer suggested that a statue of Hindu god of creation, Brahma, was needed to change fortunes.

The adherence to the counsel of astrologer changed the fortune of Erawan hotel and, it embraced prosperity since. Whereas in Bharat, story of curse to Lord Brahma devoid him of worship; in Thailand, the god of creation is worshiped across the geography, and Lord Brahma is obliging them with prosperity."

I saw endless stream of Thai devotees paying respect to Brahma in this low walled compound midst the high rise shopping malls and hotels. They would come, light incense sticks, offer flowers, bow to Lord Brahma's four faces separately with folded hands and closed eyes. Thai people offered small wooden elephants and carved dancer artifacts to Lord Brahma. By the shrine side, a group of Thai women dancers were performing in traditional dress, and they earned appreciation and money for their performance. Today, appreciation does not feed you, money does. I appreciate, appreciation of devotees to appreciate this fact. Lord Brahma is a revered God among Thai populace.

I asked Priyamwada about the relevance of 'Spirit house' across Thailand. She said "There are few around my university campus, too. You would see these beautifully tended miniature spirit house outside hotels, hospitals, buildings, conventions centers, apartments. Faith has it, that the protective spirits resides in Spirit houses, and would look after them. There are outdoor shrines all over Thailand dedicated to Lord Ganesha, Lord Shiva, Lord Vishnu. Near the Erawan Shrine, there are two more famous shrines; one dedicated to Trimurti and other to Lord Ganesha. They were brainchild of local experts in Feng Shui, the Chinese art akin to the Hindu *Vastu Shastra*."

This triggered my interest since both shrines are near to Erawan Shrine. We took the passageway towards Trimurti shrine.

A girl in red dress was praying to Trimurti when Priyamwada gently tapped her on shoulder gently "What are you expecting from the three Gods?

She turned and smiled "Only one thing -True love, and I have been granted that.

But, for now, I wanted to appease God of wisdom and obstacle remover, Ganapati whose shrine is located next to Trimurti shrine in front of Central World, Bangkok. For artistic success and accomplishment, Thai people consider invoking Lord Ganesha, a master of intellect and wisdom. I bow to Lord Ganesha, Thai people bow to Lord Ganesha!

Lord Vishnu - the Operator and Hindu- Thai Exchange

Gradually, we realised the process, method and outcome of inter connectivity of religions, faith and culture as we moved along the path. Initially, it looked herculean task to put experiences to paper.

My grandfather, a wise man, told me once that the people bind themselves to one of the three categorizes, first one, they will never start a work for risk of failure, second one, they will give up task on first sign of pressure and then third one, they would never ever give up irrespective of what difficulties beset them. Always, stay in third category, there is less competition in there.

We reached Vishnu temple located in central Bangkok which is oldest Hindu temple. This temple houses number of deities and is central place for celebration of all Hindu festivals. The main deity, Lord Vishnu is consecrated on first floor along with some shrines for other Hindu gods. This place has a meditative spirit and Hindu people as well as Thai people flock here in large number during all festivals.

Priyamawada while looking at the pictures of Gods said "Thai people keep the pictures of Hindu Gods and Goddess in their houses which increases demand of idol of Gods. Some Thai people are ardent devotees of Hindu pantheon of Gods especially Brahma who appeared before Lord Buddha while he was on penance and offered him guidance."

We sat on the bench facing the temple, and entered in a deep conversation. In fact, Priyamwada started it.

Priyamwada said, placing one leg over other, indicator of comfort level "World would be better without religion. Let no child be introduced to religion till adolescence and then, let him be free to choose his religion. In most cases, he will choose none." I confirmed to her thought, though, not in its wholeness.

I said, holding out notebook from my bag "Books, ideas, religion, knife, they all become worthy or worthless depending on who own them. Therefore, religion is neither a disease, nor symptom. It is cure of the frail human mind. Faith of a person is unquestionable and a matter beyond negotiations. He takes birth, live and die believing in that faith. He hands over credit of the grand design to the ultimate, unseen, and he believes in cosmic strength. Though, the pejorative, illogical and fanatical interpretation of the religion damages the social construct of the society."

Priyamwada came back stronger than ever, and spoke "Societal behaviour of humans is not derived from religion. It existed before religions came in to existence. Human behaviour predates religion. Since, no one has seen God. Whatever that can be claimed without evidence, can also be rejected because of lack of it. Most part of the known world has fought wars in the name of the religion, in the name of the God. Which God would like the sight of the slayed people, meaninglessly and endlessly?. (Pointing at me) God has not created man, in fact, it is other way around. And, this defines the reason for fratricide both between and among religions that has retarded the conscience of human civilization. Some day I will attempt a work of fiction which in essence would be non fiction, that is 'Gods are humans and Humans are gods'. I was amused at the name of her future book , not at the content. It was time to shift to the temple of Lord Shiva.

Devasthanam and the Giant Swing

We planed a Tuk Tuk from Vishnu Mandir to Dev Mandir. Seriously, this tuk tuk was no less than a plane, it was agonizingly short of flying. Priyawamda, who lost control over her hairs as wind caused unwinding of hair bun, came close raising her voice, not temper said "In Aug 22, Dr S Jaishankar visited Devasthanam and met Indian community in Thailand. (She opened X app, erstwhile Twitter), and showed tweet by Dr S Jaishankar dated 16 Jul 2023. The tweet highlighted following from his interaction with Indian community 1. That, it is a historical and cultural relationship of great significance. 2. That, Indian community is an important shareholder in Bharat-Thailand relations. 3. Increased trade and economic connections. And, that BIMSTEC and MGC represent our continued efforts at deepening linkages 4. highlighted Amrit Kaal and its significance for India and Indian community...and there were some other points too. But, the important one was advise to the community to maintain cultural connect and interest in learning Indian languages and arts."

Pic(s) Author. Pic(L)-replica of Ram Janambhoomi at Dev Mandir Bangkok. Pic (R) Devotees offering prayers to Lord Rama at Dev Mandir, Bangkok on eve of Ram temple inauguration in Ayodhya

I was wondering, what is the relevance of Dr S Jaishankar's tweet about learning Indian languages and culture.

She said, adjusting her position in Tuk Tuk "The Dev temple, where we are headed, runs Bhartiya Vidyalaya school in which most of the students are Thai, and Hinduism is not part of the curriculum. And you know why? On my previous visit, one of the priest at the temple told me that Hindus themselves preferred to send their children to well-known Christian schools in Thailand, Bharat and other countries. I, for one, don't find anything wrong in grabbing better opportunities, though." Tuk Tuk came to a screeching halt, and we entered the temple premises.

The temple has statues of various deities within its precincts as temple without consecrated deities is like body without soul. The temple has statues of Hindu Trinity along with other deities like Shri Sitaram, Shri Radhakrishna, Lord Bhuddha, Maa Durga and Lord Hanumana on raised platforms. The two stone slabs fixed on staircase depicts Sage Vashistha instructing Shri Ram, and other one Maharishi Valmiki along with revered saints of Hinduism. We were told an interesting story about the stone slabs. These stone slabs were consecrated in Jaipur, and were brought to Thailand on Thai airways without any charge. The sacred relics were received with deserving pomp and ceremony, and brought in decorated chariot to the temple premise. In addition to the slabs, the Dev mandir is blessed with water from the all the sacred rivers of Bharat. There was a picture of the inauguration of the temple which caught our attention. It is on 11th June 1969, their majesties the King Bhumibol Aduldayej and Queen graciously inaugurated the temple, and spent about two hours in temple learning about the Hindu religion. That must be a red letter day for the temple. The Dev temple is popular with both, the Hindus as well as with the Thai people. The Hindus have adopted to Thai ways as well. To accommodate Thai populations religious interest, temple has a statue of Lord Buddha inside its premise, and big celebration of Buddha's birthday is organized every year.

Priyamada smiled looking at the rates for various ceremonies "That, is one of the reason I have grown to detest very fundamentals of the religion. (sarcastically, with lifted eyebrows and taunting smile)The charges of the Pooja are dependent on the size of the automobile; 200 for motorcycle , 500 for car etc. They have put separate price tag on *Pooja* ceremony for different festivals. In fact, they have put Hindu pantheon of Gods in financial module of hierarchy. And, its not about Hinduism, every religion, except those who profess and propagate humanity as religion, have resorted to the commercialization of religion."

I had no logical counter to her remark, honestly "There are two aspects to your observation, one, money paid for Puja ceremony that goes to temple donations. Other, the offering to the Priest (Priest charges) for his act of invoking a particular form of divine. In all belief systems, the act of offering is considered devotion, gratitude and humility rather than a transaction. The offerings are not a tool for harboring good faith of deity, but it is a tool to help needy and less privileged. More so, Hinduism believe there is God in everyone and everyone is God in human form. You, demonize this symbolic and personal act of gratitude by calling it donation. We call it Dakshina, it does not sound like donation either in matter or manner. We neither have riches nor ill manners to insults our Gods. Everything is His! This money is collected to built community facilities, schools, hospitals, community food services, and like. At least, we believe so"

Priyamwada, in slight agreement to my penetrating remarks, interrupted in between (very unlike her) said "The priests demand and accept huge some of money from congregants before praying for them, they sell *pooja* material at exorbitant prices, put entry tickets to visit temple; there are scan points for people to offer donation. Is it not the commercialization of Gods and religion."

I knew answer to this, so I said "Einstein discovered the energy equation which could be used for helping humanity, or turning it in to a curse for humanity. Similarly, purpose of these offerings was to help needy people in society without insulting them. The vices of and in people has no end. They are limitless!"

While we were walking down to the Brahmin shrines from Dev mandir, we passed by Giant Swing. There were tourists struggling to capture the Giant Swing and themselves in one frame. But, there are limited points which facilitates the celebrated picture frame. The placard at the site informs that the Giant swing was constructed in 1784 during reign of King Rama I. The Giant swing ceremony was completely discontinued in 1935 after several fatal accidents. The major reconstruction on the Giant Swing began in 2005, almost after 45 years of last renovation. The rebuilt swing was dedicated to Thai people in royal ceremony presided by King Bhumibol Abulyadej in 2007. And, I realized the importantance of taking down notes while traveling. I immediately realized that I have seen timbers of original Giant swing preserved in Bangkok national museum. I gleefully, with a puffed up chest, told Priyamwada about the location of original timbers of the Giant Swing.

I did not understand the ceremony properly, so I quizzed "What was the genesis of the Giant Swing ceremony that lead to many fatal incidents? Was it some sort of sacrificial ceremony?

Priyamwada replied "According to ancient Hindu mythology, after Brahma created the world, he sent Shiva to look after it. When Shiva descended to the earth, Naga serpents were wrapped around the mountains in order to keep the earth in place. After Shiva came to the Earth, the Nagas shifted to the seas in celebration and made the earth completely stable. The Swing Ceremony was an enactment of this myth. The pillars of the Giant Swing represented the mountains, while the circular base of the swing represented the earth and the seas. In the ceremony, Brahmans would swing in an attempt to grab a bag of coins placed on one of the pillars. Till 1935, the Giant swing ceremony also known as Triyampavai - Tripavai was an annual affair at many major cities, and not only Bangkok. The name of the ceremony was derived from the names of two Tamil Hindu Chants: Thiruvempavai (a Shiavite hymn) and Thirupavai (a Vaishnavite hymn). Among Thai people, the ceremony was popularly known as *Lo Jin Ja* («pulling the swing»). These ceremonies were also performed during royal ceremonies. Such is intermingling of Hinduism and Buddhism in the 'Land of Smiles'."

Pic(L) Giant Swing & Pic (R) Orientation of Devasthana Shrines

I was fascinated by the legend, but scared by the prospect of a man in senses, attempting a feat so courageous and illogical. We got ourselves clicked in perfect frame, with the Giant Swing appearing less gigantic in frame as we occupied most part of the picture. Soon enough, we entered Royal Brahmin Office of Thai Court. This place is considered as the official centre of Hinduism in Thailand and links the Hinduism to the monarchy, directly and deeply. This temple is home to court Brahmins (Rameshwaram, Tamil lineage) who consummate important religious and royal ceremonies for the monarchy of Thailand. The temple is bound by white wall, and the three shrines in the temple are dedicated to Phra Isuan (Lord Shiva), Phra Phikkhanesuan (Lord Ganesha), Phra Narai (Lord Vishnu). We met a learned Brahmin near small outdoor shrine (similar in appearance to Erawan Shrine) dedicated to Lord Brahma in the temple precinct.

Learned Brahmin offered *Prasadam* and a seat to us. Priyamwada was aware about the disinterest of next generation of hindus towards priestly duties and life. She asked "Acharya (a respectful salutation), how is future of Hinduism manifesting in next generation of Hindus in Thailand?"

Brahmin in a pensive posture replied, thoughtfully "There are no easy answers, but I admit this is an issue. Youth is deeply affected by the glamour of materialism and western culture, even in Bharat. Here, still, children have the moral decency to sit down and listen to the elders and parents. Today, youth do not like superstitions. We need to convey to our future generations that Sanatana Dharma is not just a religion based on heresy but, that it is, based on science and arts. Youth asks 'How could Gods have a thousand hands and two legs? Or how can a God have elephant head? They should be dealt on scientific grounds. But, parents do not take responsibility to teach them the science about Sanatana Bharma. Hinduism has mattered to me a lot since the day I was born. Visit our Durga temple and you will see young girls in huge numbers, both Thai and Hindu, gather to worship Goddess Durga and Parwati."

Priyamwada said "Yes, but Sanatana will survive, come what may. We can't be faded in to oblivion. We can't be doused by bombs, bullets or western culture, we haven't been so far." We gently bowed to the learned Brahmin after taking his blessings, and left.

Mother Ganga (Phra Mae Khongkha)

Seating in comfort of balcony and working on project, I felt that a short introduction to Goddess of River and Earth is necessary to highlight the interconnections among the two religions.

To a Hindu, some Thai festivals would appear familiar in rituals and celebratory acts. For example, celebration and purpose of Loy Krathong is akin to Karthik Purnima Dev Deepawali, Songkran, similar to Holi, celebrated by throwing scented water on each other; tying of strings on the wrists of loved ones akin to Raksha Bandan; applying a white paste for protection from evil akin to smearing vibhuti (holy ash); and conduct of long boat race is akin to celebration of Onam. On the full moon night of the 12th lunar month, Thai and Hindu people gather along the water bodies to pay homage to Phra Mae Khongkha and her water spirits. In a way, people beg forgiveness for polluting and mistreating water. Among other deities, Goddess of river and water, Maa Ganga, is widely worshiped. Every year Thailand celebrates Loy Krathong festival to thank Maa Ganga. People make krathong (a floating vessel beautifully decorated with flowers) that are floated in rivers, ponds, or reservoirs to celebrate Loy Krathong. Nakhon Sawan (*Sawan meaning Heaven*) province is the point of confluence of two of Thailand's major rivers, the Ping and the Nan. These converge in Nakhon Sawan to form the Chao Phraya river which flows south to Bangkok, and out into the Gulf of Thailand. The point of confluence of two rivers is a place of worship and, it is their version of Triveni.

Pic (L) by Kmusser(2018) depicting merging of Nan and Ping to form Chao Phraya river. Pic(R) Author at confluence of rivers (origin of Chao Phraya river)

Mother Earth

Offerings are paid to Goddess of the Earth, Phra Mae Thorani by farmers across Thailand. They have adopted the idea from Hinduism of holy spirit of the Earth. In Hindu mythology, Lord Vishnu has two consorts namely *Maa Lakshmi* and *Maa Bhumi* (Earth). Farmers pray to Goddess of Earth at the start of the season. Though, I did not encounter big statue or shrine dedicated to the goddess of Earth except near the Grand Palace. There is a ceremony to invoke mother earth in which monks chant a hymn while people pour water from a jar to a container. This is a symbolic ritual to pass the merit and spirit to the water. Then, the water is poured under trees or temple ground, like in Hinduism to invoke Phra *Mae Thorani*.

Cult of Monkey God and Elephant headed God

Soon, Priyamwada joined me at balcony for morning coffee, and discussions over rise of Lord Ganesha and Lord Hanumana cult in Thailand and some other related subjects. That morning, the God of rain was kind. His kindness was little more profuse than we wanted. It literally poured. I served 'cutting chai' to both of us, a rarity in Thailand. We sat in balcony with a cup of tea, on a rainy morning, facing the gilded stupa on horizon, and discussing about our most cherished subjects. Those moments were rich and fulfilling.

Priyamwada sipping tea from a ceramic cup indicated to reduce volume of 'Shiv Tandav Strotam' running in background. She said in contemplative tone "I wish, people are kind in willful wish of rain, a lot of people will have to deal with mud, too."

Adjusting volume of music system, I said "People have adjusted to rain patterns around the world in last thousand of years. It is deviance from pattern that may trouble them, and we are the cause of the problem of climate change which cause deviation from the normal"

Priyamwada said "Do you really believe, humans can create anything, even climate change. I'll choose opportune moment to speak about it. Where were you in Bharat when the Ganesha idols around the world were on a milk drinking spree"

I took some to recollect "I was very young and my grandmother rushed me to a nearby Ganesha Temple where people were lined up for their turn. People were singing song in praise of Lord Ganesha 'Jai Ganesh Jai Ganesh Dev, Mata jaaki Parwati, Pita Mahadev' That is all that I remember."

Priyamwada said, placing her cup on the table in front "The contemporary boom in the rise of Ganesha's cult in Thailand is influenced by that event. In 1995, a man in New Delhi dreamt of Ganehsa craving for milk. He went to nearby temple to offer milk to stone statue of Lord Ganesha. While they fed milk to statue, both, man and priests were startled at miraculous disappearance of milk. Very quickly, the real face of globalization kicked in. And, this news spread like a bush fire to all major international media channels. The Hindu temples around the world replicated the miracle. This event set the stage for increasing popularity of Lord Ganesha around the world and more so, in Thailand because of deep linkage with Hinduism. The milk-drinking story of Lord Ganehsa became part of legend not just among Hindu community but, also among the Thai populace. This was evident in the long queues of Hindus and Thai devotees waiting for their turn to feed milk to Ganesha at the Dev temple. While this event appears insipid, it gathered media attention which led to increase in the wider public attention towards the miraculous powers, which Lord Ganesha possesses."

I exclaimed "Wow! A miracle of less magnitude and relevance happened in Mumbai and Gujarat in 2006. At that time, I was in Mumbai for an educational trip. The residents of Mumbai laid claim that the seawater has suddenly turned sweet at Mahim Creek and soon after people observed 'sweet' sea water at Tithal beach in Gujrat. This caused a similar mass hysteria among people; people flocked in large numbers to see and taste miracle. Truth be told, I also drove a long distance to taste miracle."

They both laughed in unison "Lord Ganesha and Lord Hanuman are acceptable God to both faiths. The temples and shrines dedicated to them could be found scattered across Thailand. In fact, almost nine out of ten temples enshrine has a Ganesha or Hanuman statue, which bloats the pockets of idol and amulet sellers.

I said in confirmatory tone "Absolutely! I observed during my travel through Thailand that almost every temple have s small statue or shrine dedicated to Lord Ganesha or Lord Hanuman. I saw a giant temple with a huge Ganesha Statue in remote area of Chachoengsao province where tourists are bused in to offer prayers."

She continued "Lord Ganesha is a brand. He is like Apple of Gods. Lord Hanuman is close second. The idol making market is highly competitive and therefore, you will find these Gods in many versions- those imported from Bharat, those imported and modified in Thailand by adding local features, and those made in Thailand. Even during Navaratri festival, did you observe people providing advice on how to worship Ganesha and were exchanging business cards with potential religious customers outside temple. The idols of Ganesha have been given different meanings depending on the artistic finesse of artist."

I left my chair and placed hand on guardrail "Yes, I know that. Somehow, Thai people have trademarked Lord Ganesha as their God. The worship of idol of Lord Ganesha with his two consorts Riddhi and Siddhi and two sons Subh (auspicious) and Labh (gains) is for harboring prosperity and wealth for them."

Priyamwada grinned "Have you noticed Lord Ganesha idol and amulets in Thailand? Ladoo in Ganesha hand (in Bharat) is replaced with a crystal ball in Thailand. That, is real localization of Gods. Lord Ganesha is God of veneration and commodification both. In fact, Lord Ganesha is residue of human conscience build from historical cultural legacy."

I was confused with the last part of her remarks "So, the Ganesha milk drinking miracle, economic boom following it or absence of it during financial crisis in 2008 attracted a huge fan base for the elephant headed god. But, why you labeled Ganesha as the residue of cultural legacy?"

The rain stopped and tea almost finished, Priyamwada said "Lord Ganesha is set in to every Thai people conscience because of historical backing, miracles and futuristic prosperity that the elephant headed God bring to table. And, monarchy or monks, monks or military, celebrities or commoners, it has captured everyone's unbroken devotion."

I said "But, Thailand still chose Lord Hanuman as mascot for Asian Athletic Championship tweeting (reading from paper) 'Hanuman exhibits extraordinary abilities in (Lord) Rama's service, including speed, strength, courage, and wisdom ... Hanuman's greatest ability is, in fact, his incredibly staunch loyalty and devotion."

Priyamwada said, passing hand through her silky hairs "Yes, Hanuman's tattoo and amulets are very popular among Thai people. It is believed that wearer receives strength and success in every endeavour as well as protection from evil spirits. For same reason, Muay Thai fighters, if you have noticed, also wear Hanuman amulets to get power to regain strength, when they are knocked down. The amulet is extremely popular with soldiers and police for similar reasons. Also, in 'Temple of Emerald Buddha visit, there are murals featuring monkey god Hanuman in legend of Ramakein (a Thai version of Ramayana), the most popular piece of literature in Thailand."

I went back to the Study and pulled notes from visit to 'Temple of Emerald Buddha' that read "Lord Hanuman is depicted as a white monkey and most loyal soldier with the ability to change into a giant with 8 arms and 4 heads. In one of the murals, Lord Hanuman can be seen stretching his body to make a Bridge for his fellow monkey soldiers to cross over."

Priyamwada said, referring to the tweet "That, explains relevance of every word in the tweet for selecting Lord Hanumans as mascot of Asian Athletic Championship. Also, remember, monkey god statue is common on temple grounds to guard the sacred areas, like we saw in many temples. (with a deep breathe) So, the Gods with elephant and monkey head are very venerated and commercialized in Thailand. They are the real Gods of Globalization and liberalization.

By the time we finished discussions, the rain was long gone, tea cup was under attack by small insects and the stupa in horizon was crystal clear to the naked eye.

Garuda and National Emblem of Thailand

I entered my Study room to have a detailed glance at the Thailand map on wall, which I maintained laboriously. This map had full track of my solo travels, travels with Priyamwada, work trips and name of people who contributed to the work. The map was marked sincerely and miniature photos of the trips were pinned at designated places. The sight of map bruised with thump pin and marker pen was fulfilling. I texted Priyamwada to choose a place and time that befits closure of second chapter.

She texted "there is no better sight than sight of Bangkok skyline from a rooftop bar glancing at the glittering stars above and bustling street below, while we enjoy fine food and finest Cocktails. And, if you agree, nothing better than world famous Sky bar"

We found ourselves suspended on a precipice 820 ft in air, almost dizzying. We could see meandering Chao Phraya river, the city landscape and to call it beautiful, would be under appreciation; it deserve all the hype. We occupied the best seats and ordered food after revisiting menu more than couple of times. Priyamwada understood reason for revisiting the menu "All reasonable men spend money reasonably"

Priyamwada made herself comfortable, and placed her handbag by chair side "I remember Garuda from Ramanand Sagar's Ramayana serial which still remains my favourite serial. He is portrayed in serial exactly as it is understood in large part of the world including Thailand; as a gigantic hybrid half-man and half-bird creature with a head, beak, wings and talon of an eagle and torso of man."

I said, cursorily looking at the tables around "He is not only understood in that form but, also he holds pride of place among pantheon of Gods in many countries. I have a long list, exercise patience! (smiling) In south American country Suriname, there is a radio station named after Garuda which broadcast programme from Indonesia for Javanese-Surinamese population. Nepal named their first rocket after *Garuda.* When I visited Nepal, I noticed, Nepal *Rashtra* Bank (Central Bank of Nepal) have *Garuda* in their official logo, and their ancient palaces are guarded by *Garuda* statues at the gates. In Burmese Zodiac, which is based on the days of the week, Garuda symbolizes Sunday. In Burma and Vietnam, *Garuda* is considered nemesis of the *Nagas; Garuda* is portrayed eating *Nagas* in motifs and murals in temples. In Mongolia, there is a soccer team named after Garuda, and he is the symbol of the capital city of Ulan Bator. Cambodian folklore is rich with stories of *Garuda's* wrath on Nagas. In China, it is considered one of the eight legions of *Devas* and also, a manifestation of Guanyin."

Priyamwada said "I have heard most of it. In fact, in Indonesia and Thailand, Garuda is national emblem. In Indonesia, they have artistically specified the physical manifestation of Garuda. There are 17 feathers on each wing, 8 on the lower tail, 19 on the upper tail and 45 on the neck, which together make up the date 17 August 1945, the date of Indonesian independence. The shield *Garuda* carries bears the motto *Panca Sila*, which means self-defense and protection in struggle. Their national airlines is named after Garuda. In Indonesian mythology, Garuda has the centre stage in artworks and souvenirs, logo of many universities, tourism campaigns, international games. The peacekeeping force of Indonesian National armed forces is named Garuda contingent, and is considered prestigious."

"Right that, a friend from Indonesia whom I met at Erawan Shrine, told me all about significance of Garuda. In fact, in Bharat, the Indian Army uses *Garuda* on their Guards Brigade Regimental Insignia and Indian Air force special operations unit is named Garuda force"

Priyamwada was deeply involved in discussion by now "What all of this leads to? Where are we going with this discussion? (I knew, she knew the answer). Garuda is part of Hindu as well as Buddhist mythological tradition. The Hindu majority country like Bharat, Nepal, and Buddhism dominant country like China, Thailand, Myanmar, Sri Lanka has legends of *Garuda* inscribed in their historical texts. In Hindu mythology, *Garuda* is mentioned in the Rigveda who is described as celestial God with wings. He is consort of Lord Vishnu and mentioned in *Vedas* and *Puranas*. In fact, *Garuda Purana* is named after *Garuda*."

Priyamwada has gift of articulation that often glued me to 'how she *says*' rather than 'what she *says*'. For now, sunset time approached, the landscape around bathed in reddish hue of sunset, and Chao Phraya river was glittering.

Looking at Priyamwada who was enjoying her food, I remarked "In Thailand, the mythical creature is branded as a symbol of royalty for centuries. According to Hindu mythology, the *Garuda* is Lord *Vishnu's* (Narayan) vehicle. The Thai Kings believe in concept of God king, and consider themselves incarnation of Lord Vishnu. Therefore, the *Garuda* came to symbolize the divine power and authority of the king. King Vajarivudh declared *Garuda* as the national symbol in 1911. Since then, *Garuda* is depicted on office seals, which are used by the monarchy and the Government of Thailand to authenticate official documents and ceremonies"

Priyamwada interrupted immediately as I finished last word "Would you like to include a note on ceremonials at coronation of

Thai king because the ceremony has a lot of Hindu- Thai mix." I appreciated the idea and ordered next round of cocktails.

Ceremonials at Coronation- Hindu- Thai Amalgamation

Priyamwada based on her experience and understanding of Thai coronation ceremony, shared "For starters, let me give a brief on the ceremonials at coronation (*Rajabhishek*). *Rajabhishek* is a Vedic coronation ceremony which is practised in many countries and, not limited to Indonesia, Nepal, Myanmar, Cambodia and Thailand. The ceremony of Thai monarch is divided into coronation rituals and, celebration of taking over of the Residence. The coronation rituals have component from Hindu and Buddhist traditions dating back centuries. The rituals include purification bath of the king, *Rajabhishek*, crowning of the king, and taking of royal regalia, royal utensils and royal weapons of sovereignty. The assumption of the royal residence is a in-house celebration by members of the royal family at the Grand Palace."

I asked her one final question "Since, Thai monarchs consider themselves God King and incarnation of Vishnu, they title themselves Rama. Does their coronation rituals resembles *Rajyabhishek* of Lord Rama?

Priyamwada said "Don't confuse! Thai King coronation is largely by-product of Hindu Srivijaya empire, Khmer empire and Mon Kingdom. The coronation ceremony has changed considerably since the time of Ayutthaya empire. The purification bath is performed with water from five rivers of Thailand, though, they mirror five ancient Indian rivers. Before taking bath, King make prayers to Hindu deities in uniform of Field Marshal of Royal Thai army.

After purification bath, comes *Rajabhishek.*The royal regalia for *Rajabhishek* includes sword of victory; Royal sceptre, Royal slippers, Fan and Fly whisk, royal utensils and weapons of sovereignty. The legend for sword of victory is that it was found by a fisherman in Cambodia and, was presented to King Rama I. The royal sceptre is a symbol of authority in many cultures. The importance of royal footwear can be traced back to vedic text Ramayana, when Lord Rama's sandals governed the kingdom on his behalf.

We finished second round of cocktails and second chapter,too. We looked at the star studded sky looking at the stars and thanked them for it.

Chapter III

Indian Independence Movement Saga in Thailand

*May the sacred power of the Triple Gem and,
the might of every celestial being protect His Majesty
from all afflictions so that He may be the longest reigning
monarch in Thailand and, the world. May He remain
the Golden Bodhi tree of peace and love for the
Thai people in this fair and fertile Land of the Free.*

– Professor Emeritus Srisurang Poolthupya

The relations between Thailand and Bharat are centuries old which flourished under umbrella of religion and spirituality before onset of sultanate period. By the end of the 12th century, Buddhism largely disappeared from Bharat with the exception of Himalayan region and some parts of southern India, burying relations between Bharat and Thailand in sands of time. The revolutionary moment for Indian independence and a historical visit by Gurudev Rabindranath Tagore to Thailand, then Siam, in 1927 marked the dawn of contemporary Bharat- Thai relations.

Train Trail of Gurudev's Visit to Thailand

We journeyed from Nakhon Si Thammarat, a southern province to Bangkok in train for treading route taken by Gurudev about a century ago. There is only one train per day connecting two places which reaches Bangkok at 0530 every morning. Priyamwada came with load of papers and newspaper clippings for trip to Southern Thailand. We visited beautiful and tourist-heavy Phuket and Krabi, and headed back on train from Nakhon Si Thammarat to Bangkok. We sat on window seats facing each other and expected a short conversation owing to tiredness, a by-product of traveling. What was envisaged as a short conversation, in effect stretched to four hours before we collapsed on our seats.

Priyamwada, with a pillow on her lap and a paper in her hand, started conversation with narration of a poem written by Gurudev on his sojourn to Thailand from 08-16 Oct 1927.

I came today to the living temple that is one with thee,
To the altar of united hearts
In which is seated on his lotus seat Lord Buddha,
Whose silence is peace, whose voice consolation

I came from a land where the Master's words
Lie dumb, in desultory ruins, in the desolate dust
Where oblivious ages of the pillared stones
The record of a triumphant devotion

I come, a pilgrim, at thy gate, O Siam,
To offer my verse to the endless glory of India

sheltered in thy home, away from her own deserted shrine,
To bathe in the living stream that flows in thy heart,
Whose water descends from the snowy heights of a sacred
time
On which arose, from the deep of my country's being,
The Sun of Love and Righteousness

– Kusalasaya, Karuna-Ruang Urai, 2001: 42

I have been a staunch admirer of Gurudev's literary works, I exclaimed "Master crafter of written word, a wizard of words! Gurudev showered appreciation on Thailand for maintaining Indian culture and Buddhist religion with care and affection. He admired sincere glorification of one of most cherished and celebrated sons of Bharat, Siddhartha, whose teachings were shunned in land of his birth. That is the reason for referring to Bharat as 'deserted shrine' and Thailand as 'sheltered home to the endless glory of India"

Priyamwada was multitasking; she was deeply buried in discussion while frequently glancing out to appreciate natural beauty "Gurudev's visit to Thailand had a monumental, though indirect, impact on freedom movement of Bharat. I'll unfold the riddle as we progress. In first two decades of 20th century, two events that had deep rooted impact across Asia; one was Japanese victory over Russia in 1905, and second was *Gurudev* winning Nobel Prize in literature, the first Asian to accomplish the feat. These two events harbored astounding confidence in Asians about their literature, culture and ability to win wars. *Gurudev's* purpose of world tour was to encourage synthesis of different cultures, raising funds for

Shantiniketan, and advocating a Chair of Buddhism at *Vishwa Bharti."*

Stretching myself like a tree shaken by wind, I asked "Was Gurudev successful in winning over confidence of the King of Thailand for a chair of Buddhism at *Vishwa Bharti?*

Priyamwada handed over a sheet of paper to me reflecting Gurudev's detailed itinerary of Thailand visit (**Shakti Das Gupta, Tagore's Asian Outlook**). She asked "What can you glean from itinerary." Do you have your answer, now (*emphasizing on now*)?

I nodded with a gentle swing of head and responded "Itinerary was evenly divided in to events for meeting members of the royal family and visiting places of historical and cultural significance. Gurudev was accommodated in Phyathai Palace which points to "Distinguished Guest' status bestowed on him by Thai government (**Sonakul Dhani, 1987**). And, most confusing yet captivating aspect of Gurudev's itinerary was his address on 'Child birth' during 'Chinese reception' held at Pei Ying School in Bangkok (**Lak Muang, 17 Oct 1927**)."

Priyamwada answered "Remember, at this time, the members of the Thai royal family were mostly western educated, and held key positions in supreme council of state. So, when Gurudev met Prince Damrong, Prince Boripat, Prince Naris, Prince Kittiyakorn, consequent to that, he also met father of Thai history, an expert in Thai classical music, a master of Siamese art and an expert in Pali, too. He left an indelible imprint of Bharat on mind of experts of Thai culture as well as political leadership."

Priyamwada pulled blanket respecting the strong air-conditioning in the compartment and poured herself Thai tea. Sometimes, mannerism is a subjective matter. I took my tumbler and signaled to Priyamwada to help me with most craved liquid to an Indian palate.

I was confused about Gurudev attending 'Chinese reception' event in Thailand "Why Gurudev's itinerary included address to Chinese diaspora and more so, on 'Child Birth'? At this juncture, not even demand of dominion status for Bharat was accepted by British empire and any possibility of Bharat- China relations does not existed in 1927."

Priyamwada sipped her tea, and answered "The relation between Bharat and China are millennium old. Apart from that, Asian countries have a soul, very different from rest of the world. We understand problems in similar way; our understanding about value system is identical and therefore, solution to Asian problems are unique. Most Asian countries have civilizational connection. Indian political leadership misread China on most accounts, at least till Nehruvian blunders. It was not one-off incident when Gurudev attended Chinese reception, but he was part of Chinese reception in many countries during his world tour. And, the address on 'Child birth' was about ancient relations of China and Bharat. Read this extract from his speech (handing over a green colour paper to me)"

"I suppose you know that I have a Chinese name and that they celebrate my birthday in China. It means that I have had a Chinese birth. I was born as their own, as their own friend. I had my Chinese robe that day, and they treated me like a new born child, like a Chinese child…I have the hope that China and India will draw close together in spiritual and cultural unity which is the best we can share, and contribute to the world."

Gurudev visited Chulalongkorn university (only university in whole of Thailand at that time), Lopburi, Ayutthaya and prominent temples in Bangkok. His visit to Thailand left heavy and positive impact on Thai people and royalty, alike. The king requested Gurudev to send an Indian scholar permanently to Thailand who can act as a medium for revival of Bharat Thai cultural as well as political relations. Gurudev, honoured the request and sent Swami Satyanand Puri (**Pandit Raghunath Sharma, Swami Satyanand Puri's Early Life**) who played a key role in forging strong Indo Thai relations, and a significant role in formation of Indian National Army.

The exhaustion was engulfing us minute by minute and got better of us with in an hour of finishing our tea. In hurry, Priyamwada said "We would continue the story at Indo-Thai cultural lodge, the birth place of organised Indian freedom movement in Thailand. But, Gurudev ended Thailand tour with a poem dedicated to glory of Siam titled 'Farewell to Siam' and I wish to end our conversation with this poem.

The signet ring of a primaeval friendship had secretly sealed
thy name,
O Siam, on my mind, in its unconscious depth
This is why I felt I had ever known thee,
the moment I stood at thy presence
and why my traveler's hasty hours,
were constantly filled with the
golden memory of an ancient love,
and centuries silent music overflowed
the brink of the seven short days,
that surprised me with the touch,

of an immemorial kinship in thy words,
worship and aspiration
in thy numberless offerings to Beauty's shrine
Today at this sad time of parting,
I stand at thy courtyard, gaze at thy kind eyes
And leave thee with a garland crowned from me.

Among other dissimilarities with our journey, Gurudev was received with garlands; and hundreds of people gathered to get a glimpse of great poet at Bangkok railway station.(**Siam Observer, 10 Oct 1927**) We reached Indo-Thai cultural lodge and met the Director of the Lodge at a planned time. We exchanged greeting with each other and initiated introduction.

Bharat Thailand Culture Lodge

Post exchanging pleasantries, I asked "What was the contribution of Swami Satyanand Puri to India's freedom movement?

The director, a wise and learned man, responded "*Gurudev* chose square peg for square hole. Swami Satyanand Puri established 'Dharma *Ashram*' and published a monthly paper 'Voice of the East' to connect with common people. He taught *Sanskrit* at Chulalongkorn university and delivered lectures at various schools to spread Indo-Thai brotherhood. Since, he was a *Sanskrit* scholar, with in two years, he could translate Hindu holy texts in Thai language. He translated Bhagwad Gita, biographies of

Mahatma Gandhi and Guru Gobind Singh. His ashram became a central place of congregation for Hindu and Thai people for progressing relations in right direction. A need was felt to establish a Indo-Thai cultural lodge and the idea fructified in 1940. (*Director, with a smile*) We are discussing about Indo-Thai relations at same place.

Priyamwada asked, before I could "*Gurudev's* visit to Thailand had gigantic cultural and political impact, other than symbolism. In fact, Gurudev has worldwide respect in the world of literature. I have come across his bust in many countries of the world. But, other than cultural impact, does his visit indirectly impacted the political landscape of India's freedom movement in Thailand?"

I recently read a well researched and relevant book "In his book, 'Revolutionaries-the other story of how India won its freedom', Sanjeev Sanyal is vocal about the contribution of Indian diaspora in Thailand towards India's freedom movement."

Director looking momentarily at the cultural lodge's library "I have not read this book but, the context of the book appeals to me. I am alarmed at the textbook syllabus in Bharat, which is far from best version of truth. Truth, in post truth world, is bullied by influential people. In Thailand, the first seed of Indian independence movement were sown by Ghadar Party in 1914. Two year before, an Indian named Rash Bihari Bose fled from Bharat to seek refuge in Japan. His crime, he threw bomb on British Viceroy responsible for shifting capital from Kolkatta to Delhi"

Having lived in Delhi and moving around the site of the Delhi conspiracy case, I quizzed "It was a coordinated attempt to assassinate Viceroy Lord Hardinge hatched by Anushillan Samiti and headed by Rash Bihari Bose. The aim was to kill viceroy by throwing a locally made bomb on the occasion of transfer of capital from Kolkatta to New Delhi. The plan was consummated on 23 Dec 1912 but, could not yield desired results as viceroy escaped with minor injuries."

Priyamwda knowing my comfort with contemporary Indian history and my capability for monologue, stopped me in between and said "Rash Bihari Bose contribution to formation of Indian National Army is underrated and often, misunderstood. (***K K Ghosh, 1969***) He touched base with Sikh movement in Thailand with the help of Japanese and founded 'Indian Independence League'(***N G Jog, 1969***). Japan supported this organization and treated him as leader of Indian independence movement in South East Asia region.But,....

Raising his hand and not voice, Director said "Interruption was essential and timely! (a hearty laugh) Swami Satyananad Puri did not consented to Japanese influence and was wary of it because of their treatment of people in China in particular and, Southeast Asia at large. Swami launched Indian National Council which was different from Indian Independence League in its character."

Pic(L) Royal Hotel Bangkok where Netaji stayed for two months and Pic(R) Author in front of room 118 of Royal Hotel where Netaji stayed

I said, continuing from where Professor left "Effectively, during the initial part of WWII, there were two organisations operating for Indian freedom in Bangkok. Indian Independence league comprised largely of Sikhs steered by Giani Pritam Singh and Indian National Council lead by Swami Satyanand Puri."

Holding a bottle of water close to his chest and occupying chair in absolute comfort, Director said "The aftereffects of Gurudev's visit to Thailand were experienced by freedom fighters. Swami ji had confidence of His Majesty King Rama VIII government. Swami ji got permission from Broadcasting and Publicity department to broadcast news and commentary in Hindustani language on a Thai radio station (***Pandit Reghunath Sharma, Swami Satyanandpuri's Early life p48-51***). It would be foolhardy to deny Japanese influence in Thai government's decision to allow these organizations to flourish as Thailand had a tilt towards Japan at this stage of war. Moreover, with the help of German embassy in

Bangkok, Swami ji communicated with Netaji Subahsh Chandra Bose in many long telegrams"

Out of curiosity, I asked "Can we have assess to those telegrams. Certainly, those telegrams would convey feelings, struggle and journey of Indian Freedom Movement"

PC- Author at Nakamuraya Manna restaurant,
Tokyo where Rash Behari Bose took refuge while in Japan,
and made Indian Chicken curry famous in locality.

Director took a calculated pose before he answered "Under stewardship of Rash Bihari Bose, the Indian Independence League called for a conference in Tokyo of delegates from all organizations operating in the region in Mar 1942. Swami ji, of course, was an organic member of freedom movement, and an obvious invitee to the conference in Tokyo. Swami ji was convinced to call upon Subash Chandra Bose to lead a united movement in South East Asia region. He, along with Giani Pritam Singh, boarded a military plane from Singapore to Tokyo which crashed with no survivors (**Roger Beaumont, 1999**). Swamiji could never attend the conference but his voice was heard. In 1943, Subash Chandra Bose became supreme leader of the Indian freedom movement in the region, fulfilling last wish of a dead man. This, was the mortal end of implications of Gurudev's visit of 1927."

The conversation at India Thai cultural lodge was essential for the progress of the book. In addition, I drew a lot of inspiration and satisfaction at personal level from this visit. The opportunity to visit places, where these giants of India's freedom struggle once walked and breathed, was massive accomplishment. I was itching to invite Professor Sahishanu for conversation on Netaji's visit and role played by 'Land of Smiles' in Indian freedom struggle. Professor Sahishnu, is an accomplished historian working at Chulalongkorn university for 25 years. The timing of interaction with Professor couldn't have been better, as Professor himself was compiling data for a book on 'Netaji's visit and Indian National Army's footing in Thailand'.

Royal Rattanakosin Hotel, Bangkok

We decided to meet Professor Sahishnu at Royal Rattanakosin Hotel, Bangkok. I met Priyamwada a night before and discussed the score of questions for Professor to answer. We decided to journey the trail followed by Netaji during his first visit to Thailand, and that was the reason for choosing Royal Rattanakosin Hotel. I wore Netaji Cap, round glasses, cotton shirt and black oxford shoes to imitate Netaji's look.

"I have matched attire with Netaji's trademark uniform knowing that I couldn't lay claim to any other similarity. Over last decade, there is a sudden surge of nationalistic fervor across Bharat. The lives of freedom fighters are celebrated like never before; monuments, memorials and museums have been constructed to honour their lives." I remarked as we made towards hotel.

Priyamwada said, with her usual flamboyance "You are almost there, except those round glasses and lack of crisp walking style. Other similarity with him is that you also want to see *Bharat* thrive. Many leaders around the world are recognized with their trademark clothing sense. Be it, Nelson Mandela's Madiba shirt, Che Guevara's beret with a star on front wearing unkempt beards and long hairs, Narender Modi's long jackets or Steve Jobs with blue jeans, a black turtleneck and snickers. But, Salman Bhai is a different class, he made an entire nation go crazy with 'Tere Naam' hairstyle. Though, nobody noticed that the great scientist and former President of India Dr A P J Abdul Kalam wore same hair style much before release of film 'Tere Naam'(laughingly)."

We met Professor Sahishnu in Royal Hotel's Lobby. He had visual appearance of a professor. He wore a light sweater over old buttoned shirt with a tie, gray flannels and round glasses; simple and classic attire combined to create an educated and calm look. We exchanged pleasantries. Professor sat on the centre chair flanked by us.

Priyamwada initiated conversation, like she often does "We travelled across the places to soak in the religious and political impact of Gurudev's visit. We understood the dilemma of Indian Independence League and Indian Independence Council in merging with each other to form one organisation"

Professor wittingly remarked "The seeds of Netaji's tryst with Thailand were sown while he was in Germany. I consider him one of the great leaders in human history who amassed huge unpaid army in a foreign land to fight for freedom of motherland. Netaji's escape saga to Germany through treacherous land route has a mythical standing. In Germany, Netaji inspired and raised an army of Indian PoWs. *Netaji* brought *Chankaya Niti* to life when he met Adolf Hitler purely for freedom of his country while not being influenced by Hitler and his Nazi regime."

I said, taking down crisp notes "Professor, can you briefly tell the story behind title 'Netaji' and phrase *'Jai Hind'*. The slogans *'You give me blood, I will give you freedom'*, *'Netaji'*, *'Delhi Chalo'* and *'Jai Hind'* have immortalized *Netaji*."

Professor smiled as if he knew this question was coming "Netaji inspired all Indian PoWs in Germany to join Indian legion. Among these soldiers, Sardar Surender Singh, called Subhash as Netaji for the first time. Abid Hasan, who was personal secretary cum interpreter to Netaji in Germany, out of respect for Netaji, saluted and said 'Jai hind' and Subhas immortalized 'Jai Hind' by accepting it as war cry for liberation of Bharat. Even today, all defense and police forces personnel in India greet each other by salutation 'Jai hind'. He shifted his base from Germany to Japan to lead the Indian Forces in South East Asia. On 9th Feb 1943, the submarine sailed from Germany towards the Indian Ocean. The German submarine U-180 met Japanese submarine I-29 near Madagascar, where Netaji and Abid Hassan boarded on Japanese submarine which successfully and safely took them to Japan. And, Netaji tryst with Indian National Army and South East Asia saw light of the universe. A true patriot, Abid Hasan added 'Safroni' to his name to propagate communal harmony which was a receding commodity by then."

Pic (L) Author at Hellfire Pass (maintained by Australia) and Pic (R) photo of a Lady minutes before she donated all her jewelry to Netaji to cause of INA in Thailand

Priyamwada said, referring to her notes "By this time, Netaji must have attended a fabled reputation in the eyes of an average Indian. For honour and fame are reserved for the man who left coveted Indian Civil Services, abdicated chair of congress president, engineered a legendary escape to Germany fooling an Empire, amassed a huge unpaid army for pursuing Azad Hind."

Professor appreciated Priyamwada's remarks "He led the Indian National Army but, it was founded in a small Chinese Tea Shop near Shri Guru Singh Sabha Gurudwara in Bangkok. Surprised!. I promise to take you both to the approx site. Iwaichi Fujiwara (a Japanses Military Officer) got Swami Satyanad Puri (representing Indian Independence Council) and Giani Pritam Singh (representing Indian Independence League) together in Chinese tea shop to condense their differences and it is there, that Indian National Army was informally founded. However, it was Capt Mohan Singh who founded Indian National Army in Singapore on 17th Feb 1943 while Netaji was in German submarine transiting towards Japan. Later, INA was revived by Rash Bihari Bose and he handed over leadership of INA to Netaji."

I posed a direct question to Professor "This all happened before Netaji traveled to Thailand for the first time on 25th July 1943 for 4 days. Professor, take us through the nut and bolt of Netaji's visit to Thailand"

Holding two books **'Southeast Asian minorities in the wartime Japanese Empire'** by Paul H. Kratoska and **'Netaji Azad Hind Sarkar Aur Fauz – Bhrantiyo se Yatharth ki aur'** by Professor Kapil Kumar in front of his chest, Professor said "These two books would give you detailed account of Netaji's visit as well as INA activities in Thailand but, are largely silent on contribution of Indian soldiers in construction of 'Death Railway' connecting Thailand and Myanmar. Netaji landed on Don Muang airport on 25th July 1943 and was received by Pandit Raghunath Sharma (founder of Dev Mandir, Bangkok and territorial secretary of INA) and Shri Debnath Das (General Secretary, Indian Independence League). At the airport, Netaji was given Guard of Honour by Thai military officers. Outside airport, Netaji received rousing welcome by Indian freedom movement members lead by Sardar Ishwar Singh Narula. He traveled in state provided vehicle from airport and halted at Victory Monument, 500 m from this hotel, to lay wreathe to honour the fallen soldiers and receive Guard of Honour from INA soldiers. The Guard of honour and State sponsored vehicle at airport symbolizes that the visit was officially recognized by Government of Thailand."

Priyamwada, surfed her phone to show a photograph to the Professor "I saw a picture of Indian community members gathered in honour of Netaji near Sanam Luang (Royal Ground, in front of Grand Palace), Bangkok. The the size of crowd was second only to the King's coronation ceremony. (Looking at me) We passed by 'Victory Monument' and 'Sanam Luang' a while ago."

In order to maintain continuity, Professor interrupted "Netaji was received with a traditional Thai welcome ceremony by a senior Thai official in Government House as Prime Minister Field Marshal Pibhul was out of Bangkok at that time. On same day, Netaji visited embassies of Japan, Germany and Italy strengthening friendship of convenience."

We were waiting for coffee, when Professor asked us to follow him to First Floor. We reached room no 118 and Professor, with a lump in throat, said "This is the room where Netaji stayed for almost two months and made this place functioning headquarters of INA in Thailand."

I was consumed by moment and went cold for sometime before commencing a spree of selfies. I have seen the car in Kolkata in which he successfully escaped to Germany. And, I felt same out pour of emotions back then. From room no 118, he took us to Meeting Room where Netaji met local Indian community next day. Professor sat on the only chair available in Meeting Room and we, respectfully, sat on table.

Professor said "The existence of Bharat is eternal and I will illustrate through a story that unfolded at the place where we are seated. When Netaji finished his inspiring and patriotism stirring lecture, Mr Baidyanath Tiwari sent his 8-year-old son to stage with a piece to paper addressed to Netaji. It read "*Main apna Tan Mann Dhan aapko Samarpit karta hoon* (I dedicate to you my body, soul and wealth)'. On being questioned, Mr Baidynath Tiwari happily donated 200-acre land in Chonburi, 600 cows and dedicated his 3 sons and 1 daughter to the cause of freedom movement."

I exclaimed "People like him are no ordinary men. They are massive characters whose love for motherland knows no parallels. People like him would keep idea of Sanatana Dharma and Bharat alive. I remember, late actress Savitri met Lal Bahadur Shastri and came back donating all her jewelry for PM relief fund. And, there are thousands of such examples."

Professor exited chair and continued "Same day, Netaji went to Chonburi along with Baidynath Tiwari and was impressed by location of the land. Netaji took a knife, cut three lentil plants, chanted 'Jai Mata Di', and ordered construction of INA training camp at Chonburi. Unknown to most, the training camp at Chonburi fed around fifty thousand soldiers of INA over a period of time. The Indian Independence League used 600 donated cows to start a condensed milk factory; and the milk was supplied to soldiers positioned at Myanmar and Malaysia. The wards of Mr Baidynath Tiwari joined INA with immediate effect. The sacrificial act of Baidyanath Tiwari was complete and embodies true '*aatam-samarpan*'. And, remember! I am giving you only one such example."

Carefully pulling out a paper from her Jaipur embroidered cross body bag, Priyamwada flashed a picture "She is wife of Captain Ganga Prasad Pandey, recruitment officer of the first batch of INA soldiers in Thailand. (pointing at me) We saw photograph of first batch of INA soldiers at Arya Samaj Mandir with Captain Ganga Prasad Pandey. This is her picture laden with gold, moments before she donated entire jewelry to INA treasury. And, having been brought up in traditional Indian household, I know that a women parts with her gold and jewellery only in extreme emergency or when she is dying/dead. Even today, we celebrate women joining infantry or first woman pilot or first Commanding Officers of a ship. Putting them at the front line of war shows that Netaji was very progressive, and a man way ahead of his times."

Professor started a thoughtful walk towards Coffee Shop. Each one of us pulled coffee mugs to our side, and added sugar and milk to taste. Professor was very kind to speak about Netaji's childhood, education, spiritual inclination and love- hate relationship with the Congress over coffee. Professor earmarked Chulalongkorn University, Bangkok for our next meeting. By Priyamwada's expression, I could make out she knew the reason for meeting near auditorium at Chulalongkorn University.

Chulalongkorn University Auditorium

Priyamwada precisely knew the location of auditorium inside Chulalongkorn university that assisted us to reach auditorium on time. Professor reached before scheduled time, and we found him reading a book.

We greeted Professor and Priyamwada handed over self prepared Bengali sweet box to him. Professor accepted it with grace and began "Netaji started third day of his visit with an address to local Indian community in this auditorium (pointing at auditorium). The people and their emotions, both, were overflowing. Netaji spoke for four hours without a minute's break and galvanized people to unite for the noble cause of liberating motherland from the dirty clutches of British Empire. Later on, in 1945, Netaji donated 2,50,000 Thai Baht each to Chulalongkorn University and Chulalongkorn Medical College to progress India Thai relations."

Professor handed over a copy of letter from national archives of Thailand which authenticates acceptance of 5,00,000 Thai Baht by Prime Minister of Thailand to Priyamwada. And, in this letter Netaji is addressed as Prime Minister of provisional govt of Free India. Looking carefully at letter Priyamwada said "Did INA received any benefit out of this act of generosity?"

Professor responded, immediately "Yes! When the INA troops retreated from Burma in 1945, wounded soldiers were treated free of cost at Chulalongkorn medical college. In addition, Netaji paid an additional sum to Government of Thailand for allowing smooth operations of INA from Thai soil. In fact, there was a copper plate board outside Chulalongkorn Medical college till 90's stating the donated amount. But, the old building was demolished for renovation; the copper plate board could not stand test of time and was never placed again."

As I was making notes, Priyamwada said "I cannot intelligently comment whether not reinstalling a simple copper plate was a matter of omission or commission but, matter can still be pursued for reinstalling a board as official document exists. Did the stance of Government of Thailand changed towards INA and revolutionary activities when the tide of fortune swung in favour of Allied powers?

Professor, who understand nuances of Thai diplomacy, responded "Have you ever wondered why Thailand has never been colonized? They have mastered art of perfectly maneuvering in crunch situations. After his address to Indian community, Netaji had official luncheon with German, Italian, Japanese mission heads followed by a joint press conference. In evening, Mr Witchit Wichitwathakarn, Foreign minister of Thailand hosted Netaji for an official dinner for Netaji. And, next day, that is on 28 July 1943, he left for Rangoon"

I read from my notes "Some reflections of your narrative, Professor! By this time, Netaji was commanding a huge army for liberation of India and he was accepted by governments across Southeast Asia as First provisional PM of interim Government of Azad Hind. The organization of INA was well oiled, functional and structurally strong. Did Netaji returned to Thailand soon or WWII kept him switching places for putting up a coordinated effort?"

Professor said, placing his tea cup in dustbin "He left Thailand on 28 Jul 1943 and returned to Thailand on 04 Aug 1943 for a long sojourn of two months. During his second visit, Netaji stayed in Royal Hotel for two months and made it functioning HQ of INA in Thailand. He met common people, organization heads, party leaders in Thailand and forged alliances. On this visit, he met PM Pibul, ministers and military leaders of Thai government."

Priyamwada said "There must be some key people and notable places around Netaji assisting him to run Azad Hind Fauz while he was in Thailand."

Professor replied, placing books aside "Affirm! There were countless people and places which contributed to the cause of Azad Hind Fauz in Thailand. The attempt to name all of them would be foolhardy, myopic and a gross injustice to lesser-known freedom fighters. But, Dev Mandir, Arya Samaj Mandir, Guru Singh Sabha Gurudwara, Bharat Thai culture Lodge were central to the progress of INA's vision. Arya Samaj Mandir was recruiting ground, Guru Singh Sabha Gurdwara in Little India housed Indian Independece League, Bharat Thai culture Lodge was used by Indian Independence council, Dev Mandir acted as office of territorial secretary. The key persons were Pandit Raghunath Sharma, territorial secretary, Shri Ishwar Singh Narula, Chairman, IIL and Finance Minister in INA government, Badrudeen Kapasi, Minister of Transport in Azad

Hind, Seva Singh Naamdhari, Seth Trilok Singh Chawla, Darshan Singh Bajaj"

Priyamawada, in a feat of excitement, said "Netaji, when leaving Thailand for good, handed over two pistols to Ishwar Singh Narula which are still preserved by his family. Professor, what was Thai govt response when the chips went down for Axis powers?"

I added to Priyamwada's question "Relevant to Priyamwada's question, were the freedom fighters in Bharat clutched in with the happenings in Southeast Asia?"

Professor laughed heartily and placed both his hands on table 'I am not certain whether, even today, people are cognizant of story of the freedom movement in Southeast Asia for liberation of Bharat. So, in all mindfulness, to expect freedom fighters in Bharat to understand the situation in Southeast with clarity was a far-fetched idea. But, Netaji used radio to communicate his ideas to public. The Prime Minister of Thailand, Field Marshal Pibul supported INA effort as he understood requirement of running a functioning military organization. After the failure of Imphal campaign, the soldiers were rescued from Burma with the help of Thai government and were treated free of cost at Chulalongkorn medical college. INA was allowed to run a training camp as well as military base at Chonburi. Netaji was given an hour for airing his views on radio under name 'Voice of India', but for this, Netaji paid 1,00,000 Thai Baht to Government of Thailand. You can read more about INA and Government of Thailand relations in the book 'End of Empire' by Brian Lapping."

We walked out of university and checked on spicy papaya salad. Professor said "Field Marshal Pibul brought in Thai culture revolution through 12 state mandates to pace up modernization.

These mandates encouraged people to salute flag in public places, learn national anthem, usage of standardized Thai language, wear western styled attire and eat with fork and spoon rather than with hands as was customary in Thailand. He considered these mandates necessary to change Thailand's image. In fact, he changed name of the country from Siam to Thailand. Netaji was sure to get assistance from a military nationalist like Pibul. But, fortunes changed and Field Marshal Pibul fell out of favour in 1944 as the balance of WWII swung towards allied powers. Pibul resignation was partly outcome of his plan to shift capital to a remote site in jungle near Phetchabun province in northern Thailand and building a 'Buddhist city' in Saraburi province, in times of economic difficulty for country."

Priyamwada pulled out a napkin from a box kept in front of her "May be, courtesy those mandates, that we are eating papaya salad with fork(smilingly) and not with bare hands. But, eating with hands has its origin in Ayurveda. Ayurveda proclaims that human body is composed of five elements of nature and each finger is extension of one of these elements. That is why, eating with all fingers together brings all of nature's elements to give awareness of temperature, aroma, taste and texture of the food. And, let's agree that it tastes good with hands. On 09 June 1946, King Rama VIII died in Grand Palace under mysterious circumstances leading to chaos in political domain. And, Field Marshal Pibul came back to power for a longish second stint in Apr 1948. His second stint was mired with number of failed coups against him. During his second tenure, did Thailand and Bharat build their relations?"

Professor who was enjoying his share of papaya salad remarked "Since Thailand and Bharat share strong cultural, religious and linguistic links, it was only natural that Thailand was one of the first countries to establish an official diplomatic relationship with Bharat on 1 August 1947, 15 days before Bharat became an independent country. However, long before the diplomatic relations were established, Thailand had established a Thai Honorary Consulate General in Bombay as early as 1872 followed by Kolkata in 1879. Pibul never visited Bharat except in 1960. He briefly traveled to Bharat to become a monk at a Buddhist temple in Bodh Gaya while he was in exile."

I flipped used plate in bin and jumped in with a question "But, does the failure of Imphal campaign ended Netaji's connection with Thailand? The year 1944 is also significant as Gandhi was released from jail midst chaos between Hindu and Muslim factions."

We conveyed our respect and gratitude to the Professor marking end of the meeting. Professor kindly accepted "For the final episode of Netaji story, we will meet under a tree which was once inside the training camp at Chonburi. It is witness to sweat and blood of INA soldiers who gave up everything for independence of motherland. If you speak to that tree, it replies back."

Chonburi Training Camp

We chose 23rd Jan, birth anniversary of Netaji to pay homage to the tree and most importantly, to the soldiers of freedom movement. While I was in van, I recollected a tree which speaks, too.

I said to Priyamwada who was listening to songs "Long back, I ticketed to watch 'Light and Sound show' at Cellular Jail (an infamous jail, called *Kaala Paani*, constructed by British in Port

Blair). A tree, which stands in the center of the jail compound, narrates the story of heroic acts of freedom fighters. It stands testimony to the inhumane atrocities inflicted by Britishers on freedom fighters; their only crime was fight for basic human right to freedom."

Priyamwada said, keeping her earphones in hard case "I agree, heroism is not always in men, but, sometime occasion and opportunity brings out heroism. True heroism is undramatic and silent, it is clothed in simple sobriety. Real heroes do not aim to suppress others but, come with an urge to serve people with no limits. These freedom fighters were heroes of that kind, and of that mettle."

I was impressed by her line of thought "We gave immeasurable pain to the freedom fighters by consuming 70 years to rename islands. In fact, most of the islands in Andaman and Nicobar Islands were named after British heroes of mutiny of 1857, which we proudly call our First War of Independence. Even, ruthless Major Blair has one island named after him 'Port Blair'. Prime Minister honored freedom fighters by renaming Neil Island, Ross Island and Havelock Island as Shaheed Dweep, Netaji Subhash Dweep and Swaraj Dweep respectively. On Prakaram Diwas, Government of India named 21 largest unnamed islands of A & N Islands after 21 Param Vir Chakra awardees. Honour and glory to freedom fighters!"

Priyamwada said interrupting "How could textbook in schools mention it as mutiny of 1857, where in our heroes fought for freedom of motherland and laid down their lives. What will inspire next generation of leaders to willingly and gleefully make supreme sacrifice when called upon by motherland. Utterly shameful!"

I said with a positive tenor "But, optimism is medicine, and celebrating lives of these freedom fighters is cure for bringing out the national conscience unscathed from wounds of the past. There are positive changes in sight and hope is our closest ally."

We reached the tree and could not find a single board/sign marking the significance of the area for freedom struggle of Bharat. But, that came as no surprise. When it took, Bharat, seven decades to recognize the role of revolutionaries, it would be irrational to expect a foreign land to celebrate the contribution of freedom fighters. We exchange greetings and sat for a short conversation.

Professor walked us through the area, he was conversant with "At one point in during WWII, INA hoisted tricolour at A&N Islands on 30 Dec 1943 and in Moirang area of Manipur on 14 Apr 1944. But, as the waves of war changed for INA in Jul 1944, the retrieval of soldiers and equipment back to Thailand and Singapore turned out to be a laborious and extremely perilous task. This march included long journey on legs through dense jungle and in thick of enemy air bombing. It involved crossing from Burma to Thailand via infamous "Death Railway". Netaji ensured that no soldier is left behind, either a soldier was dead or he crossed to safe waters before Netaji."

Priyamwada asked a relevant question as they came under a gigantic tree "This journey would have taken considerable time. And, what is the relevance of massive tree which is covering us from sun beating down on us, directly"

"That is the reason I called you here. *Netaji* stayed in Thailand for about a month in May 1945 after crossing over from Myanmar. And, what happened few months later, is not known to anyone.

May be, only he knows or may be, even he doesn't know! Out of INA soldiers, many were proud *Brahmins* upholding the sacred thread (*Janeu*). While going for campaign, they hung their *Janeu* on this tree and vowed to wear it back on achieving independence for Bharat. *Janeu*, left by INA soldiers, smeared branches of tree in whiteness. Most of them did not return, rather embraced diseases, bullets, bombs, and consequently death. The women of Rani Jhansi regiment were safely sent back when defeat of the Axis powers seemed certain. Curtains were raised on INA chapter in Thailand."

I appreciated this journey as pilgrimage "British India was not kind to INA soldiers for obvious reasons, and they were put to infamous INA trials. Same place where last Mughal emperor Bahadur Shah Jafar was put to trials after first war of Indian independence. In post-independence era, there was lot of resistance to recognize INA soldiers as they were considered Japanese collaborators. Two prominent INA soldiers Gurubaksh Singh Dhillon and Lakshmi Sahgal were awarded the Indian civilian honours of Padma Bhushan and Padma Vibhushan respectively by the Government of India in the 1990s. At one point, Lakshmi Sahgal was nominated against Dr A P J Abdul Kalam as presidential candidate by communist party in 2002. Netaji himself was posthumously awarded Bharat Ratna in 1992, but this was later withdrawn over the controversy regarding circumstances of his death *{Basu, Kanailal (2010)}*."

Priyamwada added "But, Netaji and his team resonates well with youth. Today, Netaji statue has pride of place in India Gate complex. The initiation of Prakaram Diwas on 23 January, renaming of Ross Island to Netaji Island, inauguration of Netaji statue at many places is bringing him back to life in his own Bharat."

Professor said in contemplation, "The story of Netaji, like everyone else, begun with an idea, passion and urge to achieve it. His simple and fundamental principle to see his people free, was the clearest expression of what all humans, and everyone else who breathes, aspires for. The worst thing about British oppression with regulated suffering as a system of governance, was that it worked so well. Netaji was one in a generation man."

Priyamwada agreed in totality with Professor's views "I couldn't agree more, Professor. The political leadership at the time of independence denigrated Netaji and his army; the INA soldiers were not accepted in Indian army. Some sights have permanent reflection in your eyes, like the image of people who stabbed national conscience by excluding revolutionaries from mainstream narrative. But we didn't responded for decades. Our culture and values have taught us all the wrong things well. So, an average Indian lay completely still, and gave no reaction at all. But, the soul of the India has no colour or expiry date. The soul is forever. And, when the Bharat had its moment of truth, her soul could not be stilled. You cannot be certain about what people have inside them until you start taking it away, one strand at a time."

After writing and rehearsing my point and with an urge to appear intelligent, I remarked "This is why oppressing and traumatizing people is wrong, not because a book tells us that it is wrong, or a law defines it for us, but because Karma is true law of nature. And, bad Karma would come to haunt, in this generation or next."

We gifted a replica of newly reconstructed Ayodhaya temple to Professor for assisting in this project and took a taxi for return.

The next chapter would be covering Bharat and Thailand relations from Cold war era to present. There exists a universe of possibilities to strengthen relations spread around domains between Bharat and Thailand. For the purpose of this book, I have to put Priyamwada to rest and stride the next part of journey all by myself.

While entering university gate, Priyamwada waved at me. Both of us knew, meeting would be infrequent from now on. I waved longer than her, that was all I could do.

Bharat and Thailand Relations and A Chinese Wedge

Chapter I

A Leaf from Diplomacy

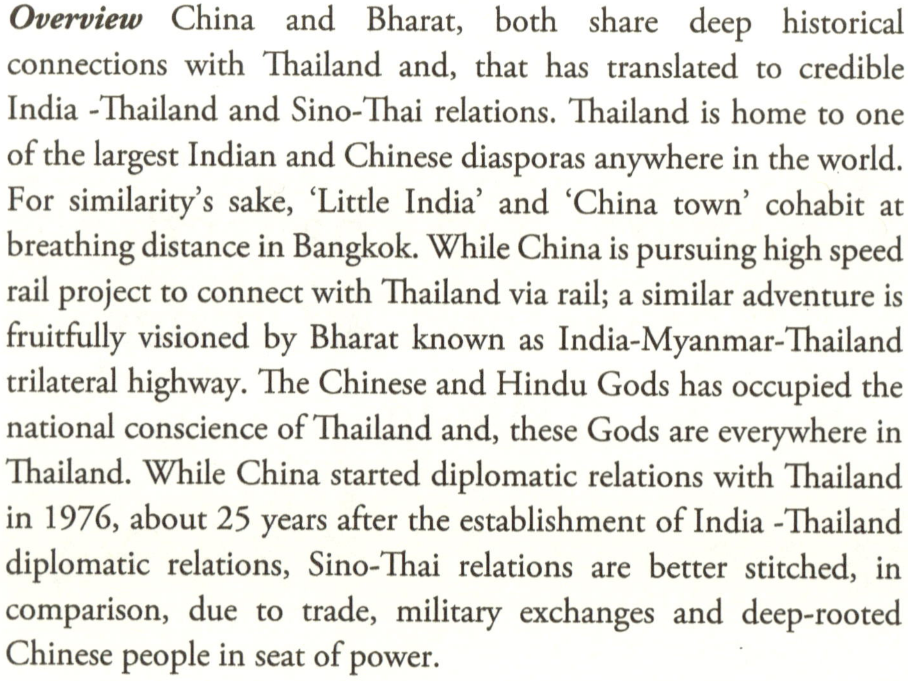

Overview China and Bharat, both share deep historical connections with Thailand and, that has translated to credible India -Thailand and Sino-Thai relations. Thailand is home to one of the largest Indian and Chinese diasporas anywhere in the world. For similarity's sake, 'Little India' and 'China town' cohabit at breathing distance in Bangkok. While China is pursuing high speed rail project to connect with Thailand via rail; a similar adventure is fruitfully visioned by Bharat known as India-Myanmar-Thailand trilateral highway. The Chinese and Hindu Gods has occupied the national conscience of Thailand and, these Gods are everywhere in Thailand. While China started diplomatic relations with Thailand in 1976, about 25 years after the establishment of India -Thailand diplomatic relations, Sino-Thai relations are better stitched, in comparison, due to trade, military exchanges and deep-rooted Chinese people in seat of power.

Thailand was one of the first countries to establish diplomatic relations with Bharat on 01 Aug 1947, 15 days before Bharat was recognized as an independent country. However, Bharat- Thailand relations did not kick off till 1976 as both countries battled their set of internal challenges. There was no state visit during 1947-1972 period between two countries. The prime reason was that, from

1948 to1973, Thailand was under the iron fist control of military regime which had affinity to one of the camps in Cold war era. (*Ganganath Jha,2010*) As the military was nudged aside with protest and coup, between 1973 to 1976, Thailand had six Prime Ministers as a result of political instability and lack of continuity, in policy matters. During Cold War, the loyalty and compromise worked hand in gloves for countries and often, countries found themselves in inconvenient position to choose sides. The frequent change of political spectrum in Thailand was result of close affinity of leaders to communist countries, or their opposites, or neutrality.(*Chris Baker and Pasuk Phongpaichit, 2009*) It requires no genius to conclude that stability is prerequisite to ensure stable policy, and lack of it in Thai government from 1947-1976 period led to stalemate in Indo-Thai relations. As far as Bharat is concerned, the political stability was hallmark of Bharat, in spite of western media literally discarding existence of united Bharat beyond few years of independence. Bharat was involved in four wars during 1947-1976 period which drained considerable resource, energy and focus of leadership. Also, Bharat's alignment with non-alignment countries left it with few options to choose from a world coloured in either Red or Blue. Though, NAM is an outdated relic, Thailand became full member of NAM in 1993, long after Cold War was over.

Thailand and Pakistan were part of South-East Asia Treaty Organisation (SEATO) with its Headquarters in Bangkok and therefore, Thailand, sometimes, supported Pakistan in international forum. However, Thailand supported Bharat by remaining neutral in United Nations on resolution of stopping India's action in support of independence of Bangladesh. The State visit of Indian President Shri V V Giri, who became the first Indian Head of

State to Thailand in 1972, was outcome of the Thailand's act of maintaining neutrality in United Nations on the subject.

A leaf from Thai diplomacy Internal political instability in Thailand, had in no way affected the shrewd diplomacy which famed Thailand as the only country in Southeast Asia to have never been colonised. The skilled and careful meandering employed by Thai diplomats saved them from the curse of colonization in 18th and 19th century and, communism in second half of 20th century. There is a reason, why phrase 'Siamese Talks' loosely means 'not to be trusted'. The colours of Thai diplomacy were at vibrant best when they signed 'Bowring treaty' with British in 1855 and saved the then, Kingdom of Thailand from British occupation. Thailand showcased diplomatic prowess during WWI and WWII when they shifted loyalties and still emerged on the right side of the history. During initial part of the WWII, Thailand proclaimed neutrality but, shifted to Axis camp to align with imperial Japan. As the winds changed in favour of Allied powers, Thailand subtly defected to Allied camp, courtesy rise of 'Free Thai movement' ***(His Royal Highness Prince Wan Waithayakon, 2022 reprinted).***

During Vietnam war, Thailand hosted American soldiers and was house to large naval bases and ensured resistance to communist movement. During this period, Thailand maintained distance with communist world. However, when President Nixon announced Vietnamisation doctrine (***US DoD, "Melvin R. Laird", Secretaries of Defense***) from US naval base Guam in 1969, Thailand sensed writing on the wall for America in Vietnam war. Warming up to changing relation between China and USA, Thai diplomacy was 'on time' to establish diplomatic relations with China on 01 Jul 1975 and with Vietnam in 1976.

In 21st century, the Chinese influence has evidently increased over the Thai internal affairs. Chinese business tycoons and entrepreneurs have deep influence in Thailand's telecommunications, agriculture, manufacturing, technology and tourism industries. And, in many ways, Thai government promotes Chinese education, language and cultural connections to attract Chinese foreign investment. During the Defense and Security event in 2023, the Chinese men and equipment presence was overwhelming and, had the biggest pavilion attributed to them. But, true to high standards of Thai diplomacy, Thailand has used their growing proximity with China to loosen the noose of diplomatic pressure from USA for advancing initiatives on human rights and democracy. Although, the influence of China has grown, but going purely by track record of Thai diplomacy, it is not a cause of panic for Thai people. With centuries of diplomatic expertise and experience, Thailand has managed not to become overly dependent or subservient to China. Thailand has developed a set of antibodies to regulate Chinese influence by forging close relations with USA, Japan and Bharat. (*Strangio, in the Dragon's shadow*)

The Chinese pressure appears minuscule in comparison to mountainous Thai sovereignty and therefore, several big projects, foreign weapon deals have been delayed or canceled, and proposal for Kra Canal deflected. Thailand rejected Chinese led security patrols near Mekong River and delayed Sino-Thai railway project to understand if these projects would jeopardize Thai sovereignty in anyway. To put it in simple words, Thai government has placed limits on rope, neither making it tight nor putting slack on it beyond a point. And, this act of fine balancing would continue in years to come.

A leaf from Chinese Diplomacy Almost no one with diplomatic acumen in world, more so in India, would disagree about the shrewd and assertive nature of Chinese diplomacy. China has displayed assertiveness in South China Sea based on historic claims and other places/ events in world under different context. It is akin to Bharat laying claim to 'Farther India' or 'Indianised states' which cover most of Southeast Asia. How arrogant, misplaced and uninformed that idea would be! Post Hu Jintao premiership, the avoidable assertiveness in Chinese diplomacy has earned their form of diplomacy title 'Wolf warrior diplomacy' (***Yuan, Shaoyu, 2023***). This approach is somersault to the diplomacy of 'cooperative rhetoric' and 'avoidance of controversy' practiced by China from 1970 to 2010. Chinese diplomats used this assertiveness to rename 'Wuhan Virus' to 'COVID 19'. Chinese diplomats engaged in Wolf warrior diplomacy over Taiwanese team's introduction as "Taiwan" instead of "Chinese Taipei" in 2020 Olympics. The Chinese diplomats in New York city complained about NBC over the usage of inaccurate map of china (not included Taiwan and South China Sea) in their coverage. On the other hand, the projection of a misplaced and unjustified China-India border in Chinese maps is considered right by Chinese diplomats. Chinese gets provoked at a correct and legal map displayed by India and they won't shake at the prospect of denying visa to a resident of Arunachal Pradesh, claiming it to be part of Chinese territory.

When Russian embassy officials posted a video on China's Weibo to celebrate anniversary of the founding of Vladivostok, a sovereign part of Russia, it received displeasure from Chinese officials. One Chinese official tweeted "This tweet of Russian embassy to China isn't so welcome on Weibo. The history of Vladivostok 'literally Ruler of the East' is from 1860 when Russia built a military harbour. But the city was Haishenwai as Chinese land, before Russia annexed it via unequal treaty of Beijing." This assertiveness in language against one of the principal allies is crude example of what they have to offer to unstable or economically weak countries. Chinese diplomacy is puzzling and comes wrapped like a Pizza. Pizza is delivered in a square box and when you open it, you realize it is round in shape. And, the cherry on cake is, when you start eating it, it takes form of a triangle.

A leaf from Indian Diplomacy Whereas, in 20th century Indian diplomacy was bound by colonial hangover, it recovered to become one of the best and respected entity in the world by end of second decade of 21st century. Today, India is the only country in the world which can claim good relations with Russia and USA, both and can talk in same vein about Israel and Palestine. Today, India's vote in UN for any resolution is considered with utter seriousness. One of the classic examples of fineness of Indian diplomacy in recent times is conduct of the biggest multilateral event in 2023 - the G20 summit. India successfully meandered between great powers (USA, Russia and China), treated its immediate and extended neighbourhood (South, Southeast and West Asia) with dignity and developing countries of Asia, Africa and Latin America responsibly to bring out a joint statement. For the first time in history of G20, India successfully convened two 'voice of the global south summit' and assimilated African union into the group. The raising of voice for the global south and inclusion of African union gave currency to G20 summit and presented an alternative to China's assertive model of outreach. A Brazilian delegate, during G20 meeting in Jaipur, told me of the high standards of hospitality and diplomacy set by India and he said 'would be difficult to emulate". The boundless respect and faith in India made PM of Papua New Guinea break protocols to honour PM Narender Modi during his visit to Papua New Guinea. Papua New Guinea has a tradition of not welcoming anyone post sunset but PM Narender Modi was given a red-carpet welcome post sunset, and was received by PM Marape by touching PM Modi's feet out of gratitude. Having discussed about the diplomatic environment of three countries, the succeeding chapters would bring out how the relations unfolded between them since the end of Cold War.

Chapter II

Dissection of Thailand's Relations with China and India

India Thailand Relations Post visit of President V V Giri, the relations remained cold until PM Rajiv Gandhi visited Thailand in 1986. He remained committed to strengthening India's relations with Southeast Asia and was considerate about Thailand's role in ASEAN. While in Thailand, PM Rajiv Gandhi asserted that India could mediate to solve the Kampuchea issue by bringing rebels and government to table. India, having a steady and strong relationship with Vietnam, encouraged Thailand to put forward views to find an amicable solution to the crisis. However, the critical events of Cold War along with Vietnam's degrading economic condition forced it to withdraw from Cambodia, thus, putting an end to the entire crisis.(***Ganganath Jha,2010***) In 1992, the then crown prince Maha Vajarilongkorn visited India indicating the importance attached to the bilateral relationship. PM P V Narasimha Rao continued momentum of relationship as he chose Thailand for his first visit outside the subcontinent in 1993. The Prime Minister's visit demonstrated the importance India attached to its relations with Thailand, which was seen as a gateway to Southeast Asia.

The announcement of 'Look East' policy in 1994 and Thailand's 'Look West' policy of 1997 made both countries converge and cooperate in multiple domains, that is, beyond the cultural and historical ties. India began formal engagement with ASEAN in 1995 as Dialogue Partner and upgraded to Summit level in 2002. In comparison, China became Dialogue partner in 1996, a year after India, but elevated the relationship to the level of Comprehensive Strategic Partnership (CSP). It offers a subtle indication that, at the turn of the 21st century, India's proximity was more than China's towards ASEAN.

There is a visible increase in the high level delegation visits to Thailand from China and India in 21st century. After Cold war, it look Thai leaders no time to understand the importance of Geo strategic location of Thailand, which they found sandwiched between collapsed communist states and emerging economies. Thailand, initiated a careful journey to maintain good relations with China and India to boost its economy. Visit of PM Atal Bihari Vajpayee in 2002 was monumental in imparting further meaning to India's 'Look East' policy, where he signed five important bilateral agreements with Thai PM Thaksin Shinawatra including 'Early Harvest Scheme'. Deputy PM L K Advani and Dr Manmohan Singh visited Thailand in 2003 and 2004 lending importance to bilateral relations. These visits by Indian PM were backed by Thailand's PM visit in 2002 and 2005. Though, these encouraging trends in bilateral relations got a jolt when Thai military staged a coup against the elected government of Thaksin Shinawatra. The period from 2006 to 2014 was mired with political disturbance, massive Red and Yellow shirt demonstrations which left a dent on Thai economy, and the speed of engagement between two countries did slow down.

However, in Jan 2012, the only female PM of Thailand and sister of ousted PM Thaksin Shinwatra was chief guest at India's Republic day parade which coincided with the 65th year of bilateral diplomatic relations. This was a landmark visit as numerous pacts on defense, security, trade, counter terrorism, piracy, services and combating terrorism were signed. This was a considerable step in casting stone for comprehensive partnership.*(Lt Col N K Chhibber and Col S K Shishodia,2013*) While, India was inching closer to comprehensive partnership in 2012, China and Thailand took their partnership to comprehensive strategic partnership of cooperation in 2012. India learned its lessons and avoided taking a stronger position against coup maker of 2014 as India did after 2006 coup, canceling a joint military exercise with Thailand. But now, stakes in bilateral relationships are high. Today, Thailand plays an important role in various regional and sub-regional groupings in Southeast Asia. It is, therefore, an important partner for India in the India-ASEAN Summit Level Partnership, the East Asia Summit (EAS), the Bay of Bengal Initiative for Multi-Sectoral Technical and Economic Cooperation (BIMSTEC), the Mekong Ganga Cooperation (MGC), Asia Cooperation Dialogue (ACD) Indian Ocean Rim Association (IORA) and Ayeyawady-Chao Phraya-Mekong Economic Cooperation Strategy (ACMECS).

To maintain tempo in relations, PM of Thailand led a ministerial delegation to visit India in June 2016. During this visit, Thai PM met Vice President, Indian businessmen from the Federation of Indian Chamber of Commerce and Industry, Confederation of Indian Industry, and Associated Chambers of Commerce of India .

A dedication to Indo-Thai relationship was evident when PM Narender Modi visited Thailand to pay respect to the longest reigning monarch of Thailand, King Bhumibol Adulyadej after his demise in October 2016. HRH Princess Maha Chakri Sirindhorn, is a regular visitor to India (almost 20 visits), a member of the International Advisory Panel of Nalanda University and recipient of Indira Gandhi Prize for Peace (2004), Padma Bhushan (2017), World *Sanskrit* Award (2016). She was awarded the first World *Sanskrit* Award by the Vice President of India on 21 November 2016. I have bragging rights of meeting Princess Sirindhorn during her visit to India in 2017 to receive an award at Rashtrapati Bhawan. Thai PM Gen Prayut Chan-o-cha visited Delhi in January 2018 for the India-ASEAN Special Commemorative Summit and as a Guest of Honour for the Republic Day Parade 2018 along with other ASEAN leaders. I had a photo opportunity with ASEAN leaders at Rashtrapati Bhawan and, was part of team which oversaw massive protocol arrangements for 10 ASEAN leaders as Chief guest for Republic parade 2018.

There were numerous high level delegation and state level visit between Thailand and China since the turn of 21st century. More so, signing of MoU for jointly promoting the construction of Belt and Road Initiative, the most ambitious undertaking by a world leader in 21st century, is a telltale sign of Thailand's proximity to China. This was further consolidated in November 2022, when they issued the joint statement on building a community with a more stable, prosperous, and sustainable future, and signed the cooperation plan on jointly promoting the construction of the Belt and Road. King (at the time crown prince) Vajiralongkorn, Princess Sirindhorn, Princess Chulabhorn, Princess Bajrakitiyabha, Princess Sirivannavari and other members of the royal family have visited China and India multiple times.

Convergence in Thailand's Relations with India and China

Defence and Counter Terrorism Cooperation At the inaugural bilateral India-Thailand Defence Dialogue in December 2001, primarily in view of infamous 9/11 attacks, both sides agreed to work together in matters related to defence and security, such as Coordinated Patrol (CORPAT), combating transnational crimes, terrorism, and maritime piracy. In Dec 2023, maiden bilateral naval exercise between two countries has been named 'Exercise Ayutthaya' after the revered cities Ayodhaya in India and Ayutthaya in Thailand. There couldn't have been a better time to name the bilateral exercise as 'Ayutthaya'; both these cities share cultural and historical linkage. The Indo-Thailand Joint Working Group (JWG) on security cooperation established in 2003 has offered a framework to tow forward cooperation in maritime domain including security cooperation, which includes counter terrorism and military cooperation.

For maritime security cooperation, India and Thailand has been cooperating through multilateral naval exercises; MILAN which is Indian Navy's key exercise which includes countries of Indian Ocean Region and beyond. In February 1995, India, Indonesia, Thailand, Singapore, and Sri Lanka were the participants in the first edition of MILAN exercise. Since then, MILAN exercise has been a successful biennial naval exercise with the list of participating countries increasing manifold since its inception. Apart from the biennially held MILAN exercise, both navies also interact in other multilateral forum such as Indian Ocean Naval Symposium (IONS), and the Western Pacific Naval Symposium (WPNS).

Among other multilateral security forum, the Royal Thai Navy and the Indian Navy have regularly participated in the Rim of Pacific (RIMPAC) exercise, which is the world's largest international maritime warfare exercise. Since 2015, India is participating in Ex-Cobra Gold, the largest Asia Pacific Military exercise as 'Observer Plus' category. The other ongoing defence cooperation initiatives comprises of Annual Staff Talks, Subject Matter Expert Exchange (SMEE) visits and training of officers at each other's institutions. Furthermore, port calls and ship docking under agreements have increased significantly for India and Thailand. Presently, India undertakes bilateral exercises with many Southeast Asian countries like *Maitree* and *Ayutthaya* with Thailand, SIMBEX with Singapore, *Samudra Shakti* with Indonesia, VINBAX and *Sahyog* with Vietnam, and CORPAT with Indonesia and Thailand, *Samudra Laksmana* with Philippines.

Needless to say, terrorism in South and Southeast Asia undermine and directly impinge on India's security, particularly with regard to a number of terrorist groups operating in Pakistan. Jemaah Islamiyah (JI) had been known to train operatives in Lashkar-e-Taiba (LeT) facilities in Pakistan, some of whom had origins in Southern Thailand. *{Acharya, A. (2006)}* While former PM Thaksin Shinawatra was unenthusiastic (out of fear of flaming the Muslim population in Thailand) in his response to international pressure, eventually, the Thai government began to change policy. The two countries share mutual security concerns over insurgent groups using Thailand as a territory for the shipment of small arms, as well as planning of and recruitment for terrorist activities.

In 2013, India and Thailand signed an extradition treaty. The bilateral treaty provides a legal framework for the extradition of fugitives, including individuals involved in acts of terrorism, economic and transnational crimes {***Published vide Notification No. G.S.R. 418(E) dated 25th April, 2017***}. Among the most crucial drivers of the bilateral security relationship between New Delhi and Bangkok is a mutual commitment to counter terrorism that has grown over the past several years. In 2014, Thailand sought and was later granted extradition of 'Willy' Naruenartwanich, who conspired to mediate a deal between Indian Naga rebels and Chinese ordinance companies for a supply of weapons estimated to be worth as much as US$2 million. (***Bangkok post, 04 Nov 2015***) In Jan 2015, Thailand also extradited Gurmeet Singh, a Sikh militant who was among the six convicted for the 1995 India bombing that killed 18 people, including Beant Singh, the Chief Minister of Punjab (***The Hindu, 07 Jan 2015***). But, true to Thai diplomacy, it has brokered such deal with China as well since Thailand has a history of balancing rising powers well. In July 2015, the Thai military ruled government deported 109 Uighurs, at China's request. Thailand also detained and deported Hong Kong democracy activist Joshua Wong before his speech commemorating the 1976 Thammasat University Massacre.

Even with burgeoning relations between two countries, there exists lot of scope for defense cooperation across the services. The Defense and Security cooperation is a vital segment of mutual understanding between two sovereign nations who are maritime neighbours. The deployment of a Royal Thai Navy officer at IFC IOR, India would swing a lot of confidence in White Shipping data for two countries. Thailand and India have immense scope of initiating new joint exercises, increasing the frequency of port visits and Coordinated Patrol (CORPAT). In 2023, Indian Navy and Singapore Navy co-hosted the inaugural India- ASEAN Maritime Exercise (AIME), in which all ASEAN members participated except Laos (a landlocked country) and Cambodia (did not participate).

Similarly, increase in number of personnel in training exchange programme would be long term investment in developing a better understanding of each other.

Bilateral Trade Thailand view India as the gateway to South Asia and beyond. As a result of the reduced tariff rates and new initiatives adopted by both the countries, trade between two countries increased manifold in recent years. In 2020, despite the pandemic situation, the trade figures stood at US$ 9.76 billion. In 2021, it reached a record high of around US$ 15 billion (*MEA official site*). To date, there is no bilateral Free Trade Agreement (FTA), although dozens of rounds of negotiations are beginning to signal the arrival of what both countries hope will be a Comprehensive Economic Cooperation Agreement. After the implementation of the 'Early Harvest Scheme (EHS)' in 2004, covering 82 products (now 83) under the proposed India-Thailand FTA, lead to both sides undertaking tariff concessions in a phased manner. Thai goods have further benefited from tax reduction under the ASEAN-India Free Trade Agreement in Goods, which came into effect from January 1, 2010, and has already resulted in substantial growth in the bilateral trade.(***Embassy of India, Bangkok***)

In terms of economic and trade relations, China is Thailand's largest trading partner among ASEAN countries, while Thailand is China's third largest trading partner. In 2022, bilateral trade between the two countries reached 135 billion USD, showing a year-on-year increase of 3%. China's exports amounted to 78.48 billion USD, marking a year-on-year increase of 13.4%, while imports reached 56.22 billion US dollars, indicating a year-on-year decrease of 8.6%. From January to October 2023, the bilateral trade volume reached 105.1 billion US dollars. Moreover, China's non-financial direct investment in Thailand reached 1.29 billion

USD in 2022, showing a year-on-year increase of 38.8%. As of the end of 2022, Chinese companies in Thailand have signed contracts worth a total of 49.71 billion USD and completed a turnover of 32.65 billion USD (***Data from Chinese Embassy of Bangkok in Kingdom of Thailand page***). The China's trade with Thailand by far exceeds in numbers comparison to India. There exists a large scope of trade enhancement with Thailand in Defense sector and Space sector

Cultural Cooperation An Indian Cultural Centre is functional in Bangkok since Sept 2009 (now renamed as the Swami Vivekananda Cultural Centre). A number of India Study Centers are operational in prestigious universities in Thailand. Regular visits of Indian cultural troupes is organized, in addition to Indian film, food and other festivals. Embassy in collaboration with Ministry of Culture and several local partners organizes festivals for strengthening cultural linkage and people to people relations. These festivals include Indian classical dances, food festivals, art and painting exhibitions, literary festival and seminars etc. Yoga has permeated conscience of the whole world since commissioning of International Day of Yoga (IDY). IDY is celebrated by EoI, Bangkok every year along with support of other organisations and, people participate in huge numbers to celebrate Indian heritage. IDY is celebrated across Thailand and notable places are Bangkok, Chiang Mai, Hat Yai, Rayong and Khon Kaen covering most part of Thailand. The Thai language translation of the Constitution of India was released by Mr. Chuan Leekpai, Hon'ble President of the National Assembly and Speaker of the House of Representatives of Thailand on 12 Mar 2021 at an event organized by the Embassy to launch the celebrations of 75th anniversary of India's independence. Without a doubt, the cultural and historical linkage of two countries is deep and appreciated by people from both countries.

On this account, China, too has strong historical linkage and deep inroads in Thai society, politics, culture and social fabric of life. The two countries are celebrating 49 years of diplomatic relations in 2024. Chinese New year Festival in one of the major festivals celebrated in Thailand with lot of vigour, meaning and regularity. The Chinese people are holding key positions in banking sector, Govt offices, ministries, education, business and other miscellaneous sectors.

Traditional Media

China's state-owned television, radio, and news media outlets that advances a favorable view of China, encourages economic investment, and suppresses or censors negative content about China has considerable influence in Thailand.(***Sarah Cook, Jan 2020***) The PRC has maintained a long-standing presence in the Thai information space, with PRC state-run media widely available in Thailand. PRC propaganda is disseminated daily through television, radio, newspapers, and online platforms, delivered in both Thai and Mandarin languages.(***Kerry K. Gershaneck, 2020***)

Over the past few decades, the PRC has invested huge sum of money to expand the capacity and reach of its state-owned media deep in to the heart of Thailand. Chinese state-owned media companies are duty-bound to propagate China's narrative and censor unfavorable content to China. More recently, PRC state-owned media outlets, including *Xinhua Thailand, China Daily,* China Radio International (CRI), and others, have become actively engaged in circulating news and producing Chinese cultural content in Thai and English, specifically targeting the local Thai audience. China state-owned media attempts to collaborate with Thai media outlets into propagating pro-Chinese narratives and coverage through advertising payments, funding of journalist associations in Thailand, sponsorship of pro-Chinese coverage by Thai journalists, financing trips for Thai journalists to China, and providing free news content.(***Ryan Loomis and Heidi Holz, 2020***)

The PRC has expanded its Chinese-language media presence to influence the substantial Chinese-speaking communities within Thailand. The Chinese speaking community is on the rise in Thailand as Mandarin is second language in large number of schools. Currently, Chinese-language media is accessible on cable and satellite television via China Central Television (CCTV), and multiple newspapers in Thailand cater to the local Chinese-speaking community.(***Loomis and Holz,2016***) This media presence empowers Chinese authorities to continuously influence the millions of Chinese speakers within Thailand. Much of this content is translated into Thai to broaden the reach of Chinese narratives.

China's investments in Thailand's telecommunication sector have also enhanced China's capacity to counter the Thai media environment. Despite, Thai regulations limiting foreign ownership of media companies to less than 25 percent, Chinese have found ways to circumvent this prerequisite by establishing local subsidiaries led by Thai nationals. For instance, the Global CAMG Group, a subsidiary of CRI, has owned Bangkok's popular 103 Like FM radio station since 2011. Like FM is registered to two Thai businessmen who subcontract the station to CAMG, broadcasting popular music and Chinese news in Thai to 10 million local listeners. (***Skaggs, CCP information warfare***)

These investments in media may not instantaneously alter public opinion in Thailand, but pro-Chinese content is increasingly disseminated to the environment which will gradually influence Thai perceptions of China over time. It is akin to a generation of Indians addressing First war of Independence of 1857 as Mutiny of 1857 and reserving praise for Britishers on account of giving railways and Post Office etc to India. They missed the point the railways were put in place for ease of exporting material from hinterlands of India.

On the other hand, *Sanskrit* has lost steam in Royal circles of Thailand and is largely reserved for chants during official ceremonies. Expectation for revival of *Sanskrit* in Thailand would be foolhardy when it is pushed against ground in land of it's origin. India Cast Media Distribution in partnership with JKN Media, Thailand runs Hindi content on an OTT Platform titled 'Bflix' for Thai viewers. Of late, people in Thailand celebrate Hindi movies a lot, likes of Bahubali and Gangubai Kathiawadi took Thai social media by storm. Gangubai Kathiawadi's fearlessness and fortitude inspired sex workers and lesser privileged in Thailand. Sex workers across Thailand posed in white saris and red dots on their foreheads like Gangubai in the movie to celebrate women's power.

Social Media

Social media serves as a tool to extend the reach of Chinese influence, magnify propaganda, monitor dissent, censor information, and directly shape public opinion. In 2022, approximately 52 million Thai citizens, accounting for 72.8 percent of the population, were active on social media. Surprisingly, TikTok, amassed more than 40 million users in Thailand by early 2023, and is projected to surpass Facebook as the most-used social media platform in Thailand. (***Bangkok Post, 24 March 2023***)

On interaction with people, it came out that Mandarin speakers in Thailand turn to the Chinese application WeChat. It finds popularity among users with connections to the Chinese community, while Chinese tourists and businesses rely on WeChat for communication and mobile payment systems. Given WeChat's centrality in China, it plays a vital role in family communication and business dealings with China.(***Kheokao and Kheokao, "Reuters Country Profile for Thailand."***)

The youth in Thailand could be find glued to the extraordinary reel world of TikTok. The effect of TikTok was on display during May 2023 elections in Thailand. The Move Forward (Kao Kla) party, a new and budding party, secured a milestone victory over established mainstream parties, riding on their effective use of filtered reality of Tiktok for engaging with the public.(***Justin Sherman, April 2020***) The deep inroads of platforms like TikTok and WeChat, in daily lives of people in Thailand, has handed over a distinct advantage to China for influencing people for her gains . This brings in grim disaster of fake information especially knowing the influence China has over these tech giants. These firms have displayed their capacity to manipulate information for the PRC government within China, including the promotion of content and suppression of supposedly inappropriate material.(***Tang, "China's Information Warfare and Media Influence."***) This influence was clearly evident when the PRC disseminated a volley of disinformation during COVID 19 crisis to shape Thai public opinion. These platforms shaped opinion of Thai people who were tricked by Chinese state media and counterfeit social media accounts in believing that the virus spread was because of US soldiers and, Wuhan was not the epicentre of the COVID 19.(***Reena Marwah and Sanika Sulochani Ramanayake,2021***)

Overseas diaspora

Thailand has the largest overseas Chinese population in the world and shares deep cultural and historical ties with China dating back many centuries. Long back, Thai people migrated from the Southern province in China to Thailand. Even in last few centuries, there have been waves of Chinese migrants to Thailand. This connection is widely recognized by both Chinese and Thai officials who often refer to the Sino-Thai relationship as relationship between old friends or family.(***Skaggs, "CCP Information Warfare"***) Out of this bonhomie, China expends significant time and energy to mobilize the overseas Chinese community in Thailand in line with China's policy of Qiaowu(***refer to book 'Qiaowu-Extra-Territorial policies for the overseas Chinese' by James Jiann Hua To***). Chinese leadership habitually emphasizes the value of the overseas Chinese community in achieving the Chinese Dream (if there is one) and, proactively desires to enlist these communities to enhance China's image, pursue Chinese policies and interests from within Thailand.(***Sivarin Lertpusit,2023***)

China's is making concerted efforts to cultivate overseas Chinese communities in Thailand including cultivating *Guangxi* networks with powerful members of the Sino-Thai community, and Chinese-funded education to connect Sino-Thais back to their Chinese ancestral roots. The Chinese strategy of *Guangxi* refers to the practice of building relationships and partnerships to facilitate successful business operations and cooperation within a region. The *Gaungxi* network is irritatingly found on display in areas where Chinese diaspora is thick. Chinese companies aim to cultivate Sino-Thai networks within the overseas Chinese community to gain local trust and credibility in foreign markets by pivoting on cultural history and similarities to navigate local marketplace, governmental barriers, and potential regulatory hurdles. Since the 1970s, multiple waves of Chinese businessmen and entrepreneurs immigrated to Thailand in search of better economic possibilities and a better standard of life. Many of these migrants opened businesses, married Thai spouses, and assimilated into Thai culture. (***Antonio L. Rappa,2022***) But the Chinese connection never dies, and Chinese cultural memory never fades!

A recent 2022 study estimated that as many as 15 percent of the total Thai population can be classified as Sino-Thai. Of this community, at least 25 percent are involved in major Thai businesses, and 53 percent of Thai prime ministers have been of Chinese descent/lineage.(***Lertpusit,2020***) These Sino-Thai community people serve as a critical nexus to connect China's business sector and investments with Thailand's economic and political organization. Many Chinese Belt and Road Initiative (BRI) investments and auxiliary projects are linked to Sino-Thai individuals and groups that advocate for increased ties between the two countries.(***Lertpusit,2021***)

Thailand's inclination towards Chinese schools is primarily linked to expanding Mandarin education to facilitate greater economic opportunities. Currently, Thailand is home to the most Confucius Institutes in Southeast Asia. Broadly speaking, a Confucius Institute (Kongzi Xueyuan) is affiliated to a national university, while a smaller scale Confucius classroom (Kongzi Ketang) is affiliated to school level. Thailand also had the most volunteer teachers with over 10,000 Chinese teachers operating in Thailand's schools and universities between the years 2003 and 2018. In 2019, a total of 36000 Chinese students were studying in Thailand, 28000 Thai students went to study in China to enhance mutual understanding between younger generation of two countries.(***Benjamin Zawacki,2021***)

The most time honoured way of altering the perception in favour is to feed young generation with distorted version of their history. These Chinese funded education programs are instrumental in promoting "official versions of Chinese history, society, and politics."(***Yujiao Wang,2019***) Though prevalent in Thai society, Chinese education is not without disapproval in Thailand. Feeding of inexperienced teachers, aiming for high turnover, and growing concerns of political influences on Thai students in schools and universities are all existent issues of aversion among the Thai people.

Although, Thailand has been experiencing a Chinese cultural renaissance for some time now, the Sino-Thai relationship is more nuanced and tangled. Currently, Thai government takes Chinese language and culture as a means of economic prosperity. All countries which have taken this route, have bottomed, but not Thailand. The amount of Chinese influence in Thailand is openly disapproved and debated, and the Thai public has pushed back on instances of perceived Chinese authoritarianism and influence in Thai domestic politics.(***Lertpusit, "China's Influence on Thai Chinese Education"***) In recent past, Sino-Thai relations grew tense when Thai celebrities and other notable persons criticized the Chinese embassy in Bangkok over the China's cruel actions against protesters in Hong Kong, threats against Taiwan's independence, and Chinese dealing of COVID-19 pandemic. However, the Chinese immigrants could be double edged sword. It is no big business to understand that many Chinese immigrants left China because of oppressing measures of China's political leadership. While overseas Chinese can be an opportunity to progress China's interests, they can also be a liability based on their insider knowledge of the system.(***Andrew Chubb,2021***) There are many authors of Chinese origin who courageously write about China's political noose over their people.

Associate of China *Associate of China* refers to the group of people/ organisations who are cultivated and harnessed by China, whether knowingly or unknowingly, to promote Beijing's interests within the local information environs. Harboring these associates function on the principle that influential intelligentsia, entrepreneurs, and political gentry within the host country are more likely to influence domestic political decisions in China's stride. The China has resorted to various deeply articulated methods to build a stronger network inside Thailand, including Chinese-funded cultural and economic associations, investment in education, political engagement, massive celebration of festivals, and carefully crafted academic institutions.(***Joshua Kurlantzick,2008***)

Some of China's most salient defenders and well-wishers in Thailand tend to be domestic business conglomerates with significant business involvement in China. For example, the Thai Chamber of Commerce in China, the Thai-Chinese Chamber of Commerce, the Chinese-Thai Business Council, and the China-Thai Cultural and Economic Association all focus on fostering closely inclined business and cultural ties between China and Thailand. It goes without saying, that all country run similar organisation for bolstering close relations with each other but none with the intention of holding the economy and polity of a country by noose. Some of Thailand's big companies are members of these organizations, and they lobby the Thai government for increasing and siding with China in economic engagements.(***Phusadee Arunmas,2023***)

Multiple groups and organizations within Thailand advocate for China's policies. A few notable examples include Thaksin

Shinawatra, the Chearavanont family (business in real estate, insurance, owner of Makro, Fresh mart and 7/11 stores across Thailand). Thaksin Shinawatra served as the Prime Minister of Thailand from 2001 to 2006 and is widely attributed with initiating a major shift and drift towards China by mobilizing ethnic Chinese. Thaksin has considerable business connections in China and entered office as one of the wealthiest men in Thailand. A few notable and landmark shift from Thaksin, Thaksin oversaw the 2003 Sino-Thai Free Trade Agreement, Thai capital investment in China, and the PRC's expanded media presence during his tenure. Thaksin was deposed in a 2006 coup after mass protests accusing him of corruption.(***Zawacki's: Shifting Ground***)

Another influential empire is the Chearavanont family. The Chearavanont family has been instrumental in successfully forging closer Sino-Thai relations for almost half a century and uses its deep connections to facilitate their business hold in China. Interestingly, Thanin Chearavanont serves as the president of the China's Overseas Chinese Business Association and honorary president of the Thai-Chinese Chamber of Commerce.(***Peggy Sito,2023***)

Geo-economic View and Opportunities in India-Thailand Relations

Geo-economic spectrum comprises of economic investments and rewards strategically applied to harness influence and control over key foreign departments and assets. The China's economic goals are key to achieving the Chinese Dream of Middle Kingdom's restoration of its past glory and pride of place in the world. In 21st century, the China has mastered the art of subtle treachery throwing countries in trap of her maligned and draconian economic activities, known to world by terms such as 'Debt trap' and 'Cheque book diplomacy'. In pursuance of this, Chinese businesses and state-owned enterprises strategically promotes the China's political and economic goals by ensuring access to key resources, controlling critical and emerging technology, and acquiring strategic assets to increase China's economic influence in key Geo-strategic regions. Economic influence creates leverage that the China uses to harness favourable deals on her own terms.(***Skaggs, "CCP Information Warfare***)

Thailand's strategic location in mainland Southeast Asia and its growing economy make it an critical partner for China's

Geo-economic ambitions. Thailand's strategic location and its economic growth have given green signal to Chinese investors to invest in the broader Association of Southeast Asian Nations (ASEAN) market and beyond. Geo-economic factors linking China and Thailand are tangled, and include trade and investment, investments in industrial sector, agricultural cooperation, and tourism that have increased exponentially over the past decade. (***Shen Hongfang,2013***)

China and Thailand have signed multiple economic exchanges to expand their bilateral trade relationship, and Thailand has been one of the most active partners for the China-ASEAN Free Trade Agreement. In addition to this, Thailand acts as a strong advocate and intermediary to link China's economic activity and investment with the rest of the ASEAN countries. Subsequently, China has become the primary trading partner for every ASEAN nation, including Thailand.(***Jiranuwat Swaspitchayaskun, 2018 and Shen,2018***) Going by hard facts, the value of Sino-Thai trade in 2022 reached 3.69 trillion baht (USD 107 billion), accounting for about 18 percent of Thailand's total foreign trade volume. As an outcome of this, Chinese BRI investments, road connectivity through Laos, have reshaped the competitive landscape in Thailand and China relations. China dethroned Japan in 2020 (first time) as the largest investor in Thailand, a position that Japan owned for the past five decades. In 2020, Chinese investments in Thailand were valued at USD 8.5 billion, while Japan's were valued at USD 2 billion. In 2020, Thailand eyed an ambitious target of converting about 30 percent of the annual vehicle production into electric vehicles (EVs) in a decade. In pursuance of this policy objective, the Thailand government courted investments from several Chinese companies to start producing EV batteries and vehicles in Thailand in 2024.(***Kitiphong Thaichareon and Satawasin Staporncharnchai,2022***)

Tourism and its Effect on Relations The changing economic trend and China's policies are primary reason for drop in number of tourist to Thailand. To add to that, the Chinese blockbuster movie "No More Bets," released in Aug 23, did not paint Thailand in a positive light. "No more Bets" is loosely based on story of Chinese citizens who were tricked into taking a work trip overseas only to be involuntarily pushed into operating illegal gambling and cryptocurrency scams in an unnamed Southeast Asian country, with clear reference to Thailand. In Sep 23, in a reckless display of spineless character, a Thai national went on a shooting spree near shoppers heartthrob, Siam Paragon shopping mall in Bangkok; three people were killed including one Chinese national. The national pride which runs deep in China and is closely guarded by state; and to guard that, the news of the shooting led around 60,000 Chinese tourists canceling their trips to Thailand, according to Thai official data.

To fix the problem of reduced tourists from China, Thailand agreed to welcome Chinese tourist without a visa for a period of 30 days. Even, a bizarre and irrational idea was floated by Governor of the Tourism Authority of Thailand (TAT) to consult Chinese embassy about commencing a joint patrol by Chinese and Thai police officers in tourist areas in Thailand for ensuring safety of Chinese tourists, in lines with Italy. There exists an arrangement between Italy and China since 2015 that allows Chinese police officers to conduct joint patrols with Italian counterparts in Rome, Milan, Naples, and other tourist centers in a bid to make Chinese tourists feel safe during the peak tourism season. However, after much backlash, idea was dropped by Thailand which could have significantly compromised sovereignty.

The tourism in Thailand is on rise since last two decades despite political instability and other internal disturbances. From 2010 to 2019. the total number of tourist arrivals in Thailand have increased from 15.94 million to 39.8 million visitors, as per official data from Tourism Authority of Thailand. However, there is an interesting pattern to number of tourists from China and India. The Chinese tourist number grew by 38.56 percent where as India tourists number skyrocketed by 91percent from 2015 to 2019 period. Notably, there is 67 percent rise in tourists from Russia in the same time period. Therefore, the Thai government, to garner more tourist from Bharat, allowed visa free entry for 30 days, likewise for China. Irony is that, Bharat, which is six times bigger in area, much richer in tradition, culture and historical places is able to attract attention of half of the number of tourist to Thailand. Even, the Buddhist pilgrimage sites in India, which could work as magnet for Buddhists from across the world, are either ill maintained or lacks global connectivity. There is no commercialisation of Harappan sites, which lay silent because of irregular or sometimes no advertisement and branding. Of late, magic of yoga has given some respite in depleting number of tourists to India.

Increase in number of tourists from China and tourists from India is very different, and is viewed differently. Increase in tourists from China has brought several challenges for the Sino-Thai relationship. Chinese tourists have been seen as rude and unpleasant, and Chinese visitors tend to support Chinese businesses in Thailand, which limits the economic benefit to the Thai economy. In addition, there has been an increase in reported crimes committed by Chinese nationals involving fraud, money laundering, gambling, drug trade, human trafficking, and unlicensed businesses, which have contributed to negative perceptions of tourists from China in Thailand.(***Nopparat Chaichalearmmongkol,2023)***

Thailand's Dilemma Unlike some of its neighbors, Thailand has the economic strength and diversity to balance Chinese influence and engage China on a equal level. Thailand and its people are concerned with becoming overly dependent on Chinese investment and has witnessed China gain control of strategic assets assertively in Cambodia, Laos, and Sri Lanka. Thailand has been able to avoid the Chinese debt trap so far by limiting Chinese BRI ventures targeting Thailand's strategic assets and hedging its bets by maintaining other partners and markets to balance Chinese investment. While Sino-Thai economic activity has significantly evolved, Thailand continues to attract significant investment from the United States and Japan, and Thailand is actively seeking to further diversify by nurturing its relationships in the Middle East, India and Europe.

Overall, Thailand's economic policy seeks to balance ties between the China and the USA to achieve the best outcome for Thai side. Because of Thailand's diverse partners, Thai businesses are set to benefit from the economic decoupling between the PRC and the United States, as Western business seek to relocate their production bases in a phased manner, out of China.(***Punyaratabandhu and Swaspitchayaskun, "Horns of a Dilemma, Bangkok Post***) In other words, Bangkok is an independent actor who has its leg on both boats carefully placed, for its own benefit.

Geo-strategic alliances

Thailand hold immense strategic importance for China and India. India and China both conduct joint exercise with Thailand and purse defence cooperation for exporting defense related equipment. China and India both participate in each other's Defence related exhibitions like Def Expo and Defence & Security exhibitions. However, the scale of frequency and intensity of joint exercises, defense exports, joint participation is tilted in China's favour.

India has put tremendous weight in order to christen Thailand -Myanmar-India trilateral highway of about 1,400-km that would link India with Southeast Asia by land and give a spike to trade, business, health, education and tourism ties among the three countries. Once the trilateral highway will get commissioned, India would be at sniffing distance to extend highway to other countries of Southeast Asia. On the other hand, China is pushing, with all its might, the construction of Kunming- Bangkok high speed railway project which is part of Belt and Road Initiative (BRI). When the project is completed, the line will see trains running from Bangkok to the border town of Nong Khai, where a bridge would connect it with the China-Laos Railway, making it possible to travel by train between Kunming and Bangkok. Thailand's economic sustainability, regional influence, and key geographic location make it a key target in the China's strategic calculations. Chinese leadership uses frequent and high-level state visits, investment and infrastructure deals, and regional organizations like ASEAN to foster close relationship and gain influence in Thailand. Moreover, the China's growing defense cooperation with Thailand also contributes massively to China's regional interests. (*Enze Han, 2018*)

The two countries have conducted joint military exercises under the Falcon and Blue Strike series since 2016, and China has become an important supplier of military equipment to Thailand. In comparison, India and Thailand too are involved in CORPATs, bilateral and multilateral exercises. However, the Thailand procure equipment, big in number and huge in scale, from China in comparison to India. This list may soon also include Yuan-class submarines; however, the deal is currently at risk due to disagreements over propulsion systems. However, Bangkok has revisited the terms and conditions of these deals in recent past due to concerns over limited training, scarcity of replacement parts, and quality of material.(*Sakshi Tiwari,2022*)

Thai Diplomacy Contrary to viewpoint of bristling against Chinese pressure, Thailand has provoked Chinese wrath by pushing back or delaying several high-profile BRI infrastructure projects, the Lancang-Mekong River project, high-speed railway project, and the proposal for almost mythical Kra Canal. Lancang-Mekong project, initially approved in 2017, involves blasting 1.6 kilometers of basin to expand river trade. Thailand suspended its part of the project when it realized that the construction of upstream dams by China is significantly affecting river flow, and China's domination of river traffic will remove the benefit for Thai businesses forever. Thailand also hurdled Chinese-led riverboat police patrols through Thai territory, threatening Thailand's sovereignty.(***Strangio, In the Dragon's Shadow***)

Next, Thailand has repeatedly put the PRC's high-speed rail project in abeyance since 2014 for right reasons. The lingering rail project has turned a sour teeth between China and Thailand. Thai officials have privately voiced their concerns over the viability of the project and potential of China to take control of the strategic asset, as they did in Laos, to settle its overdue loans.(***Crispin, "China Losing, US Gaining Crucial Ground"***)

Lastly, the envisioned Kra Canal project has the potential to dramatically reshape the strategic environment in broader indo-pacific region. It will offer China, a shorter and controlled maritime route to the Indian Ocean by cutting through the Isthmus of Kra. Despite obvious economic benefits and international recognition, Thailand has repeatedly doused the fabled project due to concerns over Chinese financing, viability and creating a debt trap that could threaten Thailand sovereignty. The canal would physically wound the country and separate Thailand's south, which has separatist voices, from the rest of the country.(***Strangio, In the Dragon's Shadow***)

These projects are key essentials of the China's ambition to skirt the United States' choke-hold on the Straits of Malacca. Both the China and the United States rely heavily on the maritime trade through the Straits to oil their economies, and a land bridge through heart of Southeast Asia would bypass this strategically important choke point to the Indian Ocean. Each of these options, however, may compromise Thailand's sovereignty, a undeniable fact Thailand is well aware and wary of. Studying the progress of these BRI projects in detail, the point comes to the fore that Thailand has willingly delayed and rebuffed BRI projects citing high costs, security and management, and sovereignty issues.(***Zawacki, Thailand: Shifting Ground***) In nutshell, Thailand is unwilling to be convinced and consumed by Chinese overambitious and assertive national security interests and will push back when Thailand would feel threat to territorial integrity, sovereignty and will of its ever free people.

Education India offers a large number of scholarships annually under various schemes to Thailand. India has also offered 1,000 Ph.D. fellowships at the IITs to ASEAN countries, including 100 slots to Thailand. Currently, there are 5 Indian Studies Centers in Thailand at Silpakorn University, Mahidol University, Chiang Mai University, Thammasat University and Chulalongkorn University. (*EoI, Bangkok site*) In addition to these India Studies Centers, 9 India Corners have been set up in Thai Institutes across Thailand. H.H. Somdet Phra Ariyawongsakhatayan, the Supreme Patriarch of Thailand, an alumnus of BHU received the Padma Shri in 2018. In 2022, Dr Chirapat Prapandvidya received the Padma Shri under category 'Literature and Education'. The two countries have opportunity to cooperate further in education sector. Thailand hold enormous scope for contributing to Buddhism studies in India, whereas India has lot of scope for nascent education and specialized domains.

Chinese funding has also shaped a deep-seated presence of Chinese ideology within Thailand's academic institutions. China uses its influence to create connections with Thailand's academic and polity intelligentsia to advance and promote China's interests. Many connections are benign and seek to promote Sino-Thai connections. For example, Huachiew Chalermprakiet University was founded by the largest Chinese charitable organization in Thailand and offers multiple degrees in Eastern Health Sciences and Chinese Studies.(*Huachiew Chalermprakiet University, 20 May 2020*) The China Studies Center at Chulalongkorn University, Thailand's prestigious university in Bangkok and Princess Sirindhorn's alma mater, receives significant funding and support from Chinese entities. The Center focuses on promoting research and understanding of China's politics with their lenses. (*Wang, "Confucius Institutes in Thailand*) However, the darker side of Chinese influence seeks to obscure the source and scale of Chinese influence, and to push policies that advance Beijing's interests over Thailand.

Embassies/Consulates: India established diplomatic relations with Thailand almost 25 years before China. However, long before diplomatic relations were established, Thailand had set up Embassy in Delhi and Consulate General in Mumbai (1872) followed by Kolkata in 1879. Thailand has one Consulate General set up in Chennai as well. In addition to the Embassy in Bangkok, Bharat has only one Consulate in Chiang Mai in Northern Thailand and it was set up as early as 12 Oct 1972. On the other hand, China has five consulate missions in Thailand commensurate with the number of Chinese diaspora in Thailand. However, China set up first Consulate General in Chiang Mai on 10 Apr 1991, almost 20 years after India set up her first Consulate General in Thailand. The Consulate at Chiang Mai was first Consulate General set up by China in Southeast Asia after China pursued reforms and opened up economy in 1991. Although, the number of Consulates has no direct connection with relations between countries, like India, America has only one Consulate General in Chiang Mai and they share 190 years of diplomatic relationship.

Opportunities in India- Thailand Relations The China has resorted to malice and an assertive approach in pursuance of its national interests in Thailand, a model which could never inspire India, and therefore would never fit India in matter and manner. China has ruffled the traditional definition of 'Soft Power' and come out with its own understanding of 'Soft Power'. Joseph Nye, coined the the term "Soft Power" to describe the ability to shape the preference of others through appeal and attraction. Whereas hard power is exercised through military and economic forces, soft power relies on the attractiveness of a nation's culture, political values and foreign policies (***Nye, 2004: 5, 11***). However, China turned definition of Soft Power on its head and went beyond traditional definition. In fact, China appears to be successful using its version of soft power to incrementally push Japan, and even the United States out of regional influence. However, there exists a stark difference between relationship of India and China with Thailand. There exists possibility to engage with Thailand on many fronts to strengthen, already strong, bilateral relations.

Sister Cities A sister city or a twin town relationship between two geographically and politically distinct cities/provinces is kind of legal,sometimes social agreement, for the purpose of promoting cultural and commercial ties. If the two cities share historical ties, these agreements help in bringing people together. Few countries have researched and utilised the concept of sister cities more than China. China's sister city relationships are managed by the Chinese People's Association for Friendship with Foreign countries(CPAFCC). The China has leveraged sister city programs with other countries to create a political and economic environment that would support Chinese interests. In April 2019, CPAFCC president Li Xiaolin himself admitted, and said, "Friendship city relations have become one of the important channels to implement the Belt and Road Initiative."{***Allen, Bethany, 1 August 2023)***} To indicate its discomfort, China canceled Shanghai's sister city relationship with Prague after Prague›s mayor signed a sister city relationship with Taipei. Thailand shares an extensive sister city program with China that have assisted massively in forging strong relationships at the provincial level.

The China and Thailand have consummated more than 39 pairs of sister cities, with considerable local exchanges in all fields (*Embassy of PRC in Thailand official website,2020*). In fact, India has a small number of sister city agreement with China, but surprisingly none with Thailand. Few years back, there were deliberations between two countries to bring Surat Thani and Surat, Chennai and Phuket in sister city arrangement, but the process was not consummated. This would be an encouraging step to bolster the strong relations between India and Thailand. The historical links, present similarities in terms of technology base, economy make many cities between Thailand and India as obvious choice for sister city arrangement. Nakhon Pathom province in Thailand, where Buddhism was introduced by mission sent by Ashoka, the great, from Dhauli Giri Hills in Bhubhneshwar. The Brahmins, who performs Royal ceremonies, at Royal Court, Bangkok are descendants from ancient lineage of priests from Kailasanatha temple, Kanchipuram, a Pallava era temple. These two cities could be better suited for sister city arrangement. Similarly, existing cultural connection, historical linkage and other such similarities offers immense possibility for two countries to converge on many sister city arrangements. This would led to start up of institutions, cultural exchange, scholarships and would bring people of two countries closer.

Tourism to Buddhist Pilgrimage Sites

On his deathbed, the Buddha advocated his followers to visit <u>four places</u> "that a pious person should visit and look upon with feeling of reverence" (*Digha Nikaya* 16.5): his birthplace in Lumbini, Nepal, the site of his enlightenment in Bodh Gaya, the site of his first sermon in Sarnath, and place of his death in Kushinagar. The Buddhist pilgrims and tourists explore Bodh Gaya as a part of the Buddhist circuit along with Sarnath and Kushinagar. Along with this pilgrim circuit, tourists and pilgrims frequently visit other sites in Bihar such as Rajgir, Nalanda and Vaishali because of their geographical proximity. These sites could be construed as a local Buddhist circuit, that attract local and international Buddhist community. These circuits are pious and important to Buddhist community around the world. The Buddhist circuit and the local Buddhist circuit in Bihar is in a way equivalent to Char Dham and Chota Char Dham pilgrimage for a person practising Hindu religion. India is a proud country which is home to birth of many religions and faiths and, has carefully protected their religious sensibilities.

This is quite evident in the new construction of monasteries and shrines within Rajgir, Nalanda, and Vaishali. A large number of countries who have Buddhist majority have constructed at least one monastery in Bodh Gaya temple complex. For instance, the only Thai temple in India, Thai monastery of Bodh Gaya was built by King Rama IX in 1956 on 2500 years of genesis of Buddhist religion. The historical trajectory of Bodh Gaya demonstrates its position at the centre of the pilgrimage site for Thailand. These Buddhist sites, other than singing songs about tolerant character of India, also shout out immense economic possibilities. There are numerous examples around the world where countries have turned religious sites in to major economic hub. This appeal of religious Buddhist sites connects India and Thailand and enhances the possibility to create a ground for soft diplomacy between India and South, South-East, and East Asia. The increase in number of flights, hotels and associated facilities is a must to attract and sustain large number of tourists and pilgrims. In addition to planned infrastructure and reasonable incentives, there exits a need to put the Buddhist circuit in the conscience of the local populace in Buddhist countries through carefully crafted programme. This Buddhist circuit has potential to be a crucial spoke of the 'Act East Policy' of the Government, that somehow remains untapped. This brings me to raise an important question; Is there a set of policies that needs to be developed to harness the potential of these Buddhist sites?. Despite Bodh Gaya's appeal to a global audience, why does Bodh Gaya continue to be undermined in the public and policy domains in India ?

Travel Accounts-
A Journey through
'The Land of Smiles'

Chapter I

Bridge over the River Kwai, Kanchanaburi

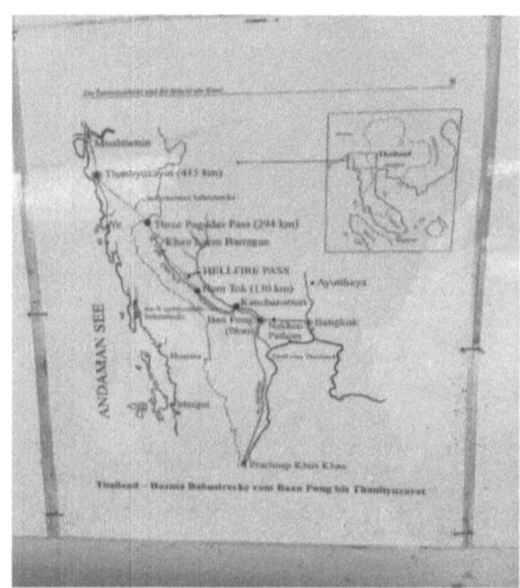

Pic(L) from JEATH War Museum, Kanchanaburi by Author.
Placed for better understanding of the scope of "Death Railway".
Pic (R) 'Death Bridge' just before Light and Sound Show

Let's delve into this picture before understanding and learning from gigantic blunder committed less than a century ago. A plan was drawn up in June 1942 by Imperial Japanese Army to link Bangkok and Yangon to march towards Bharat. The idea of cutting across thick forest and meandering mountains was not new. In fact,

British surveyed same route at the turn of the 20th century to expand their colonial adventures, but abandoned the idea as impracticable. But for the Japanese, well aware of the heavy price they would pay in case of defeat after their surprise attack on Pearl harbour, no cost was too high for victory. The Supreme Commander of Japanese Imperial Army ordered construction of one-metre gauge railway line following the same route British had surveyed in 1903. *The line from Ban Pong passed through Kanchanaburi and crossed the river Kwai where it followed the Kwae Noi river to the Myanmar border via the Hell fire pass. From Three Pagoda Pass, it travelled North-West to link up the British line to Yangon at Thanbyuzayat on the Myanmar coast (see in picture).*

The construction of the Burma-Thailand highway began at both ends simultaneously using British, Americans, Australians, Canadians, New Zealand and Dutch POWs and Tamil Indians in addition to 200,000 Asian slave workers rounded up in Indonesia, Vietnam, Malaya, Burma and Bharat. The French in the Indochina came up with a "Diplomatic Understanding" with the Japanese and were spared horrors of working on Death Railway. There were two bridges constructed across river Kwai, the original wooden bridge was completed in Jan 1943 whereas the concrete bridge, that we see today, completed in Jul 1943.

Anyone who has ever read history of WWII in some detail must have read or watched "Bridge over the river Kwai" and the iconic dialogue by Col Nicholson *"One day the war will be over. And, I hope that the people that use this bridge in years to come will remember how it was built and who built it. Not a gang of slaves, but soldiers, British soldiers, even in captivity"* Colonel's word turned prophetic; the war was over long back and people travel in large numbers and pay homage to the soldiers who laid down their lives in detention camps on tracks and midst of nowhere in forests. I got my chance to travel to Kanchanaburi with Priyamwada and I wouldn't have picked anyone else for this extraordinary train journey over Death Railways. The fact that our journey coincided with Light and Sound show festival at Bridge over River Kwai, which is an yearly phenomenon was icing on the cake.

The first sight of the Bridge from train window and that harrowing train whistle was a scary experience. The train incessantly whistled and slowed down to clear people from the Bridge on to the sides. She pinched me as we crossed "the Bridge over the river Kwai" as it was surreal experience for us to travel across bridge on Death Railway. People standing by track sides waved, photographed and sang songs which were subsided by the train whistle.

We went to WWII cemetery in Kanchanaburi province in front of railway station. Priyamwada said, as we entered "These places, they speak to us, only if we are keen to listen. Look, how dutifully they lie in tropical serenity telling us the dark story of their times. See the green rust on the copper plates, and words from their families are real and sad. This is not the only place of humans extraordinary capability of destruction. They are countless and we have seen few, and we have missed many. Remember, Jallianwallah Bagh, the Slave lodge in Capetown, Highway of Death between Kuwait and Iraq, Concentration Camps of WWII, and the list is endless. And, its not about Japanese, every country or state who ever believed in supremacy of only their ideas and felt that their way of organizing society should reign supreme, have ended up bruising and injuring the larger conscience of human race. Japanese, Britishers, Americans, Dutch, Portuguese and many others have treadled this path. While the Death railway should have taught humanity a lesson, we saw "Highway of Death" in our lifetimes"

Where it ends then? I asked her as we sat on the bench contemplating bigger and important questions.

She said "It has no beginning, and it has no end. Half of the known world is at war at any given point of time. Sadly, people are killing each other without loss of temper. Look around, Russia-Ukraine, Israel-Palestine, Armenia-Ajarbaijan, trade war between American and China (Trade wars, too kill people), many countries in Africa (internal as well as external conflicts), resurgence of Taliban; it is all happening around us. All these leaders have promised peace and laid wreath at memorials, but they also ensure enough reasons and monuments like these for future leaders to lay wreath and maintain the vicious circle. So, in nutshell, it will never end till *Kalki* dish out a favour to us - Ultimate destruction."

We moved to nearby JEATH War Museum which was the original site of detention camp. At once, I thought, JEATH is mispronounced version of Death. But, as i entered museum it was clear that the majority of the people involved in construction of the Death Railway were from Japan, England, Australia/America, Thailand, Holland. The museum is immaculately maintained and the original material findings, letters, experiences are preserved.

One young Japanese soldier writes in his diary "*The education system was re-scripted in 1890 and re-script was issued in the name of the emperor Meiji with the contents based on feudalistic ethics such as loyalty to the emperor, patriotism,obedience to fatherhood as well as dominance of men over women. Loyalty and obedience to the emperor was the essence of national constitution. Fundamental human rights were ignored….In these circumstances, I had no hesitation in volunteering for the service*" This was written by a 23 year old boy.

Priyamwada remarked, as she photographed the letter "We haven't learned our lessons. This re-scripting of the same tenor is happening in many parts of the world, even today. The world is shifting towards de-globalisation, offensive realism (Read John Meisenheimer's '*The tragedy of great power politics*') placing narcissists or pseudo nationalists in power. And, therefore there will be periodic construction of "Death Railways" or "Death Highways" in some form, and I am not trivializing the issue."

A survivor writes that Japanese, despite their propaganda, became so convinced that.. "an allied invasion was imminent'. *"They drew up plans to execute all prisoners. And, the plan was- We were to be lined up and machine gunned in pits that we dug for ourselves. The Japanese worst fears came true but, the Japanese correctly anticipated time of attack by allied forces. The Prisoners of War were conscripted to stand in a line on the Bridge so that allied drop the plan for bombing. They kept on waving to ditch plan of bombing and aircrafts dropped full load of bombs. I saw the river turned red with blood of those PsOW. The stench of the dead bodies turned river Kwai water non potable for several days"*. ..and there were other letters drenched in equal pain and misery.

Priyamwada's attention was fixed to a letter titled "Reunion at the River Kwai" from Mr Takashi Nagase who was interpreter in Japanese quarters at Kanchanaburi. He planned a gathering of ex-prisoners and ex- Japanese officers in 1976 at the Bridge over river Kwai. This news was criticized by most ex prisoners and one of them wrote *"We will throw them into the river when they turn up"* And, the Japanese ridiculed his plan with "I told you so". Finally, on 25 Oct, 1976, 3 British, 2 Americans, 18 Australians and 51 Japanses gathered on the river Kwai. The two Americans refused to walk over the the Bridge along with Japanese and said *"We would not walk together with the Japanese thinking of our friends who died in resentment"* The event was rich in emotions. Mr Nagase replied to a reporter when questioned on holding Thai national flag and not the Japanese flag during walk over the Bridge - *"Do you know how many people on earth were slaughtered under the Japanese flag for this railway track"* I was wondering what those moments would have been like for friends and foes to walk over the Bridge. Must be soul stirring experience! Touched and excited, we both walked together across the 305 m long bridge and back. We were wondering, whether they threw all enmity and hatred in river Kwai and enjoyed the pleasure of forgiveness just by seeing each other faces.

In evening, we sat on a bench made with wood which was used in making original bridge to watch Light and Sound show. As we watched the show , Priyamwada began "Do you remember, what Lin said in novel Shantaram - *'It's forgiveness that makes us what we are. Without forgiveness, our species would've annihilated itself in endless retributions. Without forgiveness, there would be no history. Without that hope, there would be no art, for every work of art is in some way an act of forgiveness. Without that dream, there would be no love, for every act of love is in some way a promise to forgive. We live on because we can love, and we love because we can forgive'."*

Chapter II

Lady Boy Saga
A Personal Narrative

*My thoughts are with the men and women who live
in any part of the world, and feel that they are
born in and with the wrong gender*

- Author

This interview was important from the context of the book as
well as for understanding life of a Lady Boy (popularly known as
Kathoey) in Thailand. They are everywhere but, most visible and
accepted in Thailand's major cities. The fact is, even today, in rural
areas they are tolerated rather than accepted. One of the first thing
that strikes mind of a young tourist from India to Thailand is easy
to find vibrant and safe night life, clubs, Go-Go bars etc. Through
this chapter, I want to throw light on the life and difficulties of
Lady Boys, whom they would encounter in plenty during their
visit to Thailand. Though, it is far from bringing together entirety
of their difficulties like body shaming, abuse and mental torture
that they undergo as they grow up in a single chapter restricted
to few pages. More so, it is interview of a Lady Boy who is proud,

open and accepted, who met with less resistance, but not of a Lady boy who is humiliated, tortured and not accepted in the society he grew up.

Note - Vanilla (name of Ladyboy) struggled with English and therefore, for better understanding of the Reader, some sentences have been changed in manner, and not matter. Also, some information have been added based on interaction with other Lady boys. I have used 'He' for a Lady boy in this chapter for the sake of original sex and to shun away any confusion.

To start with, I had no connections or indirect reference to get in touch with a Ladyboy for interview. I chose, Hit and Trial method! I knew there are plenty of bars in Bangkok, Phuket, Pattaya which only has Lady Boys workforce. Even, surprising is the fact, that these bars are further segregated between Lady Boy with female organ or Lady boy with a male organ. I chose a bar in Nana plaza with primary workforce of Lady boys with female organ aimed at knowing and understanding seemingly painful procedure of sex reassignment. To cut it short, I stumbled on half dozen of them who rejected an interview and in some cases, I couldn't differentiate a female from a Lady Boy. Similarities were startling, differences I found none!

I met Vanilla at Nana Plaza, and requested his time for an interview. Kind and thoughtful of him, he wanted more people to know story of Thailand's most misunderstood gender, and therefore he agreed. He is a beautiful, confident and no-regrets Lady boy. I told her how confusing it's to differentiate. With a warm smile, he asked me to keep these questions for interview.

We decided to meet late evening at Cafe Kudeejeen which is located in Portuguese locality. Vanilla was dressed in red dress which was revealing and hard to ignore; a perfect bosom and a curvy back. We sat across the table and ordered food to settle our palates. I was nervous! Vannila's guts knew the fact that I was nervous and therefore, he replied to the first question I asked, when we met for the first time - how do you differentiate between a Lady boy and a woman?

Vanila keeping his cutlery in order and taking first sip of beer after a half hearted cheers from my side, said "A woman generally has broad hips and narrow shoulders where as its opposite in our case. Also, you will find distinct height difference. Recognition with a distinct Adam's Apple is a bygone thing. Look, I have got the bone shaved with surgical procedures and like me, so many. A much finer distinguishing feature is a smoother and flatter forehead in case of a woman. Unlike us, a woman has more room between the eyes and eyebrows. But, you have to literally stare at them to see through these minor details. Get talking to a Lady Boy and you will find difference in the voice. Though, we try to speak in a higher voice to mask the coarse sound (*laughingly*). But, all these are subjective identification features and would vary on case to case basis. (putting his ID card in front of me) This is the only foolproof method, you see Mr someone in I card, you will have your answer. As per govt rules, we can not have the sex changed in I card."

I overcame bout of nervousness, gulped some water, thanked her for breaking ice and started with first question from my diary "Why and how come Thai society has so much acceptance for Lady boys"

Vanilla responded "Buddhism believes in reincarnation and *Karma*, according to which it is prophetic that every soul incarnates birth after birth until it reaches the ultimate- *Nirvana*. And, *Karma* is like a spiritual bank of our deeds (good and bad) from all births and it has everybody's address. (Looking at me with a smirk of shoulders) You are a Hindu, you understand these concepts better. In the cycle of births, it is believed that we, *Kathoeys*, are in debt of previous births. May be in previous birth, I did sexual misconduct, sexual abuse or abandoned a woman with my child. Since, Lady Boys are ill fated to endure suffering from birth, people here feel sad for us rather than curse us. It is against the notion in some other parts of the world where being a transexual is considered a mental disorder."

Karma and *Nirvana* are believed to be real things in Hinduism, but hypothetically speaking, even if they are not, they bind people to accomplish good deeds. I was getting distracted by Vanilla's frequent fiddling with his hairs, but I was more focused on food, cool breeze around the temple of the ears, and interviewing him. "What was life and feelings like as you were growing up?"

Vanilla's speed with beers was making me little conscious. She settled back in chair and reminiscing about his past spoke eloquently "We, *Kathoeys*, all have different upbringing, depending on the immediate society we are brought up in. It's subjective! It remain hidden in initial years, but soon our interests grows in dressing up like a girl, lipsticks, heels and dresses. My mother got to know about it much before my father. My mother allowed me to play girl games and dressed me up like a queen in my father's absence. Soon, one day the bubble bursts when he saw me dressed up like a girl with make up on. He did not react weirdly, but he was worried about my future, my old age prospects. Against the environment at home, I was bullied a lot at school. I was called by names, segregated in class seating, and I always expected a bucket of water on me while using washroom.I gave up on school and came to work in Bangkok which has a big heart. It feels suffocating to grow up female in a man's body. You can not comprehend it, you can not feel it, you can just see it (I could see a emotional lump in his throat).

I interrupted and diverted discussion to food, weather and the cruise ship passing by on Chao Phraya river. "How and when you decided to undergo surgery ? Is that a professional need or a personal choice?"

Vanilla touched my hand politely and said "It is a dreadful experience. Surgical clinics have boomed in Thailand as more Lady boys have started expressing themselves. I wanted to be a complete woman and though, was scared of surgical procedures, got so many of them, that I have lost count of them. Breast implants (Thai women lacks big breast and perfect nose), larynx surgery (for improved vocal cords), eye surgery (to resemble Japanese manga characters), upper lips surgery, surgery to level out cheekbones (for more feminine looks), butt implant surgery (to achieve curvy back). I took a large number of pills to subdue the hormonal change. I prepared myself for grand finale surgery of sex reassignment. There is nothing that excited and scared me at the same time more than sex reassignment surgery. I was one of every ten Lady boys that willingly accepts the blade on private part. Never felt Newton's third law so closely- for every time I went under blade, there was an equal and opposite reaction.(Vanilla almost grew cold thinking about that). There are things I can not explain and there are things that you will not understand. I leave it at that."

I grew very tense and numb thinking about the process. Although, chasing dream is a joy but it comes at a cost. I looked at Vanilla and tried to imagine his face and features without surgery. I mustered courage to ask next related question - "Surgery requires a huge sum of money, how and from where you managed?"

Vanilla knew this question was coming his way and he instantly replied "Most of us take a ticket to Bangkok, Pattaya or Phuket, to the areas with bright neon lights. Massage parlour, Go-Go bars, prostitution. Depending on our beauty, features, age and money required, we choose our place. I chose prostitution. It gives lot of money, but its not easy money. Whosoever calls prostitution a source of money has never followed a drunkard or a psycho in utter dark room. To most *farangs* (foreigners) who comes in search of sex because of their disgruntlement in personal lives find us mindbogglingly beautiful hyper females from another galaxy. But, prostitution is no different for women, too. They too, undergo a lot of procedural surgeries in order to appeal to men. It takes tanning, waxing very frequently, Botox procedures, dieting, facial, hair removal surgery, regular manicures, pedicures, brow shaping, exercise, facials, breast implants, liposuction and many more to stay relevant in industry. And, if that was not enough, competition is such that girls are resorting to 'V-Lighten' (to lighten the skin of the female organ) and 'V-Tighten' which involves tightening of vagina with laser. You have heard of labiaplasty surgery?"

I was not aware of the intense competition in the world of neon lights, and neither I was aware of labiaplasty surgery. Listening to all this, was so depressing and sickening.

Vanilla smiled, said "These girls chart such stupid lengths to please men. They undergo labiaplasty which is a procedure to surgically alter the inner and outer lips of vagina. You can read more, probably a surgeon can explain with more eloquence"

I could read his face. Underneath fascinating beauty lies pain and almost no clear solution to his problems. I felt that Lady boys along with the girls working unwillingly in dark rooms are true warriors. They stand bravely against fate and give us insight in to the blessed nature of our lives. I, with all my heart, expressed solidarity and asked him "What other challenges you see coming your way as you would age?"

Vanilla finishing last morsel of his meal and sipping his beer said "It takes lot of courage to come to terms with the fact that I would never mother a child. That means, I will never be a real woman. Lifelong taunts and sneers becomes part of our lives. I have heard many stories and seen few Lady boys growing up old alone. Once the beauty and charm becomes thing of the past, we are neglected and live a life in oblivion. That's why, we need money. Remember, every story is different."

I thanked Vanilla for her time, for sharing his pain, and most importantly the story. If you are reading this, you will see these angel 'Lady boys' with a lens of rationality and generosity. That was, second and last time, we ever met. I visited that bar more than couple of times to see him, but he seemed to slip away like sand of time.

Chapter III

"Little India" and "China Town"- Too Close for Comfort

China Town - China Town could be found almost across continents because of early interaction and immigration of the Chinese people to different parts of the world. Out of sheer curiosity and fate accomplice, I visited China Town in Darwin (razed to ground during WWII, only a building left), Manila, Phillipines (probably,oldest China Town) and Kolkata. Chinatown in Kolkata has a unique Chinese Kali Temple which serves noodles as offerings (*Prasadam*) to deity. That is magnanimity and cultural understanding of *Sanatana Dharma*. However, outside Asia, the China town flourish in San Francisco and Melbourne which were established during California and Victoria gold rush respectively. Fact is that Bruce lee was born in Chinatown at San Francisco.

A coffee shop is more enticing and productive place for conversation than a bar, for the sensory dilution sometimes eludes important details. This is no way preaching but experience be-told. Walking from street to street, shop to shop, cafe to cafe endlessly, with only titbit conversations was tiring and deflating. But, fate has a definite quota of surprises for everyone. I entered a bar crestfallen, and I met this gorgeous and magnetic lady Shangdi at

243

the bar counter. She held a drink in hand carefully and helped me in overcoming language barrier. These kind of sudden connections, without any expectations are soft, warm and respectful. She passed a subtle indication to me with eyes to join her. If it is not for mouth, humans could have converse with eyes as well. Anyway, fact is we smile better with eyes. In hindsight, I could tell that a person of Thai Chinese descent lodged in China town for work was perfect to help me unfold mysterious labyrinth of China town. Shangdi didn't sipped but gulped alcohol, and narrated stories like a master storyteller.

Shangdi started to share her experience of Chinatown "Chinatown is an ecosystem and like any other ecosystem balance is essential. The popular literature on Chinatown would be all mystery and dark humour. Have you ever read about 'Murder in Chinatown' by Victoria Thompson. Most of these Chinatown settlements around the world have appreciable connectivity with sea. They harbored most of these cities as immigrants, and seas kept door open for a return ticket to homeland, if such situation arise. Most Chinatown have temple dedicated to the Mazu (Goddess of Sea), Tudigong (Land God) and Kuan Yim temple for commercial success. Most Chinatowns has a prominent large red arch entrance (Chinese call it '*Paifang*') guarded by lions on either side of gate to greet visitors. At the middle of the night, we went around all the important sites in China town, and she stood before each one explaining in detail about the significance of the site.

Sensory dilution does not deter her much, and she eloquently narrated the story of the Chinatown. The migration of Chinese people increased over centuries, and their trade and business flourished. We strolled our way to the heart of China Town, the red coloured archway known as "King's Birthday Celebration Arch".

"Long Live the King" - she read the letters (written in Mandarin) on the facade of the archway.

She continued "The text is calligraphy in Mandarin by Her Higgggghhness (she stretched the word Highness while she was herself high) Princess Maha Chakri Sirindhorn to honour the ruling monarch - I think archway is only one of its kind".

We drifted towards the area tailor made for diluting human rationality, arousing hormonal imbalance and toppling men and women from the high pedestal of righteous and gracious living in to the bottomless swirl of shame and despair. China town is house to commerce as well as red light district hosting opium centers, theaters, nightclubs and everything in "Murder in Chinatown". She commenced her monotonous recitation of the briefing about Chinese migration and their relations with Thai society. She must have narrated the beautifully curated story of the mooring of Chinese people in Thailand, a thousand times. Here goes the story -

Chinese people started trading with South East Asia or Survnabhumi even before Sukhothai period using *Sampans* (small oar boats). The Ayutthaya period saw huge number of Chinese migrants. Most of them were from the south of China migrated to Thailand, and settled down for sole purpose of trade. Chinese explorer Zheng He's treasure fleet ruled the waves from 1405 to 1433, and carried out peaceful trade as far as coast of Africa. Zheng He commented that women seem to run the show, and observed large Chinese diaspora and monks in Thailand. Ayutthaya Kingdom was one of the earlier places where Chinese traveled for trade. However, the Ayutthaya was razed to ground by the Burmese in 1767. Ayutthaya was freed again by King Taksin whose father was a Chinese and mother a Thai woman. The warrior was enthroned as King of Thonburi and Chinese considered him one of their own.

They lovingly called him Tae-Oung after his father who was a Chinese. This lead to huge immigration of Chinese people as they considered Siam territory and its King favourable for their trade and settlement. And, favourable he was! Bangkok was an accomplished Chinese trading post before it became capital of Thailand and had around 9 percent Chinese population in its demography (*data from Udon Thani Thai Chinese Culture Centre*).

Taksin remained king of Thonburi from 1762 to 1782, in fact he was the only King of Thonburi. In 1782, the seat of the power shifted to Rattanakonsin, present day Old City in Bangkok, and Chakri Dynasty was established. Fate smiled on Chinese immigrants again, first king of Chakri Dynastty was married to the daughter of a rich Chinese merchant. If fate cannot make you humble, probably nothing could. Most of the migrants, during Taksin period were men, and they got married with Thai girls. The children born of inter cultural wedlock were called Chinese children.

The reign of King Rama III was period (1824-1851) where cautious treading was the need of the hour in dealing with threat to the sovereignty from foreign powers. France and Britain were engaged in vulturous act of seizing territory and resources in South East Asia, and immigrants were flocking from China. As an outcome, the nationalist Thai across the country launched anti-Chinese campaign because of oppressive tax collection, emergence of mafia and fearful of the Chinese intentions. But remember, by this time, the Chinese were controlling a sizable part of economy, and had already monopolized certain businesses. They engaged in opium trade, owned mills, acted middle men in trading and served as tax collectors. The pattern changed, and intensity of the Chinese migration to Thailand increased at the turn of the 20th century. The deep rooted sense of nationalism and immense connection to family values catalysed migration along with their family. This was very different from their prior generations who married Thai girls and integrated with Thai way of life. Chinese nationalism started growing parallel to Thai nationalism in Thailand. Today, Bangkok has credit for the largest and probably most vibrant China Town in the world.

Little India Like China Town, Little India or Mini India has footings in many countries in the world. USA, England, Singapore, Canada, New Zealand, Australia and Bangkok to list a few. The journey of the unwilling migration, struggle and establishment of a like minded community in all these countries differs a lot in letter and not so much in spirit. In fact, there are countries like Fiji, Suriname and Mauritius which has sizable population of Indian lineage. Indian lineage people have amalgamated in these societies, but still maintain a deep rooted respect for Indian culture and traditions. What more, the President of Suriname, smallest South American nation, took oath of Office in *Sanskrit* swearing by the Vedas. On another occasion, Prime Minister of Britain Mr Rishi Sunak took oath swearing by holy *Bhagwad Gita*.

China Town and Little India in Singapore and Thailand are at close proximity to each other. Other than proximity, the there exits cultural wedge and tradition differences. The 'Little India' is a cocktail of Indian lineage people migrated from Bharat at different times for different reasons, and carried different traditions from Bharat. However, majority of the migrants came to Thailand during last century of British rule. There has been many influential Indian lineage people in Thailand. Alok Lohia (billionaire businessman), Amar Siamwalla (one of the most prominent economists of Thailand), Ratana Pestonji (Thai film director and producer), Santi Thakral (Member of privy council of King Bhumibol Adulyadej),

Vidya Dhar Shukla (Chief Hindu royal priest of Thailand). Lek Nana, a Muslim of Gujarati ancestry, was a well respected Thai businessman and politician. He was one of the founders of the Democrat party at the end of WWII, and served as deputy foreign minister as well as minister of science, technology and energy. Nana area on Sukhumvit road which is home to many migrants from India, derives its name from him.

Little India's Phahurat road was constructed in 1898. This is named after son of King Rama V. Little India has labyrinth of textile, silk, grocery shops, and they offer a congested look. But, the main attraction of 'Little India' is the *Gurudwara* Shri Guru Singh Sabha constructed around 1932, one of the largest *Gurudwara* outside Bharat. I offered prayers and had Prasadam (*langer*) at *Gurudwara*. Of all the things in 'Little India', this was the sight to behold. People from all faiths sitting together for food under one roof, seemed like the most pious realization of the faith. I wondered, "food or religion, what unites us more? Empty stomach can unite human beings more than religion, but hunger can bring the beast in men out in open. Unfortunately, the beast in men is exposed because of religion. Look around the world, what laughable entity humans have become in front of other species. Other creatures must be happy in their heart that they haven't evolved as much as humans"

Chapter IV

Bangkok's Bonanza

Literature, like music and birds have no boundaries. I have been part of literary festivals, lectures, seminars, photo exhibitions, book fairs in Delhi, Mumbai, Jaipur and Bangkok. The language and settings may be different but the appreciation for literature is a constant. For literature is one of the most cherished human expression through out the world. I participated in various forms of literary buffets across Thailand and have attempted to stitched the lessons and experiences together for the good Reader.

Bangkok Literature Festival, British Club Bangkok literature festival is an yearly celebration of books and ideas in the heart of Thailand. The event was spread across 2 days (4-5 Nov 2023) and featured around 50 local and international authors, poets and storytellers, primarily from South East Asia. It was organised in one of the most celebrated and duly maintained libraries in Thailand, that is, Neilson Hays Library, British Club. Few literary sessions stood out in terms of sheer attendance, gravity of the subject, impact of delivery and ability to galvanize people to buy their work for further reading. Here is, summary of two books that I bought and got signed by authors. Both the books are well researched and meaningful works- suitable reads.

Adam Higginbotham spoke about methodology of research for his book "Midnight in Chernobyl". He traveled extensively, met people on site who were directly affected from incident, and his central idea was that he would rather prefer to live near a safe nuclear plant then a functionally safe coal plant because nuclear plant is safe for health. Chernobyl was a man made disaster created by human negligence. The book begins with the procedure for site selection, brings out lack of budget with unrealistic timelines, and extreme faith in one individual -Victor Brukhanov. Still, everything worked in tandem until the night shift in Apr 1986. He brought clinical facts regarding absence of knowledge of first respondents about the radioactivity at the site and failure of those in charge to recognise the intensity and magnitude of disaster.

Lisa Lin spoke about her book 'Surveillance State- Inside China's quest to launch a new era of social control'. She brought out the perils of digital intrusion and social engineering of state by reckless usage of AI. She was very bold and clear in what she thought of China's Communist party policy to shape will of the people through sophisticated and, sometimes brutal harnessing of data.

Sea Junction in Bangkok Art and Culture Centre (BACC)
Sea Junction in BACC hosts number of literary functions, photo exhibitions, social functions for raising funds for needy, awareness programme on a regular basis. I attended many of those functions. Just to mention one, I attended discussions on "The social life of Teak"- a book by Tim Webster and Virginia Henderson. Before this discussion, I never looked at the Teak the way the two authors did. They discussed fundamental questions - How teak has shaped people's lives, drives fortunes and impacts future? They

discussed about our role (as natures most troublesome offspring) in controlling the ecological disaster, violent repressions, animist beliefs, imperialist expansion for saving extinction of Teak. Tim Webster spoke about the legendary love Indians have for Teak. He called British imperialism visionary in declaring teak as "endangered species". There is no heroism or wisdom of any kind in endangering a priceless commodity and then declaring it as one. Audience shared anecdotes about legacy of teak furniture in their houses. Indeed, some very interesting stories!

Foreign Correspondent Club Thailand (FCCT) Though, the membership of the prestigious club comes with satisfying overwhelming list of criteria, I attended lot of functions and lectures at this cosy and reputable club as non-member. Few of them which deserves mentions - "Photo exhibition" by world famous Rauli Virtanen (his photo collection of Afghanistan is detailed and eye opening), Enforced disappearance in Laos and across Southeast Asia, Thailand's marriage inequality, Opium trade in Southeast Asia, Human Trafficking in Southeast Asia and many more. One of the notable and interesting discussion was chaired by Mr Chris Baker and Mrs Pasuk Phongpaichit (wife of Mr Chris Baker) who are dedicated historians. Both authors together were awarded prestigious Fukuoka literature prize for contribution to Southeast Asian studies.

Pic(L) Author at FCCT, Bangkok and Pic(R) a discussion at Sea Junction, BACC

Defense and Security Exhibition 2023, Bangkok The scene at Defense and Security exhibition was straight from a Hollywood sci-fi movie. For me, people bidding for best killing machines is a nightmarish idea. Which killing machine has better precision? How many people it can kill? At what range it can destroy targets? How many people required to man the equipment for delivering a killing blow? Is it the best technique to kill people? I have strong aversion to this idea at philosophical level. The Defense and Security exhibition, an important biennial ASEAN's leading tri-services event, has grown almost exponentially since its inauguration in 2003. About 45 countries put up a exquisite display of radio jammer, weapon systems, tanks, UAV's, AI based weapons, Satellites, Telecom equipment etc. In addition, there were live demonstrations, seminars/ discussions, networking and business opportunities. In the pavilion assigned to India, BRAHMOS missile system occupied the pride of place, and it was one of the cynosure of the exhibition. From the scope and aura around, it could be safely assumed that this biennial event is on a path to become of the region's one of the most cherished and dynamic exhibitions, and could no longer be ignored.

World Hindu Congress 2023, Bangkok   The World Hindu Congress 2023, a quadrennial event, was held at Bangkok from 24-26 Nov 2023 with the theme *'Jayasa Aayatnam Dharmanh'* meaning "Dharma, the Abode of Victory". This was "I was there for 3rd WHC" moment for me because I could sense that in the years to come it would turn out to be massive and decisive body for Hindu Community. The congress was aimed at discussing and deliberating upon the opportunities and challenges faced by Hindus across the world and, how to deal with them valiantly. The earlier congresses were held at Delhi (2014) and Chicago(2018). They were held under theme theme *'Sangachchhadhwam Samvadadhwam'*, meaning "Step Together, Express Together and *'Sumantrite Suvikrante'*, meaning "Think Collectively, Achieve Valiantly" respectively. I was thinking how much this religion has endured to stay relevant in its present form. They have survived it all - the years of forced conversions, fake narratives, biased regulations against them, inhumane treatment, burning of libraries and world famous Universities, destruction of scriptures and every trick up the sleeves of the oppressor. What more, Hindu faith considers the entire universe as God's and everything in the universe as God. I have grown up admiring the dialogue between Shri Mandana Mishra and Jagatguru Shri Adi Shankaracharya which lasted for days and had scope for dissent and discourse.

Marathon across Thailand   I was not new to the Marathons before my long sojourn in Thailand. I have run Half marathons (only one Full Marathon) across the length and breadth of Bharat. In fact, I have been to home of Marathon, that is, Greece in 2018. I visited the historic Panathinaiko (beautiful marbles)stadium which has been site of finishing point of first modern Olympics marathon race in 1896 and then, in 2004 and Athens Classic Marathon since 1972 (second Sunday of every November). The name Marathon, derives its origin from the legend of Philippides, the Greek messenger. The legend states that, during the Battle of Marathon in and around 490 BC, he witnessed a Persian vessel shaping course towards Athens, he interpreted this manoeuvre as an attempt by the defeated Persians to claim a false victory or raid Athens. It is believed that he ran entire distance from Marathon to Athens, which is approximately 40-42 km, without stopping, discarding his weapons and even clothes to shed as much weight as possible and burst in to the Senate naked, exclaiming "We have won !", before collapsing and dying. To honour him, the race begins in the town of Marathon, where it passes the tomb of the Athenian soldiers and statue of Philippides (the legendary messenger) before finishing at Panathinaiko stadium.

In Thailand, I participated in 5 Half Marathons namely Bangkok Marathon, Chiang Mai Marathon, Animal Rescue Trail Marathon, Mahidol University Fund Raising Marathon, Chiang Rai Marathon. There is a definite courage, excitement and passion in people for running in Thailand. Once you run a Marathon, the route and environment gets stitched in memory. There are very few acts like that. Marathon is an event which breeds mutual respect and sometimes, a long lasting relationship along the marathon route. During Chiang Mai marathon, I came across a couple who fell in love while running marathon in Germany in 1996. They have participated in around 100 marathons, literally they have reached 'Finishing Point' together, because that was the starting point of their love- the Finish Point."

Muay Thai Experience Once a good Thai friend told me that Muay (boxing) Thai to Thailand is what Cigar is to Cuba, Pizza to Italy, *Samosa* to India, and happiness is to Bhutan. He gave me two options for witnessing Muay Thai - Rajadamnern stadium or

Lumpini Boxing Stadium (run by Royal Thai Army). To experience the skilled fight of two humans within the rigid framework of rules, I went to Rajadamnern Stadium (expensive among the two options) along with Priyamwada. The environment inside stadium was magnetic and electrifying; it is Mecca of Thai boxing and any respected Muay Thai boxer would consider it epitome of honour to compete at Rajadamnern stadium.

Posing with Muay Thai Boxers before Muay Thai bout

Priyamwada told me that Boxers have finished Wai Karu tradition which is an indication for readiness to fight. I was clueless about this ceremony, I focused on sportainment, the state of art built of stadium and spacious arena. Priyamwada asked me to look at corner of the ring "You noticed, white band in corner? The Head band (*Mongkol,* meaning Holy spirit of protection) and armbands (*pra jiad*) are traditionally presented by a trainer to the fighter when he considers that the fighter is ready to represent gym in the ring. After *Wai Kru* (prayers), trainer would take off the Head Band (*Mongkol*), and place it in his corner of the ring for luck"

Long back, before going to war, young men would tear off a piece of their mother's sarong and wear it in battle for protection. She was adamant on proving the point "In ancient times, King won subjects by offering them the spectacle of a fight in massive stadiums. In Rome, they called it Colosseum. The beating heart of the Rome was sand of the Colosseum. People would put blind eye to the vices of the King and senate because he arranged the fight of the Gladiators. How different is it today? We still pay for watching humans thrash each other, this appears like sophisticated version of the same instrument".

But these fighters are fighting willfully and they are not bound to do it. May be they enjoy it!

To which Priyamwada sarcastically said "May be, they enjoy thrashing each other, right? This, I call Neo-slavery."

There exist something like this ?

She replied without blinking "Yes, there are more number of people under subjugation, of some form than any other period in history. Since ancient times, the life of common men has marginally changed; the ecosystem of oppressor and oppressed is intact. This indifference towards the oppressed will remain the most indelible characteristic of humanity. We pretend to like truth, but we have no bone to stand for it."

For whatever she said, I enjoyed experience of watching Muay Thai boxing match from which kick boxing has emerged, in land of its origin.

Chapter VI

Festivals, Festivities and Rituals

I surfed for places to celebrate Deepawali in Thailand. Intelligent search engine that google is, offered me a list of options. I knew for certain that I wouldn't have had these many options in India. Not that Deepawali is celebrated with less fervour in India, but people prefer to celebrate at home and within community rather than through social functions. Though few, the social functions to celebrate Deepawali are massive in scope and size in India. In Ayodhya, 24 lakh *Diyas* (lamps) were lit for Deepawali 2023, establishing a Guinness world record, bettering 18 lakh *Diyas* lit in Ujjain to celebrate Maha Shivratri. Undoubtedly, Diwali and Holi are two major festivals celebrated by Hindus whether in Bharat or outside. It is also celebrated by Sikh, Jain diaspora and a sect of Buddhism. In fact, Deepawali is an official holiday in Malaysia, Mauritius, Myanmar, Nepal, Pakistan (not certain, though), Singapore, Sri Lanka, Suriname and Trinidad and Tobago, Fiji and Guyana. Broadly, 4 of the 11 Southeast Asian nations has Deepawali as national holiday; Thailand is not part of the list. Thailand has 19 national holidays which are primarily dedicated to Buddhism and to honour the contribution of Thai royalty.

Pic(L) Celebrating Loy Krathong in Khon Kaen province and Pic(R) at Chinese New Year at China Town, Bangkok

Loosely speaking, Thai people does not celebrate Diwali; though they join hands with Indian expats, Indian descent Thai people, and Hindu tourists in celebration. "Little India" was lit up for Deepawali with decorative and fancy *Diyas* and festive hue was seen all over the place especially on Walking Street along Ong Ang canal. I could find people from all faith, Hindu, Muslim, Sikh, Buddhist, Christian celebrating the idea of Deepawali, victory of Light over Darkness, Knowledge over Ignorance. It was straight out of the stories, my grandfather would tell about Deepawali celebration by all communities together when he was a toddler. During his times, he saw, what is unimaginable in most part of the India today. Thai people offer prayers at home in method and manner which may appear traditional even by Indian standards. As I was witnessing the celebration, the address by Governor of Bangkok was relayed on the screen to which every one was glued. The Governor encouraged everyone to join the festival of lights and happiness, and not just

Thai people of Indian descent. On the occasion of Deepawali 2022, the Bangkok Municipal Administration officially recognised Deepawali festival for the first time, and joined hands with Indian Association of Thailand (IAT) for increasing Deepawali festival footprint. Invariably, this step would boost tourism and would swing fortunes for "Little India" . Only then "Little India" would be truly blessed by Goddess Lakshmi.

The festival is celebrated with remarkable fervour in a country faraway from the land of its origins. A kid performed on the stage to a blend of Thai and Hind songs. His father and mother were from India and Thailand respectively. His forehead was smeared with India and Thailand flag, and he exhibited equal proficiency in both languages. That for me, was a perfect content of cultural blending. The blending of cultures is not a recent phenomenon, and neither it is at national/state level only, I see and feel the result of culture mixing in my hometown. People address each other in five different ways, follow four different religions (some derived from major religions), wear different clothes with commonality, syncretism in eating habits, many ways to live and die, and different treatment with dead body. Humans shunned acceptance of other religions than their own when the realisation was forced on them that their way to God is fast and sure. The end result is - we encounter more humans, less humanity.

There was representation from Vishwa Hindu Parishad (VHP), *Dev Mandir* (Devasthan)and other temples in Thailand for Diwali celebration.

Theravada Buddhism Funeral Rites in Thailand

"May be there is after life, may be there is no life after death, both prospects are equally scary and intimidating. Do whatever good possible in this life and find pact with both prepositions."

– Author

Unfortunately, I have been part of Hindu funeral rites in India and have noted small deviations in rituals in different parts of India. Though, the essence remains same. In the Vedic context, the journey to *Shmashana Ghat* (Cremation Ground) along with a dead man's pyre is considered a *Tirtha* (pilgrimage). *Shmashana* is a *Sanskrit* word; *shma* refers to *shava* (corpse) and *shana* refers to *shanya* (bed). Death is as certain as day after night for all beings born on earth. Hinduism and Buddhism, both religions believe in reincarnation (*Poonarjanama*), Nirvana and Karma. The essence of rituals in both religions is - the family of the bereaved person along with society perform religious ceremony and rituals to bring peace and benefits to the soul in next life. The funeral rites in Thailand are mostly influenced by the traditional Hindu and Buddhist rituals which has undergone minor changes with the passage of time.

As a certain death approaches, family of the dying person call upon monks to perform a ceremony to extend his life. A similar concept of *Jamankaaj* is conducted in Hindus to pray for the long life and to celebrate his life with a feast organised by the family. At the deathbed, family members asks him to recite the name of the Buddha as it is believed that if his last thoughts are dedicated to the

Buddha, it will reap benefits to the soul in next life. Similarly, in Hinduism, the person offers last prayer to Lord Rama with eldest son supporting his head, for a better next life.

I got an cursed opportunity to attend funeral rites in Thailand. I encountered a lot of similarities and some difference in conduct of funeral rites between Theravada Buddhism and Hinduism. After death, a bathing rite, similar to Hindu traditions, was held so that family could pay respects by pouring divine water over the dead. This water is turned pure by monks who chants *Abhidhamma*. At the end of bathing rituals, some coins were put in to his mouth for use in next life. A sombre realisation came with lightening speed - *you can not even carry few coins in next life. Why is the urge to accumulate ?*

Normally, the body of a person who dies away from home or a violent death, called "*Phi Tai Hong*" in Thai, is taken straightaway to temple, and not to the house. A chanting ceremony is accomplished in temple for a period of three or seven nights depending on the wish of the family members. During this time, four monks are invited to have meal every day as part of the merit making for the dead and to chant every night. Before chanting, the family member knock on the coffin to request the deceased to listen for the chants because in case of violent death, they didn't had opportunity to remember Buddha while they breathed last.

After the monks leave, food and sweets are served to the guests. It is believed that on the third or seventh night the ghost of the dead, called "Phi" in Thai, would visit his home after wandering for a time. He would visit the places and meet the people he liked. In Hinduism, the ceremony in case of violent death or otherwise is same. Whether this holds water or not, but from my own experience, one of the thirteen days of my grandmother's *theravin* (13 day ritual after death), dogs howled in chorus and barked in a strange way. My father told me that dogs can see ghosts, and howl strangely when they see. In case of violent death only this procedure was different.

At the end of the night chanting period, in the afternoon of the cremation day a large number of monks, usually equal to age of deceased person, performed chanting for the dead. From here on, I was witness to the entire procedural rites. The relatives and family members moved in a procession carrying the coffin, led by the monks, in counterclockwise direction around the crematorium three times. All person part of the procession held the sacred thread ("*Sai Xong*"), which was attached to the coffin. The procession proceeded in silence accompanied by a traditional Thai orchestra, which acted as suppressant of sorrow and despair. There were coordinated fireworks too. Coffin was placed at designated place (not sure, if the deceased body was placed with feet facing south as in the case of Hindu rites), monks were invited to take the funeral robes offered to them by the person designated by family members, generally elder of the family (in Hindu funeral rites, eldest son takes lead in rituals). When all is done, everybody including all the monks placed wooden flowers at the base of the funeral pyre. The designated senior of family then poured coconut water over the body of the deceased. Then, relatives and family were given a very short time to have a final look at their loved one before his body is burnt by fire. Memorial books or souvenirs were distributed to all present. I made way back home from the pilgrimage after *Antyesthi* (the last rites as per Hinduism) ritual thinking about the tender existence of beings.

When the body is burnt, the ash-collecting ritual in an urn is performed by a monk and urn is taken home for one more merit-making ceremony for the deceased or in some cases, placed in a small pagoda in the graveyard awaiting the ritual post 100 day. Some relatives may take the remaining ashes to be scattered in a river, similar to what Hindus does in mother Ganga (Mae Phra Khongkha meaning Holy Ganga) and other holy water bodies. A hundred days after the death, the last ceremony is performed to seek blessings for the deceased in presence of relatives and friends. The nine monks performs this final ritual and sprinkle holy water ("Nam Mon" in Thai) on everyone after chanting. Before departing to the temple, monks sprinkle holy water on everybody. This is the final ceremony, after the deceased has returned to five elements, and he will only be remembered in prayers.

The roots of this belief for Hindus are found in the Vedas, for example in the hymns of Rigveda in section 10.16 {*Wendy Doniger (1981), The Rig Veda, chapter on Death*}

Don't burn him through, Agni; don't scorch him; don't singe his skin, nor his body.
When you will make him cooked to readiness, then impel him forth to the forefathers.
When you will have made him cooked to readiness, then deliver him to the forefathers.
When he will embark on the (way) leading to (the other) life, then he will lead at the will of the gods.
Let your eye go to the sun, your life-breath to the wind. Go to heaven and to earth as is fitting.

Or go to the waters, if it has been fixed for you there. Take your stand in the plants with your limbs.

— Rigveda 10.16

Marriage Ceremony in Thailand

This essay is included based on my experience in the preparation and participation in marriage of a Thai friend. Marriage Ceremony is one of the significant chapters in everyone's life when a man and a woman decides to hand over reign to each other for the rest of their mortal lives. Therefore, every religion reserves most finer and celebratory rituals for marriage ceremony. Like marriage in India, horoscope plays an important role in match making in Thailand. As Dr Shashi Tharoor says "What credit card is to an American, horoscope means same to an Indian". Stretching his words a bit further, horoscope has same importance for Thai people. The marriage conventions have changed everywhere in 21st century, this chapter brings in the facets of traditional form of marriage in Thailand.

For my Thai friend's marriage, astrologers found their stars compatible and auspicious day and time of the marriage was declared. In Thailand, most wedding ceremonies are held in August, which is considered to be the most auspicious month for wedding. To save money, some people plan engagement and wedding on same day. In India, as in Thailand, marriages are becoming matter of status. Who will spend more money? Who will invite more guests, and who all will actually attend?

The engagement ceremony is usually accomplished by offering an engagement ring to the girl while the wedding ceremony is incomplete without the offering of dowry (*Sin-sod*), the money given to the bride's parents by the groom's parents. Similar practise exists in India but, bride and groom are housed in opposite camps in this evil and dying practise. I found *Khan Mark* (offering items) ceremony as most fascinating part of the marriage ceremony in which a procession of relatives and friends dance their way to the house of the bride with their hands full of offerings. Though, the energy in the dance was nothing like a wedding in northern India. The wedding ceremony began in the morning with the chanting of monks. Then, the couple and relatives offered food to 52 monks who chanted again after their meal.

Senior monk went around to bless the couple and the gathering with holy water after the chants. Late afternoon, arrangements were made for the couple to receive blessings, similar to the arrangement for *seven Phere*. But, it was unlike *seven Phere* ceremony practised by Hindus where the couple takes round of a consecrated fire seven times promising each other vows with *Agnideva* as witness.

The couple sat in a crouched position with their hands in a gesture of prayer. The relatives and friends queued up to pour scented water from a conch shell on the couple's hands wishing them a life of togetherness and happiness. The blessing ceremony was followed by a grand dinner reception at the groom's house. After the reception ceremony, bride and groom were guided to the decorated room by the senior member of the family.

Monkey Festival in Lopburi (Monkey City), Thailand

I reached Lopburi, a day before the Monkey festival, to sense pulse and enjoy the setting of the festival. To my sheer astonishment, I witnessed monkeys by the thousand around the Phra Prang Sam Yot (literally meaning "Three Holy Towers". This temple was constructed to honour the Hindu trinity, Brahma, Vishnu, Mahesh during the reign of the Khmer empire. The centre Tower (*prang*) is higher than the other two, hinting a higher pedestal offered to Lord Vishnu in this temple. The temple is an important landmark and rightfully features on the official seal of the Lopburi province with Lord Vishnu occupying pride of place. King Narai, the great of Ayuthaya empire consecrated additional complex and placed Buddha statue in "Calling the earth to witness posture" in the temple complex. A legend from famous Ramakein (derivative of Valmiki's Ramayana) scripture says that Lord Rama gave this city to Lord Hanumana as a goodwill gesture for helping him win over Tosakanth (Raavan in Valmiki's Ramayana). This legend has holy and mythical standing respected by locals. I saw them bowing to monkeys as they pass by to honour the monkey God, Lord Hanumana.

The world knows about Thailand's reverence for Lord Hanumana. They made it even loud and clear by choosing Lord Hanumana as the mascot for Asian Athletic Championship 2023. The Asian Athletic Championship's official website explained the significance behind the choice of Hanumana as the mascot "As Hanumana exhibits extraordinary abilities in Lord Rama's service, including speed, strength, courage, and wisdom....Hanuman's greatest ability is, in fact, his incredibly staunch loyalty and devotion." These monkeys hold pride of place, as Lopburi province is named to honour them. Lopburi literally means City of the Monkeys (Lop means Monkey, Buri translates to City) in Thai language.

Monkey Banquet festival started in 1989 and is organized on the last Sunday of November every year. Collectively, people make a heap of fruits, vegetables, sticky rice, salads, drinks on open cart, and move it to the temple complex. The festive activities flags off in morning with an opening ceremony, dances and musical performances. The festival banquet is fed to monkeys 4 times a day on the day of the festival. At first, I saw, monkeys overwhelmed by the large number of spectators, but they soon overcome their apprehension to enjoy buffet. People from all around the world gather to witness and capture the spectacle of the monkeys contesting for food, gently occupying back or head of the visitors, literally bringing "monkey off the back" phrase to life. There was provision of ambulance and instant medication in case a monkey does, what he does best. The monkeys were not aggressive on humans, but their spirit of competence and confrontation for food basket was as real as human beings story of survival. In many ways, the monkey fighting to hoard food was the story of the most evolved species.

In certain aspects, I found monkeys possessed more wisdom in life and know more sophistication in understanding of death. Have you seen a monkey dying or dead ? I haven't. There is an ancient lore in Ramayana about death of the monkeys. Lord Hanuman asked for a boon from Lord Rama in favour of the monkeys. The boon was that before their death monkeys must be aware of it, and their dead bodies should never be seen by anybody. Lord Hanumana wanted dead bodies of the monkeys to be food of termite or some other creatures in need. Lord Rama agreed to his favourite devotee and granted him the boon. Monkeys aware of their hour of death, they isolate themselves to a place and contemplate the death. Isn't it sophistication as well as burdensome to await death? The monkeys coexist with human in many parts of the India, and almost everywhere in our stories. In Lopburi, monkeys inflict damage, but they bring in revenue to the city through out the year. The next large gathering of monkeys after Lopburi, I saw on Monkey mountain at "Chopsticks hill" in Hua Hin province. But, my attempt to search for a story, mythical or urban legend in Hua Hin, met disappointment. The population was of the monkeys at the hill is high and they share attributes with monkeys at Lopburi- Amusing, wise, courageous, energetic and sometimes, unconventional and wild.

There is no denying strange nature of this festival. In many ways, it depicts the diversity of Thai culture and historical significance of monkeys in Lopburi. And at last, if the history of ancient ruins, a lavish display of feasting monkeys from as close as your shoulders, authentic Thai food, music and culture interest you, and if you are around Bangkok in end November, add this festival to the list.

Thai Wai and Samudra Manthan

I saw a man bowing gently with folded hands, and an arresting smile greet me at the Suvrnabhumi airport, Thailand. This gesture was similar to greeting style in India, so I took him for an Indian. But then, after many such encounters on airport, I remembered my Thai language teacher who taught me various aspects of Thai lifestyle which are similar to India in method and manner. The Thai salutation to greet is Wai, a gesture of bowing with folded hands. This gesture is common in India where people greet each other with Nameste/Namaskar. In fact, Namaskar word has its roots in *Sanskrit*; the word Namaskaran also finds place in Thai language.

269

As I continued my stay in Thailand, I was often surprised by Thai people ability to smile in all situations, even when I found it out of place and context. It is close to impossible for a tourist or a non-Thai person to decipher the Thai smiles. A close Thai friend helped me by showing 10 of the 13 smiles, and he named each of the 13 smiles. While he was enacting smiles, Yim Soo smile (Smiling in face of an impossible struggle) was a constant decoration on his face. The other smiles were 'I am so happy smile', 'polite smile' (for someone you barely know), 'I admire you smile', 'I will laugh even though its not funny smile', 'smile masking something wicked', 'I told you so smile', 'I know its pretty bad smile', 'the sad smile', 'the dry smile', 'I disagree with you but you can go ahead smile', 'I am the winner smile' (to an opponent), 'one that he kept constantly on his face' (Yim Soo), 'I am trying to smile'. I have noticed people smiling as you pass by them in MRT, BTS, Bus, hospital, almost everywhere and on every occasion. The ability to understand these smiles would assist your social acceptance in "the land of the smiles".

Samudra Manthan I noticed a famous Hindu mural sculpture of the churning of ocean milk that is - *'Samudra Manthan'* on airport. I have grown up in a household where stories about *Samudra Manthan* were regularly told and retold. The monstrous and dastardly COVID 19 gave much breathing space for relishing these stories from childhood via theatrical representations like Shiv Mahapuran.

Gods and Demons were persuaded by Lord Shiva to rally hands together for churn of the ocean, and distribute the outcome among themselves. The mount *Mandara* as churning stick, and *Vasuki* serpent as churning rope were placed on tortoise back for churn of the ocean. The churn of the ocean which is immensely important and deeply connected to Hindu culture has found a place of prominence at Suvrnabhumi airport. The relation and connection of *Samudra Manthan* to Thailand does not start and end at Suvrnabhumi Airport. In fact, the tale is famous in most parts of the Thailand. The churning turned the ocean water to milk out of which came Nector, the Sun, the holy cow, other personified deities as well as elephant Airavat (given to Lord *Indra*, for which Gods and Demons both agreed). Airavat, called Erawan in Thai language, is an elephant with four tusks, seven trunks and a white complexion.

Erawan is extremely popular in Thai culture. There is dedicated museum, shrine and national park in honour of the holy elephant. In Thailand, Erawan is symbolically berthed on sphere depicting earth to save earth from bad omens. Also, a shrine named after Erawan is located in Erwan hotel in Bangkok which house gilded four faced Lord Brahma *(called Phra Phrom in Thailand, Phra means Holy and Phrom is distortion of word 'Brahma')*.

I visited shrine like many tourists and found four faced, four handed Lord Brahma sitting cross legged, gazing and guarding all four cardinal directions, precisely the way it is portrayed in the only Brahma Temple in Bharat located in *Pushkar* district, Rajasthan. In Brahma temple at *Pushkar, Savitri* and *Gayatri,* the two wives of Lord Brahma are seated on either side of idol. Having studied in Ajmer for 7 years, I have been fortunate to pay homage to the holy site on numerous occasions. I was startled by the fact that Brahma, one of the *Trimurtis* in Hindu traditions, has only one temple dedicated to him in land of temples, and he is not worshiped at same pedestal as other Gods.

I met with an Indonesian Hindu tourist, wearing a Kurta with Ram embroidered on it "My friend, why only one Brahma temple in India? We have more than one in Indonesia"

I instantly answered him "There is one temple of historic relevance dedicated to Lord Brahma. Brahma is part of Trinity and he is worshiped in all temples dedicated to Trimurti. Also, lately temples for Brahma has been constructed at many places across Bharat. The reason for Brahma missing the share of worship has been part of folklore, and holds many explanations. The most accepted one believes in a duel between Lord Brahma and Lord Vishnu for claiming superiority. Lord Shiva, to settle dispute, created a tunnel of light and expected the superior of the two to find the end of the tunnel. They both went in different directions. Lord Vishnu accepted his defeat while Lord Brahma was too proud to loose. Angered by his lie, Lord Shiva cursed Lord Brahma, and bane him unworthy of worship."

Common interest and religion, we proudly share, brought us together as close friends over a period of time.

Section V

Literature Review

Chapter I

Seminal Literature and Analysis

This section contains list of books and articles referred for writing, and their critical analysis to assist the Reader in forming an informed opinion about Thailand. I found, Chris Baker and his wife Pasuk Phongpaichit tall and clear voice on history and geopolitical underpinnings on Thailand. I was also fortunate to meet these two prolific writers during a talk on "*The five oldest Thai poems: Love, Loss and Landscape*" at the Siam Society on 02 Mar 24. Rest of the works mentioned, I have read and listened to the authors. I have attempted to put their works under scanner from my perspective. It would be befitting to start with the authors, I have met.

Author with Mr Chris Baker at the Siam Society, Bangkok

Chris Baker and Pasuk Phongpaichit - 'A History of Thailand'

Anyone with serious interest in contemporary Thai history, political spectrum and their interconnection, must chew this book for starters. The book covers early history to the founding of Bangkok in 1782, briefly, touching upon the empires of Southeast Asia from 15-18th century. The majority of the pages are consumed by Chakri dynasty in detailed, catchy and sequential manner. So exquisite is flow of writing, that reader would be confused, 'who is a Thai' because of palimpsest nature of Thai beliefs, qualities, values, traditions identity over centuries. The present generation of Thai people is increasingly in conflict with the traditional Thai people on what really means to be a Thai, in a nation stitched together from a divergent concoction of people and Kingdoms in past. All ancient countries and civilisational states are blessed and cursed with this concoction of beliefs and identities. India, is no different , that way because similar dilemma is encountered in defining "Who is an Indian?"

The books reveals that, at various points of Thai history, the minorities like Muslims, ethnic Chinese and Isan, Christians have been seen as "Un-Thai". The proud revelation is that Hindu in Thailand have never seen/treated as "Un-Thai". They have amalgamated to Thai culture and society, so neatly . The book brings out dissent with the fascination of stretching Thai history to Sukhothai era in school textbooks, only to harness authenticity for lineage of Kings.

I found "A history of Thailand" to be deeply informative, well paced and simple to read (a praiseworthy attribute for a book on political history). Highly recommended!

Paul M.Handley- 'The King Never Smiles: A Biography of Thailand's Bhumibol Adulyadej

At the outset, this book is banned in Thailand. This book has, in some measure, defamatory words for former King Bhumibol Adulyadej who is highly revered by Thai people. Handley is a Washington based journalist experienced in Asian matters for more than 20 years of which 13 years were dedicated to political events in Thailand. This extensive experience shaped his book- 'The King never smiles' which is termed by many as 'the first serious biography of perhaps the most important figure in modern Thai history'.

The kind and apolitical portrayal of the King is tossed in air and brings out his deeply political and autocratic side which together with his well-wishers in big business and corrupt Thai military, raised a dying monarchical structure to prominence. Paul Handley's book is well researched, fact based account of the king's rise to the throne, proficient political maneuverings and attempt to shape Thailand as a Buddhist kingdom.

Chris baker has praised the book at conceptual level, but he remarks that the role of Thai elite and rising middle class in re-imagining Bhumibol as a symbol and protector of democracy is neglected. The Thai middle class played an important role in casting King Bhumibol as harbinger of peace during political upheavals in 1973,1976,1992 thereby, making people believe that democracy is a gift from throne. Baker reviewed the book in *Asian sentinels,* and said that the book added a little to experts view but it did piece everything brilliantly. For the love of conspiracy and a break from mainstream view, I would suggest readers to pick this book.

Nirmal Ghosh - ' Unquiet Kingdom- Thailand in Transition

It would be icing on the cake if you read **"Jungle Book: Thailand's politics, Moral Panic, and Plunder 1996-2008"** before buying a copy of Nirmal Ghosh book. The Jungle Book is a collection of 64 columns from Asian financial crisis to Thaksin's self exile that appeared in *The Nation* newspaper. I read selective articles from the book which offered, not just facts but a deeper understanding of Thai politics.

Nirmal Ghosh, a correspondent for *The Straits Times* since 2003, has written this book as first hand account of many incidents in political and social landscape of Thailand that continue to change the political spectrum. He explains the rise in political awareness of common man which is an outcome of high economic growth (like most places, have increased gulf between elite and poor) and explosive expansion of social media. The author has put the events which followed Thaksin's unsettling from power in finer detail - the Red and Yellow demonstrations, the series of army coups, fresh elections in 2011 and election of Yingluck Shinawatra (Thaksin's sister).

I found chapter five "Monks, Money, Metta" very revealing, and consider it as core of the book. The book, with numerous examples, brings out the deepening corruption in the monk sect as most had become wise in worldly ways, and had commercialized Buddhism. Though, the commercialization of Gods is a phenomenon across the religions.

Paul Chambers and Napisa Waitoolkiat - Khaki Capitalism : The political Economy of the Military of Southeast Asia

This books brings in fresh air on military activities undertaken by Southeast Asian governments to generate income. I believe, the understanding of Thailand as a country would fall short on every account unless Military, monks and Monarchy and their interrelations are understood, holistically. I read this book to understand military part of the triad and, this book did absolute justice to time and effort. The authors exhausted a lot of pages in defining informal and formal source, and legal and illegal means of military income. The book cover sections for individual chronology of military of Southeast Asian countries but Malaysia and Singapore are not included in the analysis (reason best known to authors). I read Thailand, Myanmar and Laos with keen detail.

The authors state that Thailand's *Khaki Capital* is reason of envy for other Southeast Asian militaries. The book brings out Thai military's active involvement in capital generating activities, both legal and illegal, formal and informal which enables it to retain distrust of civilian leadership. Thai military's, hand in glove relationship with royal family, has given it unquestionable legitimacy to disrupt and uproot elected governments. Importantly, Thai armed forces have maintained absolute budgetary independence which allows it to pursue goals on their terms. Author, on comparison, says that no other country close to Thai military in operating illegal capital generation avenues, especially narcotics trade.

This book is recommended to understand the inroads of military in political setup of most of the countries of Southeast Asia.

Lawrence Osborne- Bangkok Days : A Sojourn in the Capital of Pleasure

This book is a light read and offers a peek in to dark, gray and pink world of Capital of Pleasure. I thoroughly enjoyed reading this book which takes reader through the streets and heart of Bangkok, yet not clamming to reveal hidden layers of Thai culture. The author does not claim to know Thai culture or language better, but he offers his perspective in a inquisitive and freelance way. It is a work that would keep reader busy with turning pages, should you pick this book.

Source of additional Information

Participation in numerous lectures and seminars hosted at FCCT, BACC and Royal Siam Society in Bangkok helped me a great deal to solve the maze of Thai history, culture, fighting resolve of Thai people and their acceptance of rationed freedom. All lectures and seminars are available online for better understanding of different facets of Thailand. Highly recommended!

Chapter II

Important Personalities

Abhisit Vejjajiva A career politician who was elected to Parliament at a young age of 27. He went on to become Prime Minister in 2008 toppling Thaksin led government. His government was hit by massive pro Thaksin protests which led to death of 90 people. The charges for complicity on him were withdrawn under Prayuth Chan-ocha government who was deputy army commander during crackdown. In 2011, he was defeated by Yingluck Shinawatra, Thaksin's sister. He is more of parliamentarian than a firebrand or grass root politician.

Ananda Panyarachun He was appointed Prime Minsiter for the first time in 1991 and appointed Prime Minister again in 1992 (read more) by King Bhumibol when Suchinda was rejected by mass demonstrations in Bangkok. His functioning was efficient and reformist, and therefore was favoured by Thai people. Before that, he worked as ambassador to USA, and in United Nations. He played a substantial role in drafting of constitution in 1997. Government has sought his advice on many issues particularly political reconciliation and insurgency in southern border provinces.

Ananda,King Rama VIII He succeeded King Prajadhipok who abdicated in 1935. As he was a minor, a regency council acted on his behalf. He was not even formally crowned, when he was mysteriously shot dead in 1946. His crown was consecrated after his death.

Bhumibol Adulyadej, King Rama IX When he died in 2016, he was longest serving monarch of the world. Initially, anti-royalism of Phibun Songkhram restricted role of monarchy but during Sanit Thanarat government, monarchy raised itself to a point where he could intervene in times of political crisis. He had respect of his people and his own skills gave him extra constitutional authority.

Chulalongkorn, King Rama V He reigned from 1868 to 1910. During intial years, he was restricted by nobility. He ushered in modernity, colonial administrative methods to govern his country. He believed in authority of monarchy and outrightly rejected the idea of s constitution and parliamentary system of government.

Prince Damrong Rajanuphap He was son of King Mongkut and younger brother of King Chulalongkorn. He served as Minister of Education and Minister of Interior (for 23 years) and came to be known as "father of Thai history" He was a prolific scholar who played a critical role in execution of administrative reforms during King Chulalongkorn reign. He was one of the founder of nationalist school of Thai history. He was largely sidelined by King Vajiravudh but consulted by Prajadhipok on constitutionalism . In 1932, he went into exile in Malaya until the year before his death.

Prince Nivat Dhani He has unique distinction of serving five kings from Chulalonkorn to Bhumibol for whom he acted as a privy councillor and a regent. He is well known for his contribution to strengthening kingship and other scholarly work.

Kukrit Aphaiwong A founding member of People's Party who succeeded Phibun as Prime Minister towards end of WWII. He put appreciative diplomatic acumen at display to deal with Japanese and Americans. He did two more brief stint as Prime Minister in 1946 and 1947-48. He lead Thai government around the time of India's independence.

Kukrit Pramoj He is more known for his writing as journalist rather than politician. His most famous literary work, Si Phaendin (Four Reigns) depicts court life under Kings from Chulalongkorn to Ananda (four). As Prime Minister in 1975-1976, he oversaw withdrawal of US forces from Thailand.

Mongkut , King Rama IV He reigned from 1851 to 1868 before serving as a monk for 27 years, during which he established strict Thammayut sect of Buddhism. He recognized potential benefit of engagement with West and send many of his sons for western education. He made monarchy within the reach of common people. And, traveled across the length and breadth of country uplifting Buddhist values.

Phibun Songkhram He was head of military faction of People's party and became PM of Thailand in 1938. He controlled almost all portfolios, in that, he was Army Chief, Defense Minister, Foreign Minister and then elevated himself to Field Marshal (a rank which which reserved for monarchy till then). He propagated ultra nationalism as a policy, a part of it still survives today except its anti Chinese aspect. He sided with Japanese during WWII, and allowed Netaji Subhash to set up INA training camp in Thailand. Finally, that costed him his prime minister position in 1944, Finally, riding on a coup he came back to power in 1948. He got a taste of his own medicine when he was ousted by his Army Chief in 1957 and, was forced in to exile to Japan. He held PM office more than anyone in Thai history (17 years over two terms)

Prajadhipok, King Rama VII He ascended throne in 1925 and abdicated in 1935. He did not resist for demand to end absolute monarchy but, he did not accepted any additional curb own royal powers. He inherited an unstable government primarily because of his brother Vajiravudh's excesses.

Prayuth Chan ocha   After leading a military coup in 2014, he took over PM office and pardoned himself for staging coup and ensured immunity from future prosecution. As deputy army commander, he played role in suppression of red shirt protesters. He was pro monarchy and suppressed any voice of dissent. Lost in elections in 2023.

Pridi Banomyong He was author of 1932 Handbill, which condemned absolute monarchy and Thailand's first constitution. He was accused of communist underpinnings for his radical economic plan of 1933. He founded Thammasat university. He held office of interior minister, foreign affairs and finance minister from 1934 to 1941. He vehemently opposed pro Japanese stance during WWII and organized an anti- Japanese movement 'Seri Thai'. He was major power behind the scene and briefly became PM in 1946. His opponents accused him of complicity over the unexplained death of King Ananda in 1946, especially Seni and Kukrit Pramoj. He was involved in unsuccessful coup against Phibun and, went in to exile to China and later on to France.

Sarit Thanarat He served in Shan states during WWII and played a majot role in 1947 coup against pro Pridi government. Ousted Phibun in 1957 military coup and assumed prime minister office in 1958. He used anti communist card to invite substantial funds from USA and used them to suppress his opponents brutally. He promoted himself as a paternal ruler with in Thai tradition.

Also, he raised political role of King Bhumibol, and fostered close relationship between civil and military bureaucracy.

Seni Pramoj   He was PM for three very short terms (1945-1946,1975,1976). He was Ambassador to USA in 1941 when he refused to deliver Phibun's declaration of war on USA (important decision) and cooperated with Pridi's 'Seri Thai' movement. Later on he fall out with Pridi and, accused him of complicity in unfolding mystery of King Ananda's death. In 1962, he led Thailand's case against Cambodia for Preah Vihaer (an ancient Khmer Hindu temple) in International Court of Justice. His 1975 and 1976 prime minster stint was rocked by political turmoil preceding the coup of 1976.

Thaksin Shinawatra   Thaksin served as a police officer and, mastered in criminology. Thaksin ia a highly successful businessman. He ran a highly successful campaign to take over PM office in 2001 elections. He led economic reforms, a moratorium on rural debt, funds for development of villages, a universal health care scheme, a tough stance on drugs and insurgency in Southern Provinces. His war on drugs and insurgency led to massive scale exploitation of human rights. He appointed his cousin as Army Commander. Ousted by a military coup in 2006, he chose self exile in 2008. He returned back in 2023 to Thailand and his punishment is reduced. His popularity at grass root level is intact and he continue to influence Thai politics through Pheu Thai and Red shirt movement.

Thanom Kittikhachon He was Prime Minister in 1958 and from 1963 to 1973. He was one of the tyrants whose repressive rule paved way for student led demonstrations demanding a constitution and elections. Three days of violence in 1973 forced him to exile. His return in Oct 1976 provoked unmanageable Student protests and, led to 1976 students massacre at Thammasat university. He remains Thailand's second longest serving Prime Minister (12 years over two terms).

Vajrailongkorn, King Rama X   Current Monarch of Thailand, his reign commenced in 2016.

Vajiravudh, King Rama VI   He was first western educated king of Thailand who reigned from 1910 to 1925. He is known for excesses in spending, indifference to court life and unconventional social life. He was hardwired for ultra nationalism which is reflected in his essays, literary works and translations. He firmly rejected proposal for a constitution and parliamentary form of government.

Wichit Wathakan   He immensely contributed to the design of Thailand's official national identity under Phibun and Sarit Thanarat. He strongly advocated for change of name from Siam to Thailand. He served as minister of foreign affair, minster of finance and as an ambassador, including to Japan during WWII. Other than that, he is author of prolific nationalistic plays,songs and radio programs.

Yingluck Shinawatra   She became first female Prime Minister of Thailand in 2011 and lead Phew Thai party. Her government established good relations with monarchy and military but, was highly criticized for high costs of rice subsidy scheme. In 2013, she mulled over giving amnesty to Thaksin, her brother, which provoked protests. She attempted to resolve crisis by elections but was thwarted by Suthep. She was removed from power in 2011 when she attempted to transfer a senior official paving way for her brother to become army chief. She was meted with five years in prison over rice subsidy scheme, She chose self-exile.

Bibliography

❖

Section I

Chapter I Geo history of Thai people

1. Ahom *Sarkar, J. N. (1992), "Chapter VIII Assam-Mughal Relations", in Barpujari, H. K. (ed.), The Comprehensive History of Assam, vol. 2, Guwahati: Assam Publication Board, pp. 148–256.*

2. Thant Myint-U (2001). *The Making of Modern Burma.* Cambridge University Press. p. 20. ISBN 978-0-521-79914-0.

3. Tai ethnicity in Cambodia Wolters, 1973. Jayavarman II's military power; the territorial foundation of the Angkor empire.

4. Cambodia inter censal population survey 2013 final report; UNPF; National institute of Statistics, Minsitry of Planning, Phnom Penh, Cambodia, Nov 2013.

5. Ben Kiernan (May 2014) , the Pol Pot regime : Race, Power and, genocide in Cambodia under the Khmer Rogue, 1975-79 (Third ed) p 300.

6. Jean Michaud (2000) "Turbulent Times and Enduring Peoples: Mountain Minorities in the South East Asian Massif. P 59 ISBN 0-7007-1180-5

7. Ven. Phra Rajavaramuni, Thai Buddhism in the Buddhist World (Bangkok: Unity Progress press, 1984), p.29.

Chapter II - Sukhothai Kingdom

1. Lars Fogelin (2015). *An Archaeological History of Indian Buddhism*. Oxford University Press. pp. 229–230. ISBN 978-0-19-994823-9.

2. Chris Baker and Pasuk Phongpaichit 2017 "A history of Thailand"

3. Kusalasaya, Karuna-Ruang Urai, 2001: 42

4. Early Thailand From Prehistory to Sukhothai by Charles Higham and Rachanie Thorasat

Chapter III Ayutthaya Kingdom

1. P Bilimoria (2011), "The Idea of Hindu Law", Journal of the Oriental Society of Australia, Volume 43, pp. 103–130.

2. Donald Davis (2010), The Spirit of Hindu Law, Cambridge University Press, ISBN 978-0521877046, pp. 13–16, 166–179.

3. Melvin E.; Sonnenburg, Penny M., eds. (2003). Colonialism: An International, Social, Cultural, and Political Encyclopedia, Volume 2. ISBN 1-57607-335-1.

4. Brockey, Liam Matthew (2008). Portuguese Colonial Cities in the Early Modern World. Ashgate Publishing, Ltd. ISBN 978-0-7546-6313-3.

5. James Huntley Grayson (2001). Myths and Legends from Korea: An Annotated Compendium of Ancient and Modern Materials. Psychology Press. pp. 110–116. ISBN 978-0-7007-1241-0.

6. Damrong 2001: 75): He was 8 (in his 9th year) when he went to Pegu in 1564. Six years later, he became viceroy of Phitsanulok at age 15 (16th year).

7. Chris Baker, Pasuk Phongpaichit, A History of Thailand Third Edition (p. 307). Cambridge University Press. Kindle Edition.

Chapter IV Rise of Taksin's cult and Self crafted fall

1. Steve Van Beek: *The Chao Phya*, p.39

2. Roeder, Eric (1999). "The Origin and Significance of the Emerald Buddha" (PDF). *Explorations in Southeast Asian Studies*. **3**. Honolulu: Center for Southeast Asian Studies, University of Hawai'i at Manoa: 1, 18. Archived from the original on 4 May 2019. Retrieved 22 February 2014.

3. Journal of M. Descourvieres, (Thonburi). Dec. 21, 1782; in Launay, *Histoire*, p. 309.

Chapter V Chakri Dynasty

1. Lipi Ghosh, 2017, India-Thailand Cultural Interactions: Glimpses from the Past to Present, Springer Publishing, pp. 157

2. Habegger (2014). Masked: The Life of Anna Leonowens. p. 417.

3. *Baker, Chris; Phasuk Phongpaichit (2017). A History of Ayutthaya: Siam in the Early Modern World. Cambridge University Press. pp. 192–193.* ISBN 978-1-316-64113-2.

4. India in 1872, as Seen by the Siamese. Sachchidanand Sahai. BR Publishing Corporation, 2002. 6, 2002.

5. Stefan Hell (2017). Siam and World War I: An International History. River Books. ISBN 978-616-7339-92-4.

6. Suwannathat-Pian, Kobkua (2003), Kings, Country and Constitutions: Thailand's Political Development 1932-2000, RoutledgeCurzon, p. 169

Section II

Chapter I

1. Lars Fogelin (2015). An Archaeological History of Indian Buddhism. Oxford University Press. pp. 229–230. ISBN 978-0-19-994823-9

2. Karuna Kusalasaya (2006). Buddhism in Thailand Its Past and Its Present Archived 2021-02-10 at the Wayback Machine

3. Stillness Flowing, *(pdf) pp. 57-58*

4. *Female monks barred from paying respect(Bangkok Post, 11 Jan 2017)*

5. Allen Brent, The Imperial Cult and the Development of Church Order: Concepts and Images of Authority in Paganism and Early Christianity before the Age of Cyprian (Brill, 1999)

6. Kuppuswami Sastri, S. (1984), Brahmasiddhi, by Maṇḍanamiśra, with commentary by Śankhapāṇī. 2nd ed., Delhi, India: Sri Satguru Publications

7. *de La Vallée Poussin, Louis (1976), The Buddhist Councils, Calcutt : K.P. Bagchi Lisa Miller article "We all will be Hindus now"*

Chapter II

1. Narayana Sukta or Narayana Suktam is a Hindu hymn propitiating Narayana (Vishnu), featured in the 13th anuvaka (section) of the 10th prapathaka (chapter) of Taittiriya Aranyaka, which is part of the Krishna Yajurveda generally dated between c. 1200–1000 BCE

2. The Samudra Manthana ('churning of the ocean') is a major episode in Hinduism that is elaborated in the Vishnu Purana, a major text of Hinduism. Chaturvedi, B. K. (2006). *Vishnu Purana.* ISBN 978-81-7182-673-5.

3. For Giant Ceremony, M. E. Manickavasagam Pillai (1986). *Dravidian Influence in Thai Culture.* Tamil University. p. 69.

4. Lord Ganesha Idol drinking milk, Suzanne Goldenberg, "India's gods milk their faithful in a brief 'miracle'", The Guardian, 22 September 1995.

Chapter III

1. Shakti Das Gupta, *Tagore's Asian Outlook* p 91-92,94-96, 109,114-115

2. Sonakul Dhani *"Tagore visit to Siam in Rabindranath Tagore-A centenary volume 1861-1961"* (New Delhi Sahitya Akademi, 1987, p306)

3. Lak Muang 17 Oct 1927, cited in Shakti Das Gupta, Tagore's Asian Outlook (Calcutta: Nava Bharti. 1961,p121)

4. Pandit Raghunath Sharma in '*Early life of Swami Satyanandpuri*'

5. The Siam Observer reported Tagore's interview 10 Oct & 15 Oct 1927 cited in Shakti Das Gupta, *Tagore's Asian Outlook* p104-105,114

6. K.K. Ghosh, *the Indian National Army :Second front of Indian Independence Movement in Thailand* (1999) p189

7. N.G. Jog *In Freedom's quest* (New Delhi 1969) p 219-220

8. Roger Beaumont, *The hidden truth: A tribute to the Indian Independence Movement in Thailand* (1999) p189

9. Basu, Kanailal (2010). *Netaji: Rediscovered.*

10. *South East Asian Minorities in the Wartime Japanese Empire* by Paul H Kratoska

11. *Netaji;s Azad Hind Sarkar Aur Fauz- Bhrantiyo se Yatharth ki Aur* by Kapil Kumar

Section III

Chapter I

1.   Ganganath Jha, *India and Southeast Asia: Introspection for Future Partnership*, p. 177-178 and 183.

2.   Chris Baker and Pasuk Phongpaichit, *A History of Thailand*, (2009), p. 175, 177-178, and 183- 187

3.   *United States Department of Defense, "Melvin R. Laird", Secretaries of Defense*

4.   Strangio, in the Dragon's shadow, 138-139; *Thai military suspends deals on foreign weapons while nation battles COVID 19*

5.   *Yuan, Shaoyu (18 November 2023). "Tracing China's diplomatic transition to wolf warrior diplomacy and its implications".*

Chapter II

1.   Ganganath Jha, *India and Southeast Asia: Introspection for Future Partnership*, (New Delhi: 2010), p. 190-191.

2.   The government under Thaksin had overwhelming popularity and that led him to win two landslide elections in 2001 and 2005, making him the only PM in Thai history to have served a full-four year term.

3.   Lt Col N K Chhibber and Col S K Shishodia, "India-Thailand Relations", in Sanjay Kumar (edi) *India-Thailand Bilateral Relations*, (2013), p. 124

4. Acharya, A. (2006). India and Southeast Asia in the age of terror: Building partnerships for peace. Contemporary Southeast Asia, 28(2), 297–321.

5. India Thailand Economic and Commercial Relations", *Embassy of India, Bangkok*

6. Sarah Cook's "Beijing's Global Megaphone: The Expansion of Chinese Communist Party Media Influence since 2017," Special Report (Freedom House, January 2020).

7. Kerry K. Gershaneck, *Political Warfare: Strategies for Combating China's Plan to "Win without Fighting"* (Virginia, 2020), 64, 76–77, 87–88;

8. Ryan Loomis and Heidi Holz, "China's Efforts to Shape the Information Environment in Thailand," Information Memorandum (Center for Naval Analysis, September 2020), 11–28.

9. Loomis and Holz, "China's Efforts to Shape the Information Environment in Thailand," 25–26, 28–32, 35; Kornphanat Tungkeunkunt, "China's Soft Power in Thailand Culture and Commerce: China's Soft Power in Thailand," *International Journal of China Studies* 7, no. 2 (1 August 2016), 165–66;

10. Skaggs, "CCP Information Warfare," 99–107.

11. "Forbidden Feeds: Government Controls on Social Media in China" (New York, 13 March 2018) and Bangkok Post Public Company, "CPN, WeChat Pay to Attract Chinese," *Bangkok Post*, 24 March 2023.

12. Kheokao and Kheokao, "Reuters Country Profile for Thailand."

13. Justin Sherman, "Unpacking TikTok, Mobile Apps and National Security Risks," *Lawfare* (blog), 2 April 2020

14. Tang, "China's Information Warfare and Media Influence."

15. Reena Marwah and Sanika Sulochani Ramanayake, *China's Economic Footprint In South And Southeast Asia: A Futuristic Perspective—Case Studies Of Pakistan, Sri Lanka, Myanmar and Thailand* (Singapore: World Scientific Publishing Company, 2021), xiii,p 211–12.

16. Skaggs, "CCP Information Warfare," p111–13

17. Sivarin Lertpusit, "The Patterns of New Chinese Immigration in Thailand: The Terms of Diaspora, Overseas Chinese and New Migrants Comparing in a Global Context," *ABAC Journal* 38, no. 1 (June 2018): p78–82

18. Antonio L. Rappa, "The Teochew Chinese of Thailand," *BOHR International Journal of Social Science and Humanities Research* 1, no. 1 (2022), p10–11.

19. Lertpusit, "The Patterns of New Chinese Immigration in Thailand," 82–84; Languepin, "Challenges of Doing Business in Thailand"; and Akira Yonemoto, "The 'Belt and Road' Initiative and Overseas Chinese in Southeast Asia," *Journal La Sociale* 1, no. 1 (29 January 2020), 14–15.

20. Lertpusit, "China's Influence on Thai Chinese Education," 6–7; and Aranya Siriphon and Fanzura Banu, "The Nature of Recent Chinese Migration to Thailand," *Yusof Ishak Institute*, Perspective, no. 168 (2021), 6, https://www.iseas.edu.sg/.

21. Benjamin Zawacki, "Of Questionable Connectivity: China's BRI and Thai Civil Society," *Council on Foreign Relations* (blog), 7 June 2021, https://www.cfr.org/.

22. Yujiao Wang, "Confucius Institutes in Thailand: Revealing the Multi-Dimensionality of China's Public Diplomacy," *Journal of the Graduate School of Asia-Pacific Studies* 37, no. 37 (March 2019): 104–5, 108–9.

23. Andrew Chubb, "China's Overseas Influence Operations: Disaggregating the Risks," *U.S.–China Perception Monitor*, 14 September 2021, https://uscnpm.org/.

24. Joshua Kurlantzick, "China's Global Influence Campaign: Its Effects in Thailand," *Council on Foreign Relations* (blog), 15 February 2023, https://www.cfr.org/; and J. Yin and P. M. Taylor, "Information Operations from an Asian Perspective: A Comparative Analysis," *Journal of Information Warfare* 7, no. 1 (2008): 1–23.

25. Phusadee Arunmas, "Companies Push for Deeper China Links," *Bangkok Post*, 18 April 2022, sec. Business, https://www.bangkokpost.com/; and Brian Y. S. Wong and Tidarat Yingcharoen, "How Thailand Can Draw Closer to China despite US Elephant in the Room," *South China Morning Post*, 5 August 5, 2023.

26. Peggy Sito, "Exclusive: Thailand's Wealthiest Clan Mulls Setting up Hong Kong Family Office," *South China Morning Post*, 22 March 2023, sec. Business, https://www.scmp.com/.

Chapter III

1. Skaggs, "CCP Information Warfare," 120–25; Clive Hamilton and Alex Joske, *Silent Invasion: China's Influence in Australia* (Hardie Grant Books, 2018), 143.

2. Shen Hongfang, "The Economic Relations between China and Thailand under the Context of CAFTA: An Assessment," *Chinese Studies* 2, no. 1 (2013), 52–53, https://doi.org/.

3. Shen, "The Economic Relations between China and Thailand," 52–53; and Piratorn Punyaratabandhu and Jiranuwat Swaspitchayaskun, "The Political Economy of China-Thailand Development under the One Belt One Road Initiative: Challenges and Opportunities," *Chinese Economy* 51, no. 4 (1 July 2018), 333–35, https://doi.org/.

4. Kitiphong Thaichareon and Satawasin Staporncharnchai, "Thailand Approves $1 Billion Foxconn-PTT Venture for Battery Electric Vehicles," *Reuters*, 13 June 2022, sec. Deals, https://www.reuters.com/

5. Nopparat Chaichalearmmongkol, "Return of Chinese Tourists to Thailand Has Pros, Cons," *VOA News*, 24 May 2023, https://www.voanews.com/.

6. "Horns of a Dilemma," *Bangkok Post*; Punyaratabandhu and Swaspitchayaskun, "The Political Economy of China-Thailand Development," 334–38; and Marwah and Ramanayake, *China's Economic Footprint In South And Southeast Asia*, 230–35.

7. Enze Han, "Under the Shadow of China-US Competition: Myanmar and Thailand's Alignment Choices," *Chinese Journal*

of International Politics 11, no. 1 (Spring 2018): 81–104, https://doi.org/.

8.   Sakshi Tiwari, "China Is Now Courting Thailand, A Key US Ally, With Joint Military Drills & Massive Arms Sales," *Eurasian Times*, 22 August 2022, and, Mark S Cogan, "Is Thailand Accommodating China?," *Southeast Asian Social Science Review* 4, no. 2 (2019), 38–39.

9.   (Strangio, *In the Dragon's Shadow*, 134–36; and Crispin, "China Losing, US Gaining Crucial Ground."

10. Crispin, "China Losing, US Gaining Crucial Ground"; Strangio, *In the Dragon's Shadow*, 139–40; and Cogan, "Is Thailand Accommodating China?," 40–41.

11. Strangio, *In the Dragon's Shadow*, 138–39.

12. Zawacki, *Thailand: Shifting Ground*, 312–13; and Strangio, *In the Dragon's Shadow*, 138–40.

13. The Huakiao Poatoetek Siaengteung Foundation, the largest Chinese charitable organization in Thailand with more than 80 years of operation, founded Huachiew Chalermprakiet University. An interesting observation is that *Huachiew* actually means overseas Chinese in the Teochew dialect. "Huachiew Chalermprakiet University," Huachiew Chalermprakiet University, 20 May 2020, https://www.hcu.ac.th/.

14. Wang, "Confucius Institutes in Thailand," 105–6; and "Institute of Asian Studies," Chulalongkorn University, 2023, https://www.chula.ac.th/

15. Allen, Bethany (1 August 2023). *Beijing Rules: How China Weaponized Its Economy to Confront the World*. Harper. p. 59